The Work Sampling System®

Work Sampling in the Classroom

The Work Sampling System is an instructional performance assessment system that is used in preschool through fifth grade. Its purpose is to document and assess children's skills, knowledge, behavior, and accomplishments across a wide variety of curriculum areas on multiple occasions in order to enhance teaching and learning.

The Work Sampling System consists of three complementary elements:

1) Developmental Guidelines and Checklists,
2) Portfolios, and
3) Summary Reports.

Work Sampling calls for ongoing assessment that is summarized three times per year. By reflecting classroom goals and objectives, it helps teachers monitor children's continuous progress and places children's work within a broad developmental perspective. Through documenting and evaluating individual performance of classroom-based tasks, Work Sampling strengthens student achievement and motivation, assists teachers in instructional decision-making, and serves as an effective means for reporting children's progress to families, educators, and the community.

Work Sampling in the Classroom

A Teacher's Manual
3rd Edition: for use with the 4th Edition Work Sampling materials

Margo L. Dichtelmiller
Judy R. Jablon
Aviva B. Dorfman
Dorothea B. Marsden
Samuel J. Meisels

with contributions from
Charlotte Stetson

The Work Sampling System®

REBUS INC
ANN ARBOR, MICHIGAN

For more information about
The Work Sampling System, contact
Rebus Inc
P.O. Box 4479
Ann Arbor, MI 48106
www.rebusinc.com
1-800-435-3085

Development of the Work Sampling System was supported in part by a grant from the John D. and Catherine T. MacArthur Foundation. The opinions expressed are solely those of the authors.

Printed in the United States of America.

03 02 01   10 9 8 7 6 5 4 3

Part No. 20112 (6/01)
ISBN 1-57212-202-1

List of Work Sampling System Materials............................**ix**

List of Frequently Asked Questions..............................**xi**

Foreword..**xiii**

Acknowledgements ....**xvii**

How to Use This Book ....**xix**

CHAPTER 1   **Introducing the Work Sampling System**............**1**

Authentic Performance Assessment For
Preschool–Grade 5

Introduction **2**
Performance Assessment in the Work Sampling System **4**
The Work Sampling Domains **5**
Observing, Collecting, and Summarizing **7**
Summary **8**

CHAPTER 2   **Developmental Guidelines and Checklists**..........**9**

A Structured Approach to Observation,
Documentation, and Evaluation

Overview of Guidelines and Checklists............................**10**

PART I   **Understanding Guidelines and Checklists**......................**11**

Purposes of Guidelines and Checklists **12**

Organization and Structure of Guidelines and Checklists **13**
    Grade-Level Developmental Guidelines **14**
    Developmental Checklists **16**
    Omnibus Guidelines **17**

PART II   **How to Use Guidelines and Checklists** **19**

    Guidelines and Checklist Timeline **19**

Before the School Year Begins **20**
    Gain Familiarity with the Guidelines. **20**
    Extend Your Knowledge and Understanding of Observation. **22**
    Investigate and Prepare Observation Methods and Tools. **24**

During Each Collection Period **39**
    Plan, Observe, and Record. **39**
    Review Checklists Periodically, Making Pencil Ratings **41**
    Talk with Students. **43**
    Apply What You Have Learned **44**

Near the End of Each Collection Period..........................**46**
    Review Preliminary Ratings **46**
    Make Final Ratings **46**
    Identify Examples for the Summary Report. **47**

PART III   **Frequently Asked Questions About Guidelines and Checklists** **48**

CHAPTER 3   **Portfolios** **57**
Collecting, Selecting, and Evaluating Student Work

Overview of Portfolio Collection **58**

PART I   **Understanding Portfolio Collection** **59**

Purposes of Portfolio Collection **60**

Structure and Organization of the Work Sampling Portfolio **61**

Core Items **62**

Individualized Items **66**

Comparison of Major Functions of Core and Individualized Items **68**

Total Number of Portfolio Items **69**

PART II   **How to Use Portfolios** **70**
Portfolio Collection Timeline **71**

Before the School Year Begins **73**
Create Individual Portfolios and Decide How and Where to Store Them **73**
Devise Procedures for Collecting Student Work **75**
Consider Methods to Portray Learning **77**
Plan for Core Item Collection **84**

During Each Collection Period **96**
Planning Curriculum with Portfolio Collection in Mind **96**
Involve Students in Portfolio Collection **98**
Collecting, Selecting, and Annotating Work **100**
Managing the Selection Process **112**

Near the End of Each Collection Period **113**
Student Review and Evaluation of the Portfolio **113**
Teacher Review and Evaluation of the Portfolio for the Summary Report **116**
Preparation for Sharing Portfolios with Families **118**

PART III   **Frequently Asked Questions About Portfolios** **120**

CHAPTER 4   **Summary Reports** **127**
Summarizing Performance and Progress

Overview of the Summary Report **128**

PART I   **Understanding the Summary Report** **129**

Purposes of the Summary Report **130**

Organization and Structure of the Summary Report **131**
    Structure of the Standard Summary Report **132**
    Structure of the Narrative Summary Report **133**
    Evaluation **133**

PART II   **Completing the Summary Report** **136**
    Summary Report Timeline **136**

Before the School Year Begins **137**

During Each Collection Period **137**

Near the End of Each Collection Period **138**
    Review the Information Collected for Each Student **138**
    Evaluate and Rate Student Performance and Progress **138**
    Write a Narrative for Each Student **144**
    Share the Summary Report with the Child and Family **156**

PART III   **Frequently Asked Questions About the Summary Report** **160**

CHAPTER 5   **Getting Started with Work Sampling** **171**

Tips for You as You Learn Work Sampling **172**

Gradual Implementation of Work Sampling **173**

Enlisting the Support of Colleagues **179**

Informing the Community about Work Sampling **180**

CHAPTER 6   **Special Topics** **183**

Using Work Sampling in Preschool and Kindergarten Classrooms .. **184**

Using Work Sampling with Older Elementary Students **189**

Using Work Sampling in Multi-Age Classrooms **192**

Assessing Children with Special Needs **193**

Involving Special Subject Teachers **197**

Using Work Sampling for Title I Evaluation **199**
    Translating Work Sampling Data into Title I Ratings **199**

Conclusion **200**

APPENDIX A   Suggestions for Core Items—Preschool and Kindergarten **201**

APPENDIX B   Suggestions for Core Items—Elementary Grades **207**

APPENDIX C   Example of Teacher's Letter to Parents **213**

APPENDIX D   Examples of Completed Summary Reports **215**

APPENDIX E   Glossary of Terms **217**

Index **221**

List of Work Sampling System Materials

Introductory descriptions, in many cases followed by an illustration, for the following Work Sampling System materials can be found on the pages indicated:

Grade-Level Developmental Guidelines.............................14

Developmental Checklists 16

Omnibus Guidelines..17

Wall Chart of Performance Indicators 21

Domain Process Notes form 34

Child Domain Process Notes form...................................34

General Process Notes form 35

Roster Process Notes form..36

Portfolio Domain Labels 74

Photographic Portfolio Item Record form 80

Core Item Planning Worksheet form................................91

Core Item Collection Plan form.....................................93

Portfolio Item Record self-stick note 105

"My Portfolio Item Record" form...................................105

Portfolio Collection Tally form.....................................112

"Thoughts About My Portfolio" form...............................115

Standard Summary Report form 132

Narrative Summary Report form 133

Summary Report: Student and Family Comments form 158

Special Subject Report form 167

Overview for Families 180

List of Frequently Asked Questions

CHAPTER 2   **Developmental Guidelines and Checklists**

How can I find the time to observe and record? **48**

Should I set up specific situations so that I can observe the skills listed on
the Checklists? **48**

How do Guidelines and Checklists help me with curriculum planning? **50**

How can I be sure that my observations are fair? **50**

How can I know that my Checklist ratings are valid and reliable? **51**

Why is it necessary to record observations? **51**

Is it possible for a rating to change from "Proficient" to "In Process" from
the fall to the spring? **51**

Are Checklists sent home? **52**

Can I use the Checklist during parent-teacher conferences? **52**

How can specialists or special subjects teachers be involved in completing Checklists? . **52**

Why are Checklists filled out three times during the school year? **53**

What happens to the Checklist at the end of the year? **53**

How long does it take to learn how to use the Guidelines and Checklists? **53**

How long does it take to complete the Checklist? **54**

Which Checklist should I use for children above or below grade-level expectations? . . . **54**

How can I possibly observe everything that is going on in the classroom? **54**

Should I have a documented observation for every performance indicator on
the Checklist? **55**

How are the Guidelines and Checklists used in multi-age classrooms? **56**

Can the Guidelines and Checklists be customized to meet the requirements of a
particular state or district? **56**

CHAPTER 3   **Portfolios**

What do I need to begin Portfolio collection? **120**

I prefer to create my students' Portfolios in a different way. Is it okay to use a
method different from those described in this chapter? **120**

Should all work go into work folders? **120**

What makes a Portfolio item informative? **120**

How can I find time to file the children's work? **121**

Should I keep my notes about students in their Portfolio? **121**

Should work that is included in the Portfolio be graded? **121**

As a preschool teacher, I feel that it is very important to document growth in
Personal and Social Development and Physical Development. Why aren't they
included as domains for the collection of Core Items? **122**

If the entire class has the same areas of learning in each domain, won't all the
portfolios contain children's responses to the same projects or assignments? **122**

How do I integrate Portfolio collection into my existing curriculum and classroom schedule? 123

How will Portfolio assessment influence my curriculum and instruction? 123

How can I involve specialists in the Portfolio process? 124

What happens to Portfolios at the end of the year? 124

Should I show the Portfolio to the child's new teacher before sending it home? 125

CHAPTER 4   Summary Reports

When should I start completing Summary Reports? 160

I'm ready to start completing Summary Reports. I'm surrounded by piles of Checklists, Portfolios, observational notes, and other materials. What should I do first? 160

How does performance differ from progress? 160

Should I evaluate progress in the fall? 161

Should performance and progress ratings always agree? 161

Should performance ratings be the same for the Checklist and Portfolio? 162

Why is it necessary to make a judgment, rather than just describe a child's current performance? 164

How do you know you are maintaining standards? 164

How do I know I am making objective and fair decisions on the Summary Report? . . 165

Why include comments? 166

How long does it take to complete a Summary Report? 166

How should Summary Reports be used at conference time? 167

How can specialists be involved in Summary Reports? 167

Should Summary Reports be written differently at different times of the year? 168

Foreword

The Work Sampling System has its origins in the kindergarten class-room where I first started teaching in 1970. This was an exciting time to teach young children. Head Start was still in its infancy, Piaget had just been "rediscovered," and open classrooms were capturing the imagination of teachers everywhere. The classroom I designed at the Runkle School in Brookline, Massachusetts was rich in the possibilities of learning. It had climbing structures, books, balance beams, aquaria filled with fish, reptiles and small mammals, a nest of rabbits with their young, books and counting objects, blocks, a carpenter's bench, extensive art materials, and children's work everywhere. With a very specific set of purposes in mind, I set out to create a highly active learning environment. It was one that would allow me to teach children about themselves and their world while informing me about how they were learning so that I could enhance and extend their development. The classroom I designed in 1970 and the following year when I took on a combination kindergarten/first grade sought to meet these goals. They were settings that afforded children a multi-tude of opportunities to explore their world. My interactions with students helped me set individual goals for children, making use of the extensive learning potential implicit in the classroom environment.

However, one area resisted all of my best efforts and thinking. How could I evaluate what my students were learning? The testing culture we have grown accustomed to in recent years had not yet reached down to five and six year olds at that time, but the tests that were available seemed to me to be completely inappropriate. I was look-ing for a way to tell me how well my students were doing by docu-menting what my students were doing. Nothing available seemed to answer this need, and my own efforts were not very successful.

The checklists I constructed had no structure or justification beyond my own classroom. The folders of student work that I collected became an experience of information overload, and I could not sus-tain them past the first few months of school. My reports to parents—although filled with rich anecdotal information—were unsystematic and idiosyncratic.

In succeeding years I carried my quest for a practical and meaningful classroom assessment with me to new settings. After leaving the class-room I became a faculty member at Tufts University and director of the Eliot-Pearson Children's School. The staff at Eliot-Pearson helped me gain some clarity and try out several different approaches to assessment, but the task of creating a useful mechanism for teachers to assess and document their students' classroom accomplishments remained unfinished.

I returned to this challenge again in the mid-1980s when controversy began to rage about the inappropriate uses of tests with young children. As a critic of high stakes testing and the role of tests in enrollment and promotion decisions regarding young children, my research at Michigan began to coalesce around the need for assessment alternatives. In 1990 I turned once more to this unfinished task.

With the assistance of several exceptionally gifted colleagues and numerous generous and talented classroom teachers, the Work Sampling System began to take shape. From the outset it had three elements: a checklist, portfolio, and summary report. At first it was intended only to be a kindergarten assessment. Shortly, however, we began to develop preschool versions. This was followed by extensions to grade 3, and finally grade 5. Fundamental to the development of Work Sampling was a process of field trial, reviews by teachers and staff, and revision. This cycle went on as many as five times for some elements of the system. Over a four year period, we held focus groups with teachers, interviewed principals and supervisors, met with consultants, sent out questionnaires, completed a pilot research study, and revised our work extensively. The present version of the Work Sampling System is thus indebted to the hundreds of teachers and other educators who were willing to try to make Work Sampling a useful part of their professional lives and who shared their implementation experiences with us.

It is now nearly 25 years since I first encountered the problem of documenting and evaluating children's classroom accomplishments and learning. One thing I have learned is that there are no easy answers and no simple solutions. Children are too varied and their interactions with the world of other children, adults, and materials are so complex that conventional forced choice assessment solutions are at best unrealistic estimates of the phenomena of growth and development that we are trying to document. The Work Sampling System is a means for capturing these phenomena. It does not stand on its own: it comes to life only in the hands of a teacher. Like a car it needs a driver, like a book it requires a reader, like a musical composition it calls for a performer. The Work Sampling System is a tool for teachers. It is carefully designed so that it relies on the best knowledge available, provides extensive information to parents and administrators, and captures children's knowledge, skills, and accomplishments as fully and reliably as possible. Work Sampling helps teachers keep track of their students' accomplishments in the world of learning. It makes visible the processes and products that are part of daily classroom life, thus providing teachers with the information they need to create responsive educational experiences for all of their students.

Like teaching itself, Work Sampling is constantly evolving for its developers and users. This book is designed to open new possibilities to teachers. I invite you to study this manual, learn about Work Sampling's potential, and discover how this approach to performance assessment can add to your insight and effectiveness as a classroom teacher.

— *Samuel J. Meisels*

Ann Arbor, Michigan
June 1997

Acknowledgements

This manual represents more than six years' experience in developing, implementing, and teaching the Work Sampling System. We are grateful to a large number of individuals for their contributions to this effort. At the risk of overlooking some, we wish to mention a few of the people we have relied on.

Charlotte Stetson carefully reviewed the previous edition, identified changes needed to update the text, and offered excellent suggestions for revisions. This edition would not have been completed without secretarial assistance from Paula Bousley and Patty Humphrey; editorial assistance from Frank DeSanto; graphics production assistance from Ken Arbogast-Wilson and Ryan Ringholz; and moral support from our colleagues Bess Sternberg and Donna Kehoe. During the revision process, we learned a great deal from teachers involved in large-scale initiatives in Maryland and South Carolina. Our work has benefited greatly from the Work Sampling National Faculty, who we call upon regularly to react to and talk over our ideas. In particular Gaye Gronlund has provided us with sound advice and many practical words of wisdom. Several teachers have shared their students' and their own work with us including Katy Carroll and Jenny Gadd, Pittsburgh (PA); Nancy Brooks and Lauren Ashley, Brattleboro (VT); Lesley Straley, Townshend (VT); and Barbara Moody, Marion (MA).

We thank the following colleagues for their valuable suggestions and feedback on an early draft: Lauren Ashley and Pam Becker of the Brattleboro (VT) Public Schools; Joni Block and Laura Ruhkala of the Massachusetts Department of Education; Lucy Ware, from the Pittsburgh Public Schools; and Austine Fowler, from the District of Columbia Public Schools.

Many teachers have contributed ideas, examples, and illustrations for this manual. From Brattleboro (VT) Public Schools: Jean Allbee, Pattie Berger, Deborah Hall, Janis Kiehle, Lynn Leighton, Polly Kurty, and Donna Natowich; From Pittsburgh Public Schools: Barbara Prevost; From Dexter (MI) Community Schools: Becky Wolfinger; From Flint (MI) Community Schools: Penny Butler; From Van Buren (MI) Public Schools: Cindy Israel and Melinda Mannes; From Massachusetts Project Impact: Jan Van Gieson, Barbara Moody, and Amy Rugel; From Carnegie Mellon University Child Care Center: Marsha Poster and Joella Reed; From Esteyville Preschool in Brattleboro (VT): David Bleecker-Adams, Jan Bucossi, and Joy Hammond.

Teachers and staff from the following districts shared their implementation experiences with us: Massachusetts districts of Agawam, Boston, Cambridge, Lynn, Old Rochester Regional School District, Pioneer Valley, Somerset, and Lynn Economic Opportunity Head Start; three schools affiliated with the Bureau of Indian Affairs: Canoncito, Chuska, Takini; Davison (MI) Community Schools; Dexter (MI) Community Schools; Flint (MI) Community Schools; Northview (MI) Public Schools; Van Buren (MI) Public Schools; Willow Run (MI) Community Schools; Pittsburgh Public Schools; Carnegie Mellon University Child Care Center; Fort Worth Independent School District; Brattleboro Public Schools; and the Valeska Hinton Early Childhood Center, Peoria, IL.

Others without whom the work could not have taken place include Jan Blomberg, Sue Kelley, Sally Atkins-Burnett, Pat McMahon, and Dorothy Steele for her contributions to the original formulation of the Work Sampling System. A special thanks to Donna Bickel whose readiness to consider a problem, answer questions, and share her experience was invaluable. Finally, we offer appreciation and thanks to Tiff Crutchfield of Mode Design whose aesthetic sense and knowledge of the Work Sampling System enrich our work every step of the way.

This work was supported in part by a grant from the John D. and Catherine T. MacArthur Foundation awarded to Samuel J. Meisels, School of Education, University of Michigan. The opinions expressed are solely those of the authors.

— *Margo Dichtelmiller*

   Judy Jablon

   Aviva Dorfman

   Dot Marsden

   Sam Meisels

How to Use This Book

This book is written for teachers who are implementing the Work Sampling System and for those interested in learning more about it. The book is divided into six chapters and appendixes, including a glossary. Chapter 1 provides an overview of the Work Sampling System and an introduction to performance assessment. Chapters 2–4 explain the three elements of the Work Sampling System—Developmental Guidelines and Checklists, Portfolios, and Summary Reports. Chapter 5 offers practical suggestions for getting started with Work Sampling, including information about starting gradually. The final chapter discusses a number of issues that are central to Work Sampling, such as using Work Sampling with preschool and kindergarten children, special needs students, and working with specialists.

Structure of the Element Chapters

Each of the chapters that focuses on the Work Sampling System elements has a common structure intended to help teachers rapidly find the information they need. The chapter begins with a one-page overview of the element. Part I of each of these chapters describes the element and consists of an introduction, an explanation of the purposes and structure of the element, and discussions of the important concepts and terminology. Part II tells how to use the element. It begins with a timeline, then describes what teachers must do before the school year begins, during each collection period, and near the end of each collection period in order to use this element successfully. Part III uses a question/answer format to address specific issues that have been raised by teachers who have used Work Sampling in the past.

Using the Book

If you are just beginning to implement Work Sampling in your classroom, we suggest that you start by reading through Chapter 1, Part I of each of Chapters 2–4, and Chapter 5. After you have decided on the part(s) of the Work Sampling System that you will begin to use, read Part II of the related element chapter(s). When you have some experience with the element(s), read Part III of the chapter(s) to find answers to some of your questions. By this time, some of the issues raised in the special topics chapter may be relevant to you. Scan the topics and read those that respond to your particular situation. Most teachers find it helpful to return to Part II several times because with each reading they gain new insights and strategies. If you are using an implementation plan that focuses on using one element initially, return to this book as you add a new element of the Work Sampling System.

Two Final Points

From teaching Work Sampling to many teachers, we have learned two important lessons. First, it is essential that you begin to use Work Sampling gradually (see Chapter 5). Because Work Sampling has three elements, is very comprehensive, and requires a systematic approach, it is not a program that is learned overnight. We strongly encourage you to identify one part of the system to begin with, and add other parts as you gain confidence.

We feel equally strongly that this system is not one to be learned in isolation. As discussed in Chapter 5, we encourage you to collaborate with your colleagues. Although we have offered many suggestions and practical ideas, focused discussions with colleagues is essential for gaining deeper understanding of the Work Sampling performance indicators, devising areas of learning for Core Item collection, learning how to write effective narratives, and determining the most effective strategies for managing the practical details of using a comprehensive system of performance assessment in your classroom.

Staying Current with Work Sampling

To receive the most recent information about Work Sampling, check out our web site at: www.rebusinc.com

Enclosed with most Work Sampling System materials is a return postcard that, when mailed, will register a teacher to receive updates, information about follow-up, and Work Sampling publications. Also available for those who register is information about staff development workshops that are offered periodically throughout the year. If no postcard is available, send your name, address, and a request to be placed on the mailing list to:

The Work Sampling System
P.O. Box 4479
Ann Arbor, Michigan 48106-4479

or call 1-800-435-3085, or e-mail us at mail@rebusinc.com

CHAPTER 1
Introducing the Work Sampling System

Authentic Performance
Assessment For Preschool–
Grade 5

Introduction

The Work Sampling System is an authentic ***performance assessment.*** *
Its purpose is to help teachers document and evaluate children's skills,
knowledge, and behaviors using actual classroom-based experiences,
activities, and products. As a ***"curriculum-embedded"*** assessment,
Work Sampling enables teachers to learn about their students by encouraging students to show what they know and what they can do when
solving problems, writing in journals, constructing with blocks, painting
with various media, doing experiments, or simply interacting with peers.

Unlike group-administered, norm-referenced, multiple-choice achievement tests that are designed to rank and compare children, the Work
Sampling System is an instructional assessment: its primary focus is on
helping teachers make instructional decisions in their classrooms. Key to
any successful classroom is the method that teachers use to find out what
their children are learning and how well they are learning it. Without this
information teachers may overlook the problems of some children while
underestimating the skills available to others. Effective instructional
assessment does not rank children; it helps teachers better understand
what they are teaching, what they need to work on, what children are
learning, and what children have begun to master.

Work Sampling is an instructional assessment that is sensitive to classroom context. Teachers differ in their approaches to teaching, just as
learners differ in the ways they learn. Because of these differences,
assessments, similar to the classrooms they are intended to be used in,
should be dynamic, open to change, and relevant to a wide range of
learning styles and experiences. Work Sampling meets these criteria. It is
a comprehensive means of monitoring children's social, emotional, physical, and academic progress. It is based on teachers' observations of students who are actively working and creating products within the context
of their daily classroom experience. And it is designed to provide meaningful feedback to teachers, students, their families, and other educators
and professionals.

The advantages of the Work Sampling System are many:

♦ It enhances student motivation by emphasizing what children can do
  instead of what they cannot do, and by involving students in the
  process of assessment.

♦ It helps teachers gain perspective on how their students learn by evaluating and documenting all areas of growth and development and
  many diverse learning styles.

---

* See the Glossary in Appendix E for definitions of terms shown in ***bold italics.***

♦ It is an effective means of reporting children's progress to families because it captures information that is specific to the child and that is familiar and meaningful to the family.

♦ It accommodates a wide range of children, including those with special needs and those from diverse cultural and socio-economic backgrounds.

♦ It is based on national standards of curriculum development for children from age 3 to grade 5, and relies on three overlapping forms of documentation that give teachers a common language and a set of shared criteria for assessment and for collaboration with other teachers, with administrators, and with families.

Designed for students in preschool through fifth grade, the Work Sampling System consists of three interrelated elements:

♦ ***Developmental Guidelines*** and ***Developmental Checklists***
♦ ***Portfolios***
♦ ***Summary Reports***

These elements are all classroom-focused and instructionally relevant, reflecting the objectives of the classroom teacher. Instead of providing a mere snapshot of narrow academic skills at a single point in time, the Work Sampling System is an ongoing evaluation process designed to improve the teacher's instructional practices and the student's learning.

The continuous assessment format of the Work Sampling System has several important benefits. First, teachers and families can gain perspective on the development of skills and accomplishments over an eight-year period. Second, schools that are committed to mixed-age groupings, to K–3 Early Childhood Units, or to establishing a unified approach to the elementary curriculum will now be able to use the same assessment over a pupil's entire preschool and elementary career. Third, schools with demonstration projects that must show the year-to-year progress of their students will be able to do so using the longitudinal design of the Work Sampling System. Fourth, because the system addresses a wide range of skills and abilities, the progress of diverse students can be monitored within the same approach. Finally, the Work Sampling System demystifies assessment. It makes easily understood information available to all participants in the teaching/assessment process—children, families, teachers, and administrators. This minimizes the risk of assessments being used to track, label, isolate, or harm individuals or groups of children.

Figure 1 shows the principal elements of the Work Sampling System and illustrates several fundamental features of the system: seven ***domains,*** or categories, of classroom learning (e.g, Personal and Social Development,

Introducing the Work Sampling System

Language and Literacy, etc.) and their use throughout the system; three documentation elements (Checklists, Portfolios, Summary Reports); three *collection periods* (Fall, Winter, Spring); the involvement of teachers, students, and families; and the eight age/grade levels available (Preschool-3–Fifth Grade).

FIGURE 1
Diagrammatic overview of the Work Sampling System

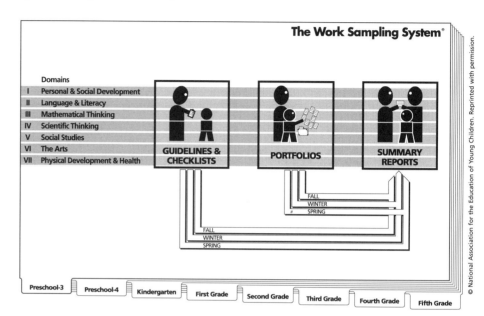

Performance Assessment in the Work Sampling System

Performance assessments are designed to document children's daily activities, to provide a means of evaluating the quality of their work, and to be flexible enough to allow a teacher to take an individualized approach to academic achievement. They are also designed to evaluate abilities that conventional standardized tests do not capture very well. Children are active constructors of knowledge. This means that they are capable of analyzing, synthesizing, evaluating, and interpreting facts and ideas. Performance assessments that focus on classroom activities allow teachers to learn about these processes by documenting how children interact with materials and peers in real-life, "authentic" situations.

All performance assessments require that students demonstrate specific skills and competencies, and that they apply the skills and knowledge they have mastered. The Work Sampling System is an authentic performance assessment, one that focuses on the context in which the student is asked to perform. The context, therefore, must be a "real-life" context, one in which students perform chosen tasks as they would in the process of general instruction.

The Work Sampling System is comprehensive in design. It goes well beyond the many performance assessments that try to assess student competence by exposing children to "on-demand" performance tasks in which choices are severely restricted for both students and teachers. In Work Sampling, competence is not assessed on the basis of a single performance. Rather, a student's work is assessed repeatedly through Guidelines and Checklists, teacher observations, and a structured Portfolio. Over time and in the context of numerous performances, teachers can observe the patterns of student learning—what students' strengths are, and where their weaker areas might be. These patterns constitute the evidence on which the evaluation is based. Comparisons between students are minimized, since students are evaluated according to how their level of performance conforms to the standards that are built into the Work Sampling System.

Comparisons of a student's performance to a norm often undercut student motivation and are not informative about a student's capabilities. Rather than producing assessments that are the same for everyone, the Work Sampling System is sensitive to the different instructional, cultural, social, and personal backgrounds of individual students. It enables teachers to follow children's development over time, within and across domains, in order to create rich profiles or portraits of children's accomplishments and approaches to learning.

The Work Sampling Domains

The Work Sampling System is based on seven categories, or domains, of classroom learning and experience, each of which is carried across all three elements of the system. The seven domains are as follows:

I Personal and Social Development

This domain emphasizes emotional and social competence. A teacher learns about children's emotional development — their sense of responsibility to themselves and others, how they feel about themselves and view themselves as learners — through ongoing observation, conversations with children, and information from family members. Teachers learn about children's social competence by interacting with them, observing their interactions with other adults and peers, and watching how they make decisions and solve social problems.

II Language and Literacy

This domain organizes the language and literacy skills needed to understand and convey meaning into five components: Listening, Speaking, Reading, Writing, and Research. Students acquire proficiency in this domain through extensive experience with language, print, and literature in a variety of contexts. Over time students learn to construct meaning,

Introducing the Work Sampling System

make connections to their own lives, and gradually begin to critically analyze and interpret what they hear, observe, and read. They begin to communicate effectively orally and in writing for different audiences and purposes.

III Mathematical Thinking

The focus of this domain is on children's approaches to mathematical thinking and problem-solving. Emphasis is placed on how students acquire and use strategies to perceive, understand, and solve mathematical problems. Mathematics is about patterns and relationships, and about seeking multiple solutions to problems. In this domain, the content of mathematics (concepts and procedures) is stressed, but the larger context of understanding and application (knowing and doing) is also of great importance.

IV Scientific Thinking

This domain addresses central areas of scientific investigation: inquiry skills, physical, life, and earth sciences. The processes of scientific investigation are emphasized throughout because process skills are embedded in—and fundamental to—all science instruction and content. The domain's focus is on how children actively investigate through observing, recording, describing, questioning, forming explanations, and drawing conclusions.

V Social Studies

Encompassing history, economics, citizenship, and geography, the domain of social studies emphasizes social and cultural understanding. Children acquire this understanding from personal experiences and from the experiences of others. As children study present day and historical topics, they learn about human interdependence and the relationships between people and their environment. Throughout social studies, children use a variety of skills, including conducting research, using oral and visual sources, solving problems systematically, and making informed decisions using the democratic process.

VI The Arts

The emphasis in this domain is on children's engagement with the arts (dance, dramatics, music, and fine arts), both actively and receptively, rather than mastery of skills and techniques related to particular artistic media. The components address two ideas: how children use the arts to express, represent, and integrate their experiences, and how children develop an understanding and appreciation for the arts. It focuses on how opportunities to use and appreciate the arts enable children to demonstrate what they know, expand their thinking, and make connections among the arts, culture, history, and other domains.

VII Physical Development

The emphasis in this domain is on physical development as an integral part of a child's well-being and educational growth. The components address gross motor skills, fine motor skills, and personal health and safety. A principal focus in gross motor is on children's ability to move in ways that demonstrate control, balance, and coordination. Fine motor skills are equally important in laying the groundwork for artistic expression, handwriting, and self-care skills. The third component addresses children's growing ability to understand and manage their personal health and safety.

Observing, Collecting, and Summarizing

The purpose of the Work Sampling System is to document and assess children's skills, knowledge, behavior, and accomplishments across a wide variety of classroom activities and areas of learning on multiple occasions. It consists of three complementary elements: 1) observations by teachers using Developmental Guidelines and Checklists; 2) collections of children's work in Portfolios; and 3) summaries of this information on Summary Reports.

One of the Work Sampling System's strengths is its systematic structure. It is based on collecting extensive information from multiple sources, and using all of this information collectively to make evaluative decisions about what children know and can do. In its reliance on *observing, collecting,* and *summarizing,* Work Sampling organizes the assessment process so that it is both comprehensive in scope and manageable for teachers and students. Teachers observe students, collect information, and summarize student performance on three occasions throughout the school year: in the fall, winter, and spring. The mechanisms for observing, collecting, and summarizing are as follows.

The **Developmental Guidelines** provide a framework for observation. They give teachers a set of observational criteria that are based on national standards and knowledge of child development. The Guidelines set forth developmentally appropriate expectations for children at each age/grade level. In using the Guidelines as the basis of their professional judgments, teachers in different settings make decisions about children's behavior, knowledge, and accomplishments using identical criteria. Teachers' observations are recorded on the **Developmental Checklists.**

Portfolios are purposeful collections of children's work that illustrate children's efforts, progress, and achievements. These collections are intended to display the individual nature and quality of children's work and progress over time. Work Sampling advocates a structured approach to portfolio collection through the collection of two types of work samples: *Core Items* and *Individualized Items.* Core Items are designed to show growth over time by representing an area of learning within a domain on three occasions during the school year. Individualized Items are designed to portray the unique characteristics of the child and to reflect work that integrates many domains of the curriculum. Children and teachers alike are involved in the design, selection, and evaluation of Portfolios.

Summary Reports are completed three times a year. Teachers combine information from the Developmental Checklists and Portfolios with their own knowledge of child development to make evaluative decisions about student performance and progress. They summarize their knowledge of the child as they make ratings and write brief comments describing the student's strengths and their own areas of concern. Summary Reports take the place of conventional report cards.

Work Sampling not only provides the teacher with clear criteria for evaluation but also incorporates the teacher's expertise and judgment. An evaluation system that does not dictate curriculum or instructional methods, it is designed for use with diverse groups of children, in a variety of settings. The Work Sampling System is a flexible framework for assessment that helps teachers structure their assessments systematically and that encourages teachers to devise techniques best suited to their styles, their students, and their contexts.

Summary

The three elements of the Work Sampling System form an integrated whole. Checklists record a student's growth in relationship to teacher expectations and national standards. Portfolios graphically display the texture and quality of the child's work, as well as his or her progress over time. Summary Reports integrate this information into a concise record that the student's family can understand and that administrators can use.

Work Sampling draws upon teachers' perceptions of students while informing, expanding, and structuring their perceptions. It assesses students' development and accomplishments—rather than their test-taking skills—in meaningful, curriculum-based activities. It enables children's unique learning styles to be recognized and nurtured, instead of rigidly classifying children as high- or low-achievers based on simplistic assessments. It enables families to become actively involved in the assessment process. And, finally, by objectively documenting what children learn and how teachers teach, the Work Sampling System provides for meaningful evaluation and genuine accountability.

CHAPTER 2

Developmental Guidelines and Checklists

A Structured Approach to Observation, Documentation, and Evaluation

This chapter explains the Work Sampling System's Developmental Guidelines and Checklists and is divided into three major sections:

PART I Understanding Guidelines and Checklists

PART II How to Use Guidelines and Checklists

PART III Frequently Asked Questions About Guidelines and Checklists

Overview of Guidelines and Checklists

What are they?	◆ **Developmental Guidelines** are a set of reasonable expectations used to evaluate student performance and achievement at different ages
	◆ **Developmental Checklists** are lists of grade-specific performance indicators that are described in the Developmental Guidelines and are used for summarizing and interpreting your observations

What are their purposes?

1 To focus observation on particular knowledge, skills, and behavior

2 To summarize, record, and interpret observations

3 To provide a set of criteria for observation and evaluation based on national standards of curriculum and child development research

4 To help plan appropriate curriculum and instruction

What are their features?

◆ **Grade-Level Guidelines** contain the Guidelines for a single age/grade level and are designed for efficient classroom use with Checklists

◆ **Omnibus Guidelines** present Guidelines for six grade levels side-by-side to show continuous progress of performance indicators

◆ Checklists list performance indicators for a single grade level and provide space to rate students on each indicator three times per year

How do I use Guidelines and Checklists?

Before the school year begins:

◆ Gain familiarity with the Guidelines for your age/grade level
◆ Extend your knowledge and understanding of observation
◆ Investigate and prepare observation methods and tools
◆ Set up an organized storage system

During each collection period:

◆ Plan, observe, and record
◆ Review Checklists periodically, making pencil ratings
◆ Talk with students about observation and expectations
◆ Apply what you learn to daily/weekly planning

Near the end of each collection period:

◆ Review preliminary ratings
◆ Make final ratings
◆ Identify examples for the Summary Reports

Related Materials

■ Reproducible Masters of Process Notes forms

■ Wall Charts of Performance Indicators

Part I **Understanding Guidelines and Checklists**

Children engage in many different classroom activities every day. They construct block buildings, participate in class meetings, solve problems using manipulatives, talk with their friends, and write in their journals. Systematic observation of students' behavior, actions, and language enables you, the teacher, to gather information about children's skills and knowledge. For example, a block structure may show a child's understanding of symmetry and sense of order. Comments during a class meeting may reveal a child's understanding of human similarities and differences. A child's solution to a math problem may demonstrate how she uses problem-solving strategies.

Using observational assessment effectively requires that you know what to look for, how to recognize features of children's learning at different ages, and the criteria to use to evaluate students fairly and reliably. The Work Sampling System Developmental Guidelines outline developmentally appropriate expectations for students and help you focus your observations on significant skills, knowledge, and behaviors. They incorporate extensive research into national, state, and local standards and reflect widely-accepted expectations for children of different ages.

Effective observational assessment also requires an organizational tool that helps you manage your observations. The Developmental Checklist helps you organize what you have observed (the content of your observations) and your interpretations or evaluations. Without a Checklist, it is nearly impossible to focus on and remember the actions, behaviors, and language of 20 or 30 students for six or eight hours a day. The Checklist enables you to document and evaluate students' classroom activities by creating a detailed profile of each child's skills, knowledge, and behaviors.

Together, the Work Sampling System Guidelines and Checklists provide a framework for observation, documentation, and evaluation. They can help you focus on students you do not yet know very well; remind you to observe all areas of your curriculum; assist you in determining when your instructional strategies are working and when they are not; and help you chart children's continuous progress in order to plan curriculum that reflects individual growth and change.

Purposes of Guidelines and Checklists

1   **To focus observation.** Guidelines and Checklists direct your attention to students' acquisition of particular knowledge, skills, and behaviors. The Guidelines and Checklists list and describe what you should look for at particular ages or grade levels.

2   **To summarize, record, and interpret observations.** Over a period of some months you will collect many observational records. Periodically, you review these records and give meaning to them, look for patterns, and assess what you know and do not know about each child. Every time you review and rate a student using the Checklist, you transfer a mass of observational data into a more manageable profile of the child's knowledge, skills, and behaviors.

3   **To provide valid criteria for evaluation.** The Guidelines describe reasonable expectations for children within a particular year so that teachers know what to expect of children at a given age or grade. These criteria, or standards, are based on information from numerous national curriculum groups, state and local scope and sequences, and child development research. A complete list of references is available in each volume of the ***Omnibus Guidelines.*** In addition, the Guidelines reflect the provisions of the National Education Goals Panel and the principles of Developmentally Appropriate Practices as defined by the National Association for the Education of Young Children. When you use these criteria, your evaluations of children will be more reliable and valid than when you use individual, possibly inaccurate, ideas about what students should be able to do at different ages.

4   **To support curriculum and instruction.** Repeated review of the Guidelines is an excellent way to ensure that you are addressing all aspects of the curriculum in your classroom. Periodic review of children's Checklists ensures that some children are not being overlooked or missing out on instructional opportunities. This type of ongoing monitoring of students' performance can remind you to use the information you acquire about children's skills and knowledge to plan and individualize instruction.

Organization and Structure of Guidelines and Checklists

The Guidelines and Checklists identify and describe a set of developmentally appropriate skills, knowledge, and behaviors for each age/grade level across the seven Work Sampling domains. They are organized into domains, functional components, and performance indicators.

DOMAIN   A **domain** is defined as a broad area of a child's growth and learning. The following seven domains appear throughout all age/grade levels covered by the Work Sampling System:

◆ Personal and Social Development
◆ Language and Literacy
◆ Mathematical Thinking
◆ Scientific Thinking
◆ Social Studies
◆ The Arts
◆ Physical Development & Health

FUNCTIONAL COMPONENT   Each domain is divided into sub-sets or **functional components.** For example, the domain of Mathematical Thinking is composed of the following functional components:

◆ Mathematical processes
◆ Number and operations
◆ Patterns and functions
◆ Geometry and spatial relations
◆ Measurement
◆ Data collection and probability (appears only in grades K–5)

Within each domain, most functional components appear throughout all eight age/grade levels of the Work Sampling System. Some components, however, are appropriate only at particular grade levels. For example, in the domain of Mathematical Thinking, the component of data collection and probability appears only in grades K–5 because it is not developmentally appropriate for three and four year olds. In other cases, components are introduced in order to highlight their curricular importance at certain grade levels. For example, the component of listening in the domain of Language and Literacy goes from three indicators in P3–K to only one indicator in grades 3–5.

PERFORMANCE INDICATOR   Finally, each functional component is composed of a set of **performance indicators.** Performance indicators state the skills,

Understanding Guidelines and Checklists

behaviors, attitudes, and accomplishments you will be teaching and assessing in the classroom. Performance indicators and the expectations described for them are specific to each grade level, changing gradually from grade to grade. Figure 1 shows the relationship among domain, functional components, and performance indicators for Language and Literacy. The performance indicators shown are from the first-grade Guidelines.

FIGURE 1
Relationship of domain, functional components, and performance indicators for Language and Literacy, first grade

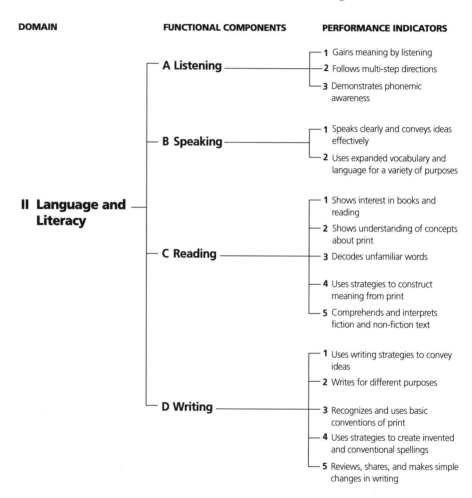

DOMAIN	FUNCTIONAL COMPONENTS	PERFORMANCE INDICATORS
	A Listening	1 Gains meaning by listening
		2 Follows multi-step directions
		3 Demonstrates phonemic awareness
	B Speaking	1 Speaks clearly and conveys ideas effectively
		2 Uses expanded vocabulary and language for a variety of purposes
II Language and Literacy	**C Reading**	1 Shows interest in books and reading
		2 Shows understanding of concepts about print
		3 Decodes unfamiliar words
		4 Uses strategies to construct meaning from print
		5 Comprehends and interprets fiction and non-fiction text
	D Writing	1 Uses writing strategies to convey ideas
		2 Writes for different purposes
		3 Recognizes and uses basic conventions of print
		4 Uses strategies to create invented and conventional spellings
		5 Reviews, shares, and makes simple changes in writing

Grade-Level Developmental Guidelines

Each of the Work Sampling System's eight grade-level Developmental Guidelines (age 3 to grade 5) provide an overall view of what children can be expected to learn each year. Each performance indicator is elaborated with a ***rationale*** and several ***examples.*** The rationale explains the meaning of and justification for the performance indicator and briefly outlines reasonable expectations for children at a given age or grade.

The three to five curriculum-embedded examples that follow each rationale show several ways children might demonstrate the skill, knowledge, or behavior within the context of the classroom. It is important to remember that these are only examples. Children have many ways of showing us what they know and can do. These examples are intended as a reminder of this diversity and as a catalyst for thinking about how individual children demonstrate their learning. You should not expect to see children perform all (or even any) of the examples given. Rather, the examples illustrate and give additional meaning to the performance indicators so that they will be interpreted similarly in different classrooms by different teachers.

The Developmental Guidelines are *criterion-referenced.* This means that a student's work is compared to specific criteria in each domain rather than to other students' work. During the pilot years of the Work Sampling project, teachers, curriculum specialists, and administrators from around the country contributed extensively to shaping the content of the Guidelines.

The domain is identified, followed by a brief description

Components are labeled with letters

Performance indicators are listed numerically after component names (indicator text matches that used on the Checklist)

Each indicator is followed by a detailed rationale that describes age/grade-level expectations

Each indicator also includes several examples that illustrate some ways children might demonstrate the indicator in daily classroom activities

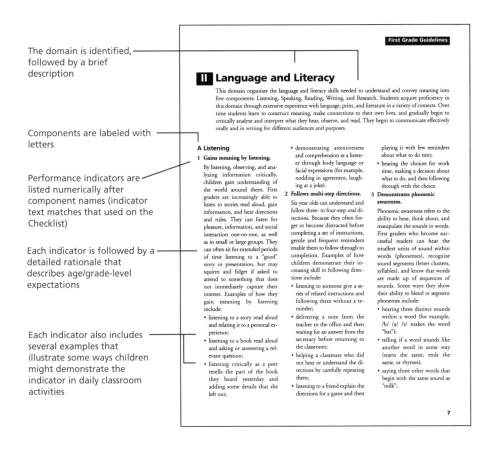

First Grade Guidelines

II Language and Literacy

This domain organizes the language and literacy skills needed to understand and convey meaning into five components: Listening, Speaking, Reading, Writing, and Research. Students acquire proficiency in this domain through extensive experience with language, print, and literature in a variety of contexts. Over time students learn to construct meaning, make connections to their own lives, and gradually begin to critically analyze and interpret what they hear, observe, and read. They begin to communicate effectively orally and in writing for different audiences and purposes.

A Listening

1 Gains meaning by listening.

By listening, observing, and analyzing information critically, children gain understanding of the world around them. First graders are increasingly able to listen to stories read aloud, gain information, and hear directions and rules. They can listen for pleasure, information, and social interaction one-on-one, as well as in small or large groups. They can often sit for extended periods of time listening to a "good" story or presentation, but may squirm and fidget if asked to attend to something that does not immediately capture their interest. Examples of how they gain meaning by listening include:

• listening to a story read aloud and relating it to a personal experience;

• listening to a book read aloud and asking or answering a relevant question;

• listening critically as a peer retells the part of the book they heard yesterday and adding some details that she left out;

• demonstrating attentiveness and comprehension as a listener through body language or facial expressions (for example, nodding in agreement, laughing at a joke).

2 Follows multi-step directions.

Six year olds can understand and follow three- to four-step oral directions. Because they often forget or become distracted before completing a set of instructions, gentle and frequent reminders enable them to follow through to completion. Examples of how children demonstrate their increasing skill in following directions include:

• listening to someone give a series of related instructions and following them without a reminder;

• delivering a note from the teacher to the office and then waiting for an answer from the secretary before returning to the classroom;

• helping a classmate who did not hear or understand the directions by carefully repeating them;

• listening to a friend explain the directions for a game and then

playing it with few reminders about what to do next;

• hearing the choices for work time, making a decision about what to do, and then following through with the choice.

3 Demonstrates phonemic awareness.

Phonemic awareness refers to the ability to hear, think about, and manipulate the sounds in words. First graders who become successful readers can hear the smallest units of sound within words (phonemes), recognize sound segments (letter clusters, syllables), and know that words are made up of sequences of sounds. Some ways they show their ability to blend or segment phonemes include:

• hearing three distinct sounds within a word (for example, /b/ /a/ /t/ makes the word "bat");

• telling if a word sounds like another word in some way (starts the same, ends the same, or rhymes);

• saying three other words that begin with the same sound as "milk";

7

Developmental Checklists

Developmental Checklists are double-page spreads showing all the domains, components, and performance indicators for a single age/grade level. Using a Checklist for each student, you review your observational data, make an interpretation, and then make evaluative ratings. This process is completed formally three times during the year (fall, winter, and spring). You rate each indicator using the ratings "Not Yet," "In Process," or "Proficient." These ratings will be discussed more fully later in this chapter (see page 42).

Identifying information about the child is along the side

Domain names appear in black

Component names appear in black type on a colored bar

Indicators are listed for each component

Each indicator includes a page reference keyed to the grade-level Guidelines

Each indicator includes space to make one of three ratings ("Not Yet," "In Process," "Proficient") during the fall, winter, and spring (F, W, S)

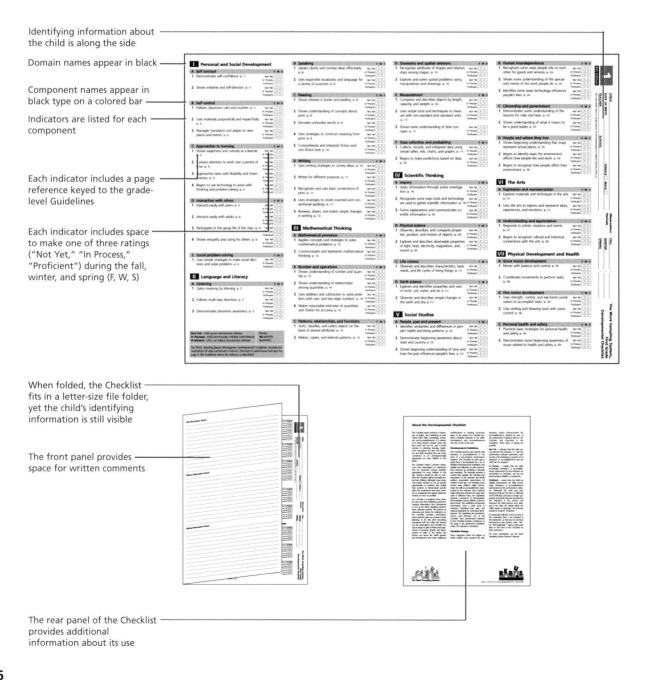

When folded, the Checklist fits in a letter-size file folder, yet the child's identifying information is still visible

The front panel provides space for written comments

The rear panel of the Checklist provides additional information about its use

Along the right hand edge of the Checklist, there is space for identifying information about the child and the dates of the collection period. Information on the back cover of the Checklist describes the Guidelines and Checklist and explains the ratings. This information is useful when a student transfers to a new school where teachers are unfamiliar with Work Sampling. The front cover of the Checklist includes space for you to record optional comments.

Omnibus Guidelines

To illustrate and highlight the continuum of development, the Omnibus Guidelines combines six levels of the individual grade-level Guidelines into a single volume. Each pair of facing pages shows the changes over time in a set of related performance indicators. There are two volumes of the Omnibus Guidelines:

◆ Vol. 1: Preschool–Third Grade
◆ Vol. 2: Kindergarten–Fifth Grade

Many performance indicators appear consistently throughout all age/grade levels. However, in some cases performance indicators do not appear at each age/grade level. This may occur for one of several reasons.

◆ Sometimes a skill is not developmentally appropriate for a particular age/grade level. For example, in the component of Data Collection and Probability within the domain of Mathematical Thinking, the first performance indicator at the Kindergarten level is "Begins to collect data and make records using lists or graphs." However, this skill is not an age-appropriate expectation for three or four year olds. Therefore, in these locations in the Omnibus, you will see the text "Not expected at this age/grade level."

◆ In some cases, although a skill is not assessed at a particular age/grade level because it is not yet age-appropriate, it is suitable to expect that children will have begun to work on related skills. When this is the case, reference is made to related indicators (coded in terms of Domain, Component, and Indicator). For example, in the component of Research within the domain of Language and Literacy, while there is no comparable indicator for three and four year olds (because doing research is not a reasonable expectation for children this age), at kindergarten, first, and second grades the reader is referred to other indicators that draw upon skills related to research. In second grade, the text reads "See IC4: Uses technology to assist with thinking and problem solving, IIC5: Reads for varied purposes, and II D2: Writes for different purposes in different formats." Experience with these related

Understanding Guidelines and Checklists

indicators prepares children for doing research in a more formal way at third grade.

♦ Sometimes a performance indicator does not appear at an age/grade level because it is no longer a unique curricular focus, but is embedded within another indicator. For example, in the component of Number and Operations within the domain of Mathematical Thinking, the second indicator at first grade is "Shows understanding of relationships among quantities." However, from second through fifth grade the text says "See IIIB1: "Shows understanding of number, quantities, and their relationships." This is meant to suggest that at these age/grade levels, understanding of relationships among quantities is included in indicator IIIB1.

Each domain appears in the Omnibus Guidelines in its own section and begins with a brief description

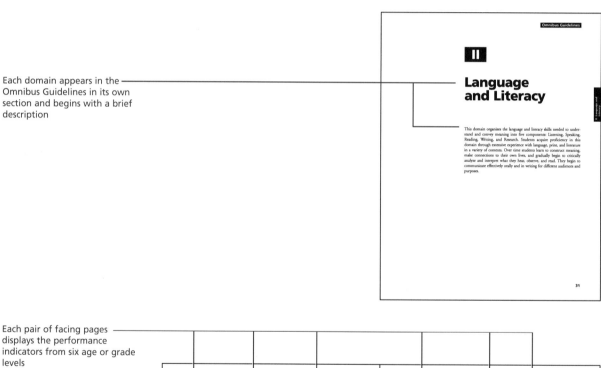

Each pair of facing pages displays the performance indicators from six age or grade levels

Functional component

Each indicator is followed by the same rationale and examples that appear in the grade-level Guidelines

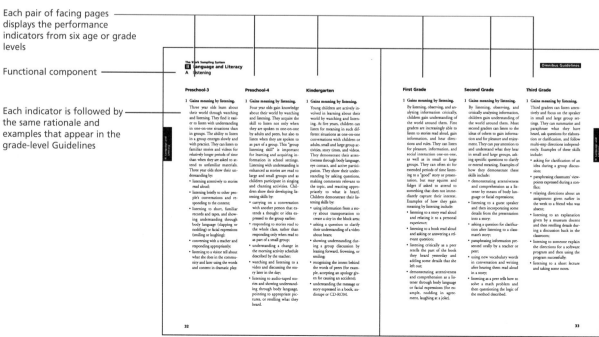

Part II How to Use Guidelines and Checklists

Using Guidelines and Checklists involves different tasks at different times of the school year, all directed toward making observation and recording an integral part of your classroom life.

Guidelines and Checklist Timeline

The timeline depicts the schedule for activities associated with the Guidelines and Checklist for a single collection period.

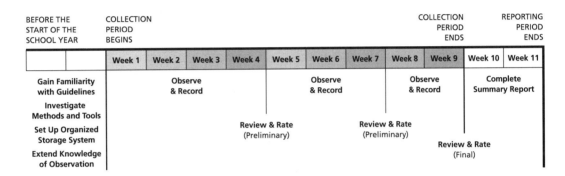

- ◆ **Before** the school year begins, four preparatory steps will require your time and attention, including becoming familiar with the Guidelines and the process of observation, and setting up organizational and observational systems.

- ◆ **During** each collection period, you maintain routines of observing and recording, periodically reviewing students' Checklists so that your observations stay focused and your curriculum is responsive to each student.

- ◆ **Near the end** of each collection period, you turn your attention to summarizing your knowledge about students and to identifying examples for Summary Reports.

Before the School Year Begins

Before the children arrive in the fall, we recommend that you begin the following activities. These are significant tasks when you are learning to use Work Sampling System, but will require less of your time after the first year of implementation.

- Gain familiarity with the Guidelines.

- Extend your knowledge and understanding of observation.

- Investigate and prepare observation methods and tools.

- Set up an organized storage system.

Gain Familiarity with the Guidelines

Familiarizing yourself with the Guidelines for your age/grade level is a first step to integrating Work Sampling into your life as a teacher. Once familiar with the Guidelines, you can plan curriculum and instruction with confidence that you have the information needed to assess your students. Many teachers report that their understanding of the Guidelines helps them to be more focused in their curriculum planning. As you assess students using observation, knowing the Guidelines will make it easier to decide what to look for and pay attention to. You develop clearer expectations for students, leading to greater consistency in your observations and judgments about children. There are many ways to become more familiar with the Guidelines. We suggest these four:

- Read one domain at a time
- Discuss the Guidelines with colleagues
- Add your own examples
- Use the Wall Chart

READ ONE DOMAIN AT A TIME Reading and studying the Guidelines repeatedly is the primary way to become familiar with them. One or two complete readings can be followed by focusing on one domain at a time until you feel comfortable with the content. Teachers have invented many unique ways of keeping the Guidelines in the forefront of their minds. A common approach is to read them as you do weekly curriculum planning.

DISCUSS THE GUIDELINES WITH COLLEAGES Discussing the Guidelines with colleagues offers many benefits. Conversation about the Guidelines leads to a shared understanding of the contents of each domain. Teachers of different grade levels gain an appreciation for the subtle developmental changes that occur as children grow. Moreover you will better recognize and appreciate commonalities among curricula at different age/grade levels. A fifth-grade teacher, for example, may come to recognize that early experiences with math manipulatives lay the groundwork for more sophisticated understanding of numerical concepts and operations.

Groups of teachers often study each domain collectively and compare their own local or state curriculum guides with the Work Sampling Guidelines. Another benefit of discussing the Guidelines with colleagues is that the group will develop a more consistent understanding of expectations for children; Checklist ratings from teacher to teacher will become more consistent and reliable. These collegial conversations are crucial when an entire school or system is working to implement Work Sampling.

ADD YOUR OWN EXAMPLES Adding examples of your own to those listed in the Guidelines will help you internalize the performance indicators and rationales and make them more useful in your classroom. Remember that the examples listed are not comprehensive. They show only some of the ways that children demonstrate their knowledge and skills. One way that teachers have personalized the Work Sampling Guidelines is by adding examples that reflect the cultural backgrounds of the students in their setting. We encourage you to add examples from your students that show how they demonstrate their knowledge and skills.

USE THE WALL CHART Using the Wall Chart of Performance Indicators that accompanies each set of grade-level Guidelines is a convenient way to keep the domains, functional components, and performance indicators in your frame of reference. Post it in a place where you, students, and families can see and refer to it easily. It is a way of saying, "This is what is important to learn in this classroom. These are the things I teach, and these are the things I expect children to learn."

Extend Your Knowledge and Understanding of Observation

Before the school year begins, teachers new to Work Sampling can prepare themselves to use the Guidelines and Checklists by becoming knowledgeable about the processes of observation and recording. These processes are essential to using the Work Sampling System successfully, and especially to using Guidelines and Checklists. Observation provides the evidence that you will use to support your evaluations of students.

In this section, we will discuss five key ideas:

♦ Definition of observation
♦ What you can learn from observing children
♦ Why classroom-based and ongoing observation is important
♦ Reasons for recording observation
♦ Differentiating between fact and interpretation

DEFINITION OF OBSERVATION Observation is defined as watching or regarding with attention or purpose in order to see or learn something. Observation allows us to learn about children by carefully watching them, listening to them, and studying their work. The following are some ways that you can observe students to learn more about them:

♦ ask questions that encourage them to describe their thinking

♦ listen to them as they describe how they made decisions and solved problems

♦ watch them as they play and work with materials and other children

♦ hold conferences with them about their work

♦ listen as they talk with others informally and during group discussions

♦ study their work (e.g., projects, writing, drawings, reports, learning logs, journals)

WHAT YOU CAN LEARN FROM OBSERVING CHILDREN Children tell us a great deal about who they are, what they know, and how they think by their actions and language. Careful observation over time can reveal important information about children's individual strengths and difficulties. It can also reveal not only what children know but how they came to know it—their process of thinking and learning. Observation helps you answer myriad questions you have about each student:

♦ How does this child approach tasks?

♦ How does this child use language to express thinking?

♦ What is this child's typical method of expression (e.g., drama, drawing, verbal language, body language)?

♦ How does this child use materials?

♦ How does this child engage in social tasks with others?

The answers to these questions are most readily obtained from classroom-based observation.

WHY CLASSROOM-BASED AND ONGOING OBSERVATION IS IMPORTANT Observational assessment gives a representative and complete view of a child because it is classroom-based and ongoing. Because classroom observation occurs in a context that is familiar and comfortable for the child, you are likely to acquire an accurate picture of this child as a learner. Children's behavior is not influenced by "test anxiety" or misrepresented because the child misunderstands the directions to a task, as can happen with other types of assessment. The information you collect from observation reveals not only whether or not the child solved a problem correctly, but also illustrates the manner in which the child approached the task and solved the problem.

Moreover, observation is a valid way to assess children. It provides you with repeated opportunities to witness children practicing skills, demonstrating knowledge, and exhibiting behaviors in real—not simulated—learning activities. For example, one day you might photograph the castle a preschool student constructed in the block area. On another day, you might draw a quick sketch of the pattern block design she made in the math center. On yet a third occasion, you might save the collage she made by gluing shapes into a design. When you are ready to evaluate her performance and progress, your judgments about her sense of balance and symmetry will be based on these and many other observations rather than on a single example of her work.

REASONS FOR RECORDING OBSERVATIONS Recording your observations of children is important for at least four reasons. First, records help you remember and keep track of what children know and can do. Second, your documented observations provide the evidence to support your evaluations of children. Third, observations recorded over time enable you to see patterns in children's behaviors and their approach to learning. These patterns are often evident to us only when we reflect on collections of observational notes. Finally, records of observations will help you plan instructional activities that are responsive to children's interests, strengths and needs.

DIFFERENTIATING BETWEEN FACT AND INTERPRETATION Documenting observations effectively requires that you differentiate between what you actually see and hear and your own opinions and interpretations of these actions.

How to Use Guidelines and Checklists

Language that describes the actions of children at work and play is more informative than words that convey judgment. For example, Jeremy, a first-grader, is working with Cuisenaire rods to solve a series of math problems. Examples 1 and 2 show how two teachers might document his work.

EXAMPLE 1 11/4 10 a.m.—Jeremy is scattered and too distracted to do his work.

EXAMPLE 2 11/4 10 a.m.—Jeremy has worked on math for 15 min—completed one problem of five. Builds with rods. Talks continually w/others about baseball. Walked to and from pencil sharpener and water fountain many times.

Although both records convey that Jeremy is not actually completing his math work, the first gives only the teacher's impressions. The second record describes Jeremy's actions and provides enough detailed information to explain why he is not completing his work. It allows you to ask questions about how to support Jeremy's success as a learner: Is Jeremy distracted? Is his interest in baseball absorbing his attention? Would it help to engage Jeremy's interest by relating the math problems to baseball? Would he be more successful if he could work collaboratively on the problems with others? Questions and interpretations/impressions can be included in the documentation of an observation, but should be clearly identified as such. As shown in Example 3, some teachers divide their records into two parts. On one side they write observations. On the other side they note questions, concerns, and interpretations of behavior.

Notes	Interpretations
11/4: 10 a.m. Jeremy has worked on math for 15 min—completed one problem of five. Builds with rods. Talks continually w/others about baseball. Walked to and from pencil sharpener and water fountain many times.	Distracted? Why?

Investigate and Prepare Observation Methods and Tools

Although you have experience informally observing your students, observing systematically and recording your observations may be less familiar to you. Before you begin to observe and record we encourage you to consider three issues:

- The context for observation
- How to record observational information
- Tools for recording observations

The Context for Observation

Teachers observe and record children's learning in three different situations:

♦ Participating in the action
♦ Stepping out of the action
♦ Reflecting on the action after the fact

PARTICIPATING IN THE ACTION   As a teacher, you are typically in the midst of classroom action. You might be conferring with a single student, guiding a small group through a lesson, or having a discussion with the entire class. At the same time, you are watching children, listening to them, taking mental notes about who is working with whom, and asking questions that extend children's thinking. Clearly, you are gathering a wealth of information as you interact in the classroom. Perhaps the biggest challenge of using the Work Sampling System is finding effective, efficient methods to create a written record of important information so that you do not have to rely solely on memory. A thorough discussion of the options available for recording your observations begins on page 28.

It is essential to establish realistic expectations about how much is possible to record as you observe in the action. You should not expect to meaningfully record every behavior or word. The records you make may seem brief and lacking in detail compared to the records you make when you step out of the action or reflect on the action at a later time. When you are working or talking with one child, you may be able to record sentence-length comments and anecdotal notes. But when you are leading a class discussion or working with a group of children, you have to limit your recording to shorthand notes or checkmarks and other symbols that have meaning to you.

Figure 2 shows how a third grade teacher documented her observations when observing during the action. This teacher was leading a class discussion about a conflict that occurred on the playground. During the discussion she noted the students who participated and when relevant, she added a quick comment describing their participation.

How to Use Guidelines and Checklists

FIGURE 2
Teacher-created matrix
allows the teacher to
monitor children's
participation during
class discussions

Class Meeting Observations   Date: _4/12/99_

Topic: _Discuss playground conflict/soccer_

NOTE: P   -participated somewhat
Nick and Victor had argument   PA -participated actively
Nick requested the meeting   Q   -quiet

Names		Comments and Reflections
Alex	PA	V and N argued last year
Bonita	P	"this happens w/ other kids too" suggested 2 play areas
Carla	Q	
Collin	P	
Devan	PA	related personal stories
Ekker	P	sug. N & V write apology ltrs.
Frank	PA	asked N & V qstns for details
Horace	abs	
Ingrid	Q	
Kate	PA	volunteered as note taker
Lara	P	"Nick, maybe you and Victor should play in different games"
Marcus	PA	
Nick	PA	told conflict clearly - owned responsibility
Paul	Q	seemed focused -
Rajit	P	
Roxanne	PA	begins all w/ well, I think... many comments not related
Shayna	P	
Trina	abs	
Victor	P	hesitant to speak much - shrugs w/ ideas, I'll try it...to L's idea

Whether you are working with a single child or a group, planning and focusing are important keys to successful observational recording. Thinking ahead of time about the purpose of an activity and what you expect to observe will help you devise recording methods and tools that will facilitate the observation process.

STEPPING OUT OF THE ACTION   Stepping out of the action to observe is an extremely effective way to learn about children. It allows you to focus on one child at a time. You may watch how the child interacts with others or how the child approaches a learning task. When you are in the midst of classroom action, you do many things simultaneously—motivating children, communicating information, keeping children engaged, providing materials, and teaching skills. By stepping out of the action, however, you can suspend these tasks for a few moments and be completely observant of the activities around you.

Stepping out of the action to observe does not require large amounts of time. Take three to five minutes to step back and observe one or two children. You will be surprised by how much data you can collect in a short time. Rather than being overly ambitious and setting aside large amounts of time, it is more effective to develop the habit of observing out of the action for just a few minutes three or four times each week. Example 4 shows anecdotal notes taken by a preschool teacher while stepping out of the action:

EXAMPLE 4

4/6 Recci: Dramatic Play
As I approach the house area, Recci is playing with the doctor's kit. He silently administers oxygen to a doll, takes its temperature, and tests its reflexes. He uses the stethoscope and says, "I can hear his heart for real." He uses the blood pressure cuff, asking for help from Lisa in attaching it to the doll's arm.

Iola enters the house area, and asks Lisa who is also playing in the house, "Who are you being?" She replies, "Doctor." Iola then asks Recci. He says, "A nurse." Iola asks, "What can I be?" Recci says, "You're the mom." He hands her the doll and gives the doll a shot. He says, "Ouch!"

REFLECTING ON THE ACTION AFTER THE FACT Reflecting after the fact suggests two different types of teacher actions. The first involves taking a moment after an event occurs or at the end of the day to document what transpired. The second entails reviewing children's work as a way to reflect on their learning.

You probably make mental notes in the midst of classroom action all the time. By taking a few minutes during a break in the day (for example, during rest time, quiet reading, or journal time) or at the end of a day or week, you can record some notes about events that occurred. Recall a math period and some of the strategies children used, or a discussion and some comments children made. It is both unnecessary and unrealistic to think about recording something about every child or every event in the day. However, when you get in the habit of making a few notes about one or two children or events each day or every few days, these records add up to a substantial written record of what children know and can do.

When you review children's work at the end of the day or week, the notes you make about children's learning inform the Checklist. What does the work show? What skills and knowledge are expressed in the work? Does the work reflect the assignment? Looking at children's work also will remind you of the context in which the work was created. What was the child doing? What was the activity? How did the child approach the task? Did the child show interest in the task? What else was going on in the classroom at that time? By jotting down these reflections you will have valuable information to help you complete the Checklist. These notes will

How to Use Guidelines and Checklists

also come in handy when you write Summary Reports and prepare for conferences. Reviewing a domain of the Guidelines or Checklist prior to looking at children's work can help to focus your reflection. Example 5 illustrates a preschool teacher's reflection after the fact.

EXAMPLE 5

> Nkrumah is currently working on controlling the mouse on the computer. He understands that he needs to put the cursor arrow on an object to activate it, but has difficulty coordinating movements to do so. When using the keyboard, he presses the screen occasionally instead of pressing a key.

How to Record Observational Information

RECORDING METHODS Teachers find many ways to record observational data in the classroom. Each technique makes different demands on a teacher's time and energy, and each provides a different type of information. Most teachers find that they use multiple methods. Deciding upon methods to use depends on the type of information you are trying to capture and the amount of observation time you have during classroom activities.

For example, if you are interested in how a child thinks, solves problems, uses materials, and interacts with others, select a method that allows for some descriptive writing. On the other hand, if you simply want to know whether a child is speaking during class meetings or the materials a child chooses during math time or the colors a child names accurately, select a method that involves checking or tallying.

When you are working with one child, in a reading or writing conference for example, you are able to take notes that describe what the child is doing quite clearly. However, when you are circulating around the classroom guiding children's involvement in a science project, making quick checkmarks on a matrix is easier to manage.

Selecting a documentation method depends on several factors: what you want to learn, the activities children are engaged in, and your responsibilities at the time of observation. Descriptions and samples of several different recording methods follow.

♦ **Brief notes** are quick written records that serve as a reminder of observed events. In Example 6, the teacher jotted a brief note that described how R.L., a third grader, showed his understanding of a story through his participation in his reading group.

EXAMPLE 6

1/15 R.L.
skit of Mrs. BEF w/TW, GK, ES
org. grp into roles
R acted w/express—phys + verb
repeated reminders to grp that seq. of skit follow story

♦ **Anecdotal notes** are more detailed narrative accounts that describe a particular event factually. Often they are created by jotting down brief notes and adding details later. They provide rich, detailed information. Example 7 is an anecdotal record from a preschool teacher who stepped out of the action to observe Dwight's participation in a cooking activity.

EXAMPLE 7

11/5 Dwight
Dwight is at the table cooking cranberries with Brian and Nancy (assistant). He is seated on his chair leaning over the table with his elbows on his chin. His lips are pursed and he is frowning a little bit. He watches. B stirs with the wooden spoon. D says, "I see smoke." Suger, water, and cranberries are heating on the hot plate. N says, "This is steam, Dwight. Not smoke." D says, giggling, "Brian that steam's getting on your face." He sits up on his knees, his two hands on the table. "I want to stir now. I want steam in my face." He takes the spoon and begins to stir, putting his face near the pot.

♦ **Running records** are detailed narrative accounts of behavior recorded in a sequential manner, just as it happens. They include all behavior that occurs within a given time frame. Like anecdotal notes, they provide rich information, but require you to step out of the action.

EXAMPLE 8

Nikki and Josepha are standing side-by-side at the water table, Josepha is pouring water from a cup measure into a small-mouthed bottle. Much of the water spills into the water table instead of going into the bottle. Nikki gives Josepha a funnel saying, "Use this so the water won't leak out of the bottle." Josepha takes it and puts it onto the top of the bottle; it's too big to fit down into the bottle. She wraps her right fist around the seam between the funnel and the bottle and continues to pour with her left hand. Nikki watches. After four more cupfuls, crouches down and looks on the shelf under the table. He finds a bottle with a wider mouth and brings it up, saying to Josepha, "The funnel will definitely fit in this one and then you can use both of your hands."

Interpretation: Nikki—expressive language, problem solving

Josepha—works silently, exploring

♦ **Rating scales** are tools that indicate the degree to which a student possesses a certain skill (Figure 3).

How to Use Guidelines and Checklists

FIGURE 3

Simple check marks are
sufficient to record
detailed information
using rating scales

Child: _Tony_____ Date: _2/16/00_____ Time: _2:00 PM_

Observer: _Mrs. R._____

Behavior	Rating			
	Always	Usually	Never	N/A
Makes contribution to discussion		✓		
Contributions relevant to topic			✓	
Looks at person speaking	✓			
Asks questions of other contributors	✓			

♦ **Matrices** provide a way to write very brief notes or make a simple rating of a skill or set of skills for a few children or for the entire class. Names of students are listed on the left-hand side of a page. Specific skills, concepts, or behaviors are listed across the top. Figure 4 illustrates a matrix created by a kindergarten teacher for use during small group activities. She fills in children's names and the skills she plans to observe during the activity. In this example she added some notes below the matrix.

FIGURE 4

The teacher created this
matrix to be used for
observations during
group activities

Math Activity: _Spin a Step_____   Date: _12/18/99_____

I -Independently
H -with help
N -no

Names	Shows interest in the game	Follows rules	Plays cooperatively	Maintains focus	Counts accurately	Adds to solve problem
Ben	I	H	H*	I	I	I
Elise	H	I	I	H	I	H*
George	N	H	H	N*	H	H
Patsy	I	I	I	I	H*	N*

Notes:

Ben didn't want to give up the spinner when it was the next person's turn
Held it, kept spinning it, put it on the floor

Elise read the numbers on spinner, moved correct # of spaces, needed cubes to do addition

George wandered off between turns; said I hate this game when the spinner landed on a number he couldn't use

Patsy needs practice with numbers to be successful w/game. Others gave her help

♦ **Tallies** are used to count the instances of a particular behavior or event during a predetermined time interval. Figure 5 shows an example of how a kindergarten teacher used a tally to record children's choices during the course of a week. Each week she monitored the activities of five children during "free choice time." Each day of the week she noted the choice the child made at the beginning of the period. If they moved to another choice, she noted it with an additional mark in a different column. The information she gathered from this documentation method helped her learn about children's interests and their willingness to select different activities within the classroom. She used this information to make instructional decisions that build on and extend children's interests.

FIGURE 5
A tally provides an efficient method for recording children's choices

Choice Record

Week of: 4/8–12

Names	Blocks	Table Toys	Art	Computer	Dram. Play	Writing Ctr	Library
Annie	I			II	III		
Brian		P / I	PPP / III				II
Maya	II		C / I	I		II	I
Shayguan			DCC / III	I	II		
Tyrell	III	LL / II		II			

L - Lego   D - Draw
M - Math manip   p - Paint
P - Puzzles   C - Collage

♦ **Time samplings** are used to record the frequency of a behavior over time. Time samplings can be helpful when you need very specific information about a particular aspect of a child's behavior. Figure 6 illustrates how a teacher used a time sampling to monitor a student's ability to sustain attention on a task. She will use the information she gains from this documentation method to help establish a behavior plan for the child.

FIGURE 6
A time sampling helps teachers monitor a student's abilities

Time Sample

Child: Samantha   Date: 3/12   Time: 2:00 PM

Activity: Group Project Work

1:00	1:05	1:10	1:15	1:20	1:25	1:30
OT	I	OT	OT	I	I	I

I – Involved (focused on activity, working with others on the task, contributing to the group's work)
OT – Off task (wandering around the room, engaging with others unrelated to the task, sitting alone and not working)

♦ **Diagrams, sketches, and photographs** capture the details of certain types of activities and projects, yet do not require lengthy writing. Older students can create these types of records themselves. In Figure 7, Ms. Q. sketched Oliver's response to the house building task.

How to Use Guidelines and Checklists

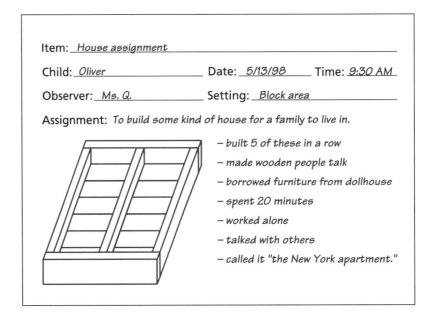

Item: _House assignment_

Child: _Oliver_   Date: _5/13/98_   Time: _9:30 AM_

Observer: _Ms. Q._   Setting: _Block area_

Assignment: _To build some kind of house for a family to live in._

– built 5 of these in a row

– made wooden people talk

– borrowed furniture from dollhouse

– spent 20 minutes

– worked alone

– talked with others

– called it "the New York apartment."

♦ **Audiotapes and videotapes** are excellent ways to capture children's language. Skits, puppet shows, story telling, and reading aloud lend themselves to this method of documentation.

TOOLS FOR RECORDING OBSERVATIONS   Depending on the recording methods you choose, you will need a variety of tools to carry out your observations efficiently and effectively. The possibilities range from simple materials like note pads and index cards to sophisticated electronic devices. It is critical to think ahead and prepare what you are apt to need so your tools are ready once you begin your observations. Consider the following possibilities:

♦ **Mailing labels**   Attach a strip or sheet of labels to a clipboard. After jotting notes on a label, remove it and put it in the child's Teacher File. These labels can also be pre-printed and dated using a computer. (Teacher Files are described beginning on page 38.)

♦ **Legal pads**   Use large ones to accommodate a whole class list or place smaller ones in several key locations around the classroom so there is always one nearby. Attach a pen or pencil to the pad. Figure 8 shows how one teacher modified a legal pad to fit her observation needs.

FIGURE 8
A teacher-created method for recording observations over time. The left margins of all pages but the last are cut away. The class list is written on the last page. Each day, a new page is used to record observations.

♦ **Index cards** Attach a card for each child to a file folder with tape so that the cards overlap. Alternatively, color-code them by domain and store on a ring or file them in a box.

♦ **Calendars** Some teachers keep a calendar for each month for each child on a ring or in a notebook. They keep daily notes on as many children as possible and then, at the end of a month, file the calendar in each child's Teacher File. Weekly calendars and large desk calendars have also been used for recording observations.

♦ **Butcher paper** Hang butcher paper around the room and make notes directly on the paper or attach post-its to it.

♦ **Masking tape** Make notes on the tape, tear pieces off, and file in the child's Teacher File.

♦ **Self-stick notes** These come in a variety of colors and sizes and can be used on calendars, Work Sampling Process Note forms, or placed directly in students' Teacher Files.

♦ **Carpenters' aprons** Wearing a carpenter's apron enables some teachers to have post-its and pens ready to record spontaneous as well as planned observational notes.

♦ **Tape recorders** Use a tape recorder to dictate your observations. The disadvantage of this tool is that the taped information must be transcribed.

♦ **Still cameras** Many teachers find taking a photograph a quick way to capture a record of an event or product. You can solicit your school's parent organization, media center, or your classroom parents to help pay for film and processing. Some teachers ask for rolls of film as part of the required school supplies at the beginning of the school year.

♦ **Video cameras** These are useful tools for documenting active work.

♦ **Hand-held computers** Teachers are beginning to use these to input observational data. These systems generally allow data to be sorted by student, date, and domain.

WORK SAMPLING PROCESS NOTE FORMS The Work Sampling System provides several forms designed to facilitate the documentation process. Use of these forms is entirely optional. Provided in the booklet of Reproducible Masters, they can be reproduced or adapted to meet your specific needs.

The **DOMAIN PROCESS NOTES** form (Figure 9) has three columns and shows all seven domains. You can use this form to record observations for all developmental domains either for three children or for one child at three different times.

FIGURE 9
Domain Process Notes
Form

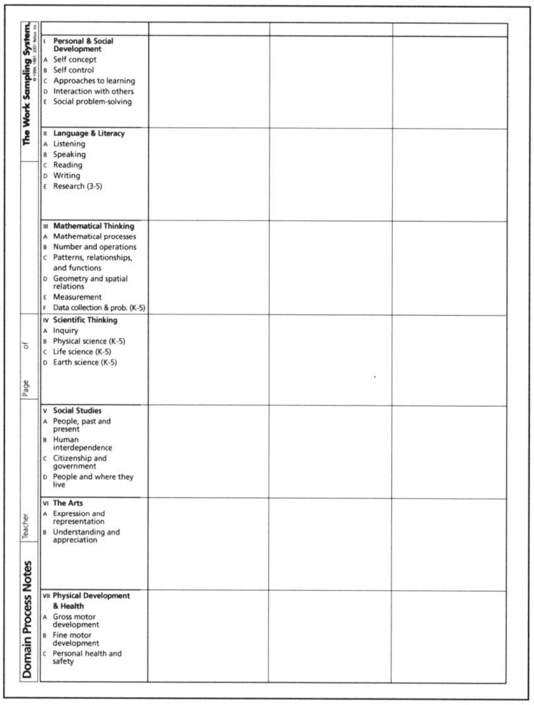

The **CHILD DOMAIN PROCESS NOTES** form (Figure 10) is divided into eight boxes of equal size, one for each domain and one for additional comments. It is designed to document observations for all seven domains for one child.

FIGURE 10
Child Domain Process
Notes form

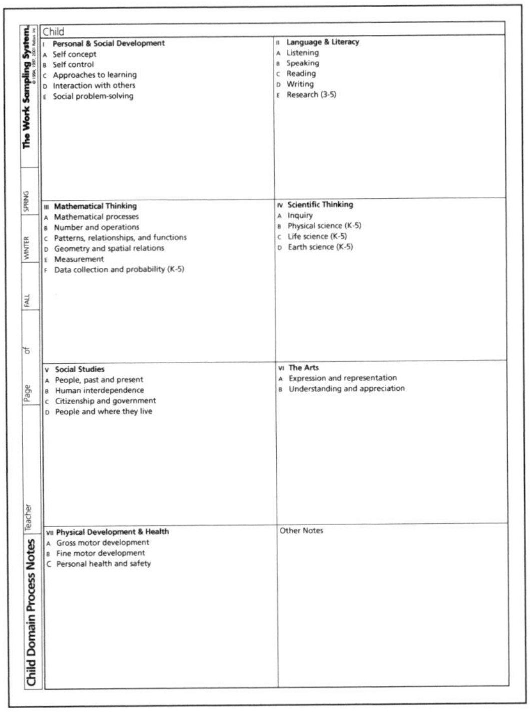

The **GENERAL PROCESS NOTES** form (Figure 11) consists of a 20-box grid with space to write children's names or dates of observations at the top of each box. It is open-ended and can be used in many ways, for example, to observe 20 children once, or five children at four different times, or four children during the course of a week. The boxes are the size of a small self-stick note (1½" x 2"). Using these notes will enable you to transfer the notes to a child's folder easily and effectively. Some teachers write directly on the forms; after the forms are completed they are cut up and placed in children's observation folders.

FIGURE 11
General Process Notes
form

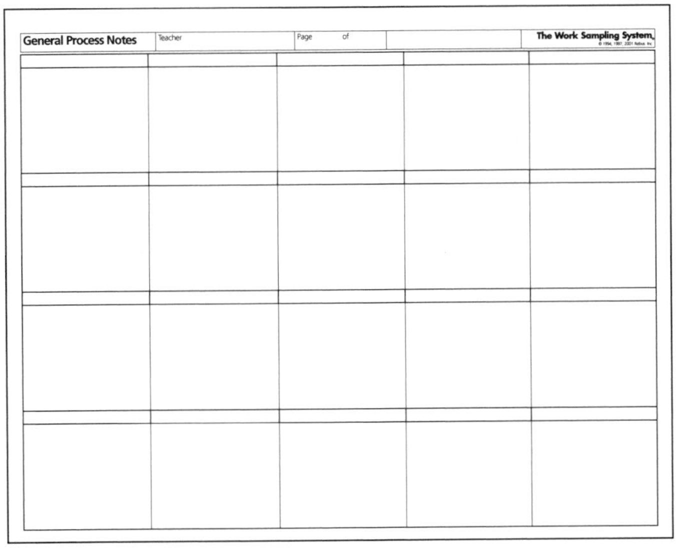

How to Use Guidelines and Checklists

The **ROSTER PROCESS NOTES** form (Figure 12) provides a basic matrix used for recording brief notes, coded entries, or other information for up to 30 children on one sheet.

FIGURE 12

Roster Process Notes form

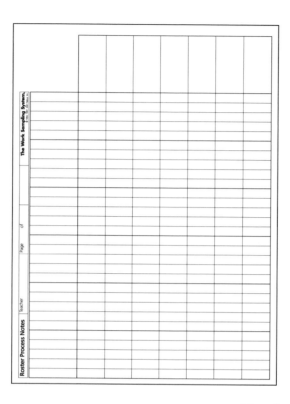

USING WORK SAMPLING PROCESS NOTES   The figures that follow illustrate several ways that teachers have used the Work Sampling Process Notes. Figure 13 shows how a second grade teacher used the Domain Process Notes form to record her observations on two children. She used the same form for one week.

FIGURE 13

Part of a second grade teacher's completed Domain Process Notes form

Week of 2/14	Juanita	Whitney	
II Language & Literacy A Listening B Speaking C Reading D Writing E Research (3-5)	2/15 worked w/B.G. & R.T. on book skit; came to me 4x for help dealing with B & R	2/16 org. puppet show during choice stayed w/it for 45 min. presented it to the class	
III Mathematical Thinking A Mathematical processes B Number and operations C Patterns, relationships, and functions D Geometry and spatial relations E Measurement F Data collection & prob. (K-5)	2/14 wrote long story in journal — wanted to count total p. said "I can count the p. and times it by 2 to get all my sides."	2/15 3 color pattern AAB-CAABC w/unifix 2/16 reversals w/numbers	
IV Scientific Thinking A Inquiry B Physical science (K-5) C Life science (K-5) D Earth science (K-5)	2/16 Observed guinea pig w/Nikki - spent time making detailed record of how g.p. eats	2/15 commented on layering of snow & ice in playgrd. Predicted it would take longer to melt than reg. snow because it was "packed so tight"	

Figure 14 shows how a third grade teacher used the Child Domain Process Notes form to document observations about one child during a two-week period.

I **Personal & Social Development**	II **Language & Literacy**
A Self concept	A Listening
B Self control	B Speaking
C Approaches to learning	C Reading
D Interaction with others	D Writing
E Social problem-solving	E Research (3-5)
3/9 in a fight w/Rodney about rules for soccer— came in from recess sweating and frowning— stomped around, would not sit down to talk	3/7 conf. w/him about story, he revised the ending to make it clear. He identified some spelling errors 3/18 conf. interested in Nolan Ryan-checked out book about Famous Pitchers said he knew N.R. would be in it. read 2 ch. for contract
III **Mathematical Thinking**	IV **Scientific Thinking**
A Mathematical processes	A Inquiry
B Number and operations	B Physical science (K-5)

Figure 15 shows how the same third grade teacher recorded observations about her students' writing.

General Process Notes	Teacher	Page of	
Nikki	Jennifer	Albert	
3/11 Conf. to brain-storm gymnastics story. Shared her Xmas story. Good character development. Humorous "Book language" used to make transitions	3/7 Shared "The Cat, the Dog, the Bird, and Their Incredible Adventure." Works well from brain-storm. Learning to use quotation marks.	3/8 Conferenced with him about Jill or Owen story. He made revisions to make ending more clear. Also identified some spelling errors (3/7 computer)	

Figure 16 shows how a teacher monitored children's skills in recounting events in their writing. After deciding on certain skills to teach during writers' workshop for a week, the teacher set up the Roster Process Notes form with each child's name along the side and the skills to look for along the top. To record more detailed information, the teacher devised a rating code and noted it in the upper left corner of the form.

WRITERS' WORKSHOP Week of 3/17 4 = Proficient ✔ = Not Yet ~ = Emerging	Independently selects topic	Establishes time and place	Recounts events in logical sequence	Includes relevant characters and details	Uses complete sentences	Uses some conventions of print
Amanthe	4	~	~	✔	✔	✔
Bobby	~		~	N		
Devon	~	✔	✔			
Gina	~	N	✔	~	✔	~

How to Use Guidelines and Checklists

Set Up an Organized Storage System

Teachers repeatedly say that one of the greatest challenges of using Work Sampling is staying organized. Once you have decided on observation methods and tools you think will work for you, we strongly urge you to set up a system for organizing the data you collect.

We suggest creating a Teacher File for each child. At the end of the year, the Teacher File will contain the following:

♦ the child's Checklist
♦ all the observational data the teacher collects about that child
♦ notes from other teachers
♦ notes from the child's family
♦ health information

We do *not* recommend keeping such information in the child's Portfolio (see Chapter 3) because the Portfolio is a collection of student work. The Teacher File is a collection of the teacher's data about the child.

How you create Teacher Files is up to you. Choose a plan that works for you. Here are some ideas:

♦ Set up one folder for each child containing the types of records listed above

♦ Use a large three-ring binder with a separate section for each child. You can punch holes in the Checklist and include it, along with all the other observational data and notes, in each child's section

♦ Store all students' Checklists together in one folder and keep observational data for the whole class in a binder organized by domain

Above all, it is important to make this organizational system match your personal work style. If you are a visual learner, you may want to keep your Teacher Files displayed so that you can see them easily. If you are a teacher who must have a clean, orderly desk top, you'll probably want to store your Teacher Files in a file cabinet. If you already have a method that works for you, there is no reason to change it just because you start to use Work Sampling.

During Each Collection Period

There are four ongoing processes to incorporate into your routines during each collection period:

- Plan, observe, and record.

- Review Checklists periodically, making pencil ratings.

- Talk with your students about observation and expectations.

- Apply what you have learned to daily and weekly planning.

As you begin to use the Guidelines and Checklists, your focus will be on planning for observation, observing and recording, and reviewing the Checklist to narrow your observational focus. With continued use of Work Sampling, you will gain comfort talking with your students about the expectations on the Checklist and using Checklist information to guide your instruction.

Plan, Observe, and Record

Although you should read the Guidelines before school begins, mastery of the Guidelines comes as a result of returning to them throughout the year as you plan curriculum and focus your observations. We recommend that you think about and plan for observation before school begins. However, making observations and recording part of your daily experience as a teacher may be one of the most challenging aspects of using the Work Sampling System. Many teachers find that creating specific, concrete plans for observation enables them to effectively incorporate observation and documentation into their teaching. Planning for observation involves four considerations:

- Decide what to observe
- Identify when and where to observe
- Prepare appropriate documentation methods and tools
- Enlist support from your colleagues

Decide What to Observe

As you plan activities and projects each week, add one question to your planning process: "How will I focus my observations this week?" This means identifying the questions you are trying to answer about individual learners and small groups of learners in your classroom.

For example, in a review of Checklists for your class, you may realize that you lack information about students' questioning and predicting skills.

How to Use Guidelines and Checklists

You may decide to schedule some open-ended science activities so you will have opportunities to observe and record this component of Scientific Thinking. Alternatively, your review of Checklists may have revealed some very specific questions about particular students that will shape your observations for the week.

Teachers have found many ways of breaking down the task of observing all students in all seven domains into manageable parts. You may want to focus on a fifth of your class each day of the school week, alternating the day you focus on each fifth so that you are watching children on different days each week. Another method is to choose one domain, a few components, or a particular group of performance indicators and observe all children in relation to that focus for a week.

Identify When and Where to Observe

Once you have identified a focus, review your curriculum plan for the week and decide the times of the day, routines, and activities that are most likely to reveal information that answers your questions. For example, suppose your question is, What do the children in my class already understand about patterns? You plan an activity or series of activities that will enable you to observe small groups of children exploring patterning. In addition, note other times when you might spontaneously see children using patterns.

It is important to remember that finding several opportunities to observe for brief periods of time is more manageable, realistic, and productive than stepping out of the action for longer periods of time.

You may prefer to record observations when they are still fresh in your mind at the end of each day. If so, create and protect a short period of time after students leave your room for you to reflect and record your observations.

Prepare Appropriate Documentation Methods and Tools

Your observation time can be used more efficiently if you devise documentation methods that fit the question and the setting. For example, anecdotal records on index cards work well when you have the luxury of stepping out of the action and have time to write, but a class list for jotting quick notes is more appropriate when you are facilitating group activities.

By taking into account the type of information to be gathered, the demands on your attention, and the students' activities, you will be able to determine the documentation technique best suited for recording your observations.

Enlist Support from Your Colleagues

Consider enlisting other teachers and staff members in your school to help you learn more about your students. You might ask a special subject teacher to observe for specific indicators. Or the reading specialist might give you some valuable observations related to a student's reading strategies. The school's guidance counselor could make observations as she works with a small group from your class. A parent volunteer during math work time might give you valuable information if you specify the skills and behavior to observe. Observation from others can reinforce your interpretations of students' behaviors or prompt you to look at a student in a new way.

In addition, you can work with other teachers in order to get more time for observing and organizing Checklist data. Take turns supervising recess and use the extra time to complete and organize observational records. Alternatively, you might team teach with another teacher. Then, while one of you leads a large group activity with your combined classes, the other observes and records.

Review Checklists Periodically, Making Pencil Ratings

You observe children continuously in the context of daily classroom activities. You regularly document what you see using various methods of recording. Periodically, you review the Checklists and make preliminary ratings based on the documentation you have collected.

A 5-minute monthly scanning of the Checklist and your observational data for each child is a valuable way to see what you have learned about your students and the questions that remain unanswered. Making some quick, tentative pencil ratings also alerts you to the instructional needs of individual children.

As you engage in this process, what you need to find out becomes apparent and you return to the task of observing and recording with a clearer and narrower focus. You are continually asking yourself, "What do I know? What do I need to find out?" If you are unsure of the rating for a performance indicator, it probably means you need more information. You now have a new observational focus for this child.

It is not necessary to scan all of your students' Checklists at one sitting, but by the midpoint of the collection period, it is a good idea to have reviewed all children's Checklists at least once.

How to Use Guidelines and Checklists

This cycle of observing and recording, reviewing and rating the Checklist, then returning to observing with a sharper focus should be repeated once or twice during each collection period (Figure 17).

FIGURE 17
Ongoing process of observing, recording, reviewing and making Checklist ratings

Observe & Record

Review & Rate

As you review the Checklists, you make ratings based on your observations using a three-point scale that describes performance mastery. The rating categories should reflect the degree to which students have acquired the skill, knowledge, or behavior, and/or demonstrated the accomplishments delineated by each performance indicator described in the Guidelines and listed on the Checklist. Three types of ratings are possible:

♦ **Not Yet** indicates that the skill, knowledge, or behavior has not been demonstrated

♦ **In Process** indicates that the skill, knowledge, or behavior is emergent, and is not demonstrated consistently

♦ **Proficient** indicates that the skill, knowledge, or behavior is firmly within the child's range of performance

You can review Checklists in different ways. Some teachers review each child's entire Checklist. Others review one domain at a time for all of the students in their class. To illustrate the process of reviewing and rating, let's assume a method of organization that uses one folder for each child. In this case, with information from the Guidelines in mind, the process of review would be as follows:

1   Select a child's folder.

2   Read through the observational notes.

3   Scan the Checklist. This may trigger memories of children's behaviors that you have not formally documented.

4   Using a pencil, make preliminary ratings for those performance indicators about which you have sufficient information. Expect to find indicators for which you do not have enough information to make a rating.

5   Make notations to yourself to focus your subsequent observations on these less-observed indicators.

6 Write questions, concerns, and strengths in the comments space on the front of the Checklist if it helps you organize your thoughts. This information will be helpful when completing the Summary Report (see Chapter 4).

Talk with Students

Although children's involvement in the process of observation and Checklist completion is indirect, it is important nonetheless. Observation of children should not be kept hidden from them. When you let children know that you are observing and when you share your observations, children can become more responsible and independent learners. You can involve children in the Checklist assessment process in two ways. First, make explicit to children what they are learning and why they are learning it. Second, discuss with children what is being assessed and how the assessment process occurs.

Make the Purpose and Expectations of Learning Activities Explicit

Helping children understand the reasons and expectations for what they learn during the school year often results in a marked increase in student motivation. How you help your students understand depends on the developmental level of your students. You may want to post the Wall Chart of domains, components, and performance indicators that comes with your grade level Guidelines. If your students can read, refer them to it at appropriate times. If your students cannot yet read, you can use it when conducting class discussions about why students are learning particular skills or knowledge.

When children have a clear idea of what is being evaluated, they are likely to perform at a higher level. Too often we fail to make the criteria we intend to use for evaluation explicit to our students. They do not have the chance to make the specific type of effort needed in order to be successful. For example, a class of third grade students are given the following assignment.

EXAMPLE 9

Write a report about an animal of your choice. Do research using at least two books, take notes on index cards without copying the book's exact text, write a first draft in your own words, proofread your work for spelling and punctuation, conference with a peer and then the teacher, make final revisions, and then, write a final draft. You will be evaluated on each step of this process.

If children understand these expectations in advance and are given clear guidance about how to proceed, they can be successful with the assignment.

Talk with Children About the Assessment Process

It is extremely valuable to have discussions with students about how you find out what they know. For example, you might pose the question, "Why do you think I take notes during a reading conference?" or "Why do you think I write down some of what you say during meeting time?" When children are made aware of your role as observer and recorder, they are more likely to understand why there are times when you are not available to them.

You might consider sharing the responsibility of recording student learning with your students. For example, in one classroom, the teacher assigns each child a steno pad. The child has responsibility for keeping track of the steno pad. During reading and writing conferences, the child brings the steno pad and both the teacher and the child write in it. This helps to place the responsibility for learning in the hands of the student. When completing the Checklist, the teacher reviews the observational data recorded in the steno pad along with the other types of observational data stored in the Teacher File.

Teachers have developed many ways to share the responsibility for observation with their students. One teacher, who wears a special hat when she is observing, procured a plastic "observer's hat" for her students to wear when it is their turn for this particular classroom job. She gives them a specific behavior or skill to watch for and a chart to record their observations. She adds these data to her collection to use when completing Checklists.

Apply What You Have Learned

Observing and documenting children's learning regularly in the context of ongoing classroom activities and making preliminary Checklist ratings reveals information that will guide your decisions about curriculum and instruction. You may find that you become a more effective teacher because you are watching and listening to children closely, discovering the diverse ways children show what they know and can do, and incorporating this information into your instructional planning, thus making your teaching increasingly responsive to the children in your classroom.

Regular scanning of the Guidelines and Checklist and a review of them when planning each week enables you to keep track of whether all curriculum goals are being addressed. You can identify whether certain domains, components, or indicators are being overlooked and can structure activities to address these areas.

Additionally, this process helps ensure that you don't overlook someone. When reviewing Checklists, you may discover that you have very little observational data on a particular child. Discovering this early in the collection period allows you to focus on that child. You will also recognize children's strengths and vulnerabilities and make plans to further their growth and learning in those areas.

Near the End of Each Collection Period

Preparations for completing Summary Reports begin about two weeks before the end of each collection period. Before you begin Summary Reports, you have three tasks to accomplish:

- Review preliminary ratings.

- Make final ratings.

- Identify examples for Summary Reports.

Review Preliminary Ratings

For each child, consult your observational notes, any other relevant information in the Teacher File, samples of the student's work, and your general knowledge about the child. Using all of this information, decide whether tentative ratings made in pencil on the Checklist still stand or if some ratings have changed, based on more recently acquired information.

Make Final Ratings

We strongly encourage you to make final ratings on the Checklists a week or two before beginning to complete Summary Reports. You are apt to feel overwhelmed if you try to make Checklist ratings, organize Portfolios, and complete Summary Reports simultaneously.

As you make the final ratings, be sure to have the Guidelines readily available so you can consult them when the meaning of an indicator is unclear or if you are unsure of expectations for a particular indicator. Take a minute to refresh your memory of the meaning of the three Checklist ratings (see page 42).

Remember that a rating reflects a child's performance based on what has been taught. A fall rating is not made based on how you expect the child to perform in the spring; it is based on how you expect the child to perform in the fall.

Make the final ratings in pen. They are now final and will not be changed. Stopping the clock in this way enables you to compare ratings from one collection period to the next.

Identify Examples for the Summary Report

As you review the Checklist data and make final ratings, highlight specific examples from your observational records that you can use to illustrate strengths and areas of concern in the Summary Report. You might use the space on the front cover of the Checklist to note these examples so they are easily accessible when you complete the Summary Reports.

Part II Frequently Asked Questions About Guidelines and Checklists

Q How can I find the time to observe and record?

A First of all, it is very important to have realistic expectations about how much time you can spend observing and recording. Classrooms are busy places and even if you observed all day long, it would be impossible to record everything that goes on. However, spending a few minutes each day doing some type of observation and recording can result in a great deal of assessment data.

Sometimes teachers dread observation and recording because they think that recording observations means stepping out of the classroom activity, sitting for long periods of time, and writing lengthy anecdotal notes. We recommend that you observe both in and out of the classroom action, and that you select a recording method that best captures the information you are trying to gather. In fact, teachers who are successful observers and recorders of children's learning use multiple ways of observing and recording. They schedule observation time into their daily activities, plan who and what they will observe, and prepare methods and tools for recording in advance. With advance planning, observing a few minutes each morning and afternoon provides sufficient evidence for making Checklist ratings confidently. (Refer to the discussion beginning on page 28 for specific ideas about how to observe and record student learning.)

Q Should I set up specific situations so that I can observe the skills listed on the Checklists?

A The Work Sampling System is a curriculum-embedded assessment. This means that observation for Checklist ratings takes place in the context of regular classroom activities. Children should not be asked to perform tasks simply for the purpose of evaluation.

Effective teacher planning plays a critical role in successful observation, making it possible for you to observe all of the performance indicators on the Checklist. As you do your daily and weekly planning, consider all the different skills, knowledge, and behaviors children might exhibit during specific activities and lessons. Consider the many ways children demonstrate what they know and can do.

Teachers plan activities so that children can be introduced to or practice a skill and, of course, they hope to observe children's performance in relation to this skill during the activity. This scenario, however, does not always happen as planned. As you plan activities, be expansive in your thinking and consider all the possible skills children are learning and demonstrating. During a math activity, for example, children are likely to display many different aspects of mathematical thinking, as well as fine motor skills, language skills, and possibly skills related to the arts. This type of planning will help to make your teaching and your assessment more efficient, as illustrated in the following example.

A kindergarten teacher puts out pattern blocks during center time and introduces two-color patterns. She hopes to observe the Mathematical Thinking indicator "Recognizes, duplicates, and extends patterns." One child immediately copies the teacher's pattern and extends it. Another child, using pattern blocks for the first time, eagerly builds a wall of yellow hexagons. A third child places blocks on the table, first a red one, then a green, then a red, and then a yellow and proceeds to form the blocks into the shape of a flower.

The teacher in the above example noted that the first child copied and extended a two-color pattern. She also noted that the second child built a wall of yellow hexagons. She asked this child to describe what he had built and added his answer to her observational record. He said, "I got all yellows—they are all the same shape." His answer gave her information for the performance indicator "Sorts objects into subgroups, classifying and comparing according to a rule." Later the same day during a game of musical chairs, the child who built the wall commented that the chairs were set up in a pattern. Children demonstrate what they are learning in many ways, though as teachers, we are often tuned into only those demonstrations we expect to see.

Effective observation calls for widening your focus and observing more broadly, in different situations, at different times of the day, and when children are interacting with different materials. If you are having difficulty observing particular indicators, consider the following questions:

♦ Have these children been provided with adequate opportunities to learn this skill?

♦ Is this skill one that I have addressed in my teaching?

♦ Have I observed for this skill in many different situations?

♦ Have I given students different ways to express their knowledge?

Frequently Asked Questions About Guidelines and Checklists

Q How do Guidelines and Checklists help me with curriculum planning?

A Developmental Guidelines and Checklists can help with curriculum planning in three different ways.

♦ The Guidelines remind you of the breadth of the curriculum. They address seven domains and include a wide range of activities typical of developmentally appropriate classrooms.

♦ Systematic observation and documentation highlight areas of the curriculum that you may be overlooking.

♦ Carefully observing children and documenting what you see gives you in-depth knowledge of children. This helps you plan instruction that is more responsive to individual children as well as to the class as a whole.

Because the Guidelines and Checklists emphasize continuous progress across ages and grades, you gain a sense of what your students can do now as well as where they need to go in the future. Familiarity with the Guidelines and Checklists can help both you and your students set learning goals.

Q How can I be sure that my observations are fair?

A To make a fair determination about whether a child knows or can do something, it is essential that you observe the child more than once and in more than one situation.

For the assessment to be fair, students should be evaluated only on indicators that have already been addressed in the classroom. It is unfair to hold children responsible for demonstrating skills, knowledge, and behaviors that have not been taught. Moreover, bear in mind that children may have certain skills, even if they do not exhibit them in the particular contexts you have chosen. It is the teacher's responsibility to provide varied experiences within the classroom in which all students are likely to demonstrate their achievements and accomplishments.

Using an observational assessment requires you to collect factual data before making judgments. People have a tendency, however, to form impressions quickly. For example, when you have difficulty with a particular child's behavior, it is not uncommon to generalize your impressions to all encounters with that child. A child who is extremely talkative or who tends to dominate social interactions with peers may be strong in mathematics or a very talented artist, but the child's behavior may interfere with your ability to observe his strengths. Observing as fairly as possible requires that teachers look at all children through the same lens. We recommend that you get in the habit of reserving judgment. Try to observe what the child is doing now, and how the child is approaching this task, rather than how the child may have behaved or performed in a very different situation at a different time.

Q How can I know that my Checklist ratings are valid and reliable?

A The Work Sampling Guidelines provide a set of criteria for performance based on national and state standards and child development research. The Guidelines also provide teachers with a set of shared expectations for children's learning. Your Checklist ratings will be valid and reliable only when you interpret your observations and make ratings consistent with the expectations described in the Guidelines, rather than ratings based on personal opinions. If you are having difficulty making a child's ratings, it may be helpful to discuss them with a colleague.

Q Why is it necessary to record observations?

A Observational records are the evidence or the data upon which evaluations are based. The documentation process in the Work Sampling System has two steps. The first step is the informal note-taking or data-gathering that you do on a regular basis. The second consists of the ratings you make on the Work Sampling Checklist in response to your informal observational notes. Recording observations is important for four reasons.

♦ Written records help you monitor what children know and can do. They remind you of a child's strengths and weaknesses.

♦ Written records collected over time enable you to see patterns in behaviors and approaches to learning.

♦ You can use your observations of children to plan instructional activities that are more responsive to children's interests and needs.

♦ Recorded observations provide evidence to support your judgments in the assessment process.

Without careful documentation, the reliability of Checklist ratings decreases and the validity of your judgments is compromised.

Q Is it possible for a rating to change from "Proficient" to "In Process" from the fall to the spring?

A Yes. Although the Guidelines describe developmental expectations for performance indicators in broad terms, you complete Checklists based on your expectations for a particular time of year. For example, when evaluating a child's performance for the Checklist in November, you consider what you have taught and your expectations of children at that time, and then make your ratings accordingly. A child who was using several reading strategies in the fall of second grade to read simple books might be rated "Proficient" on the Checklist because that was the fall expectation. By spring, however, the expectation is that children will be reading more difficult material. If the child is still reading only simple books, his rating at this time will be "In Process."

Q Are Checklists sent home?

A Checklists are not designed to be sent home. They are written in language for teachers. However, parents always have access to the Checklist should they request it, and you may wish to use the Checklists during conferences to help families understand how their child is doing in a particular domain.

Q Can I use the Checklist during parent-teacher conferences?

A Although reviewing the entire Checklist during a conference would take too much time, sometimes teachers find it helpful to refer to particular sections of the Checklist as a way to offer specific information about a child's strengths or weaknesses or to illustrate a rating on the Summary Report. Keep in mind, though, that Checklists are written in professional language and that the amount and organization of information recorded there is complex and may be overwhelming to a parent in the context of a brief conference.

Q How can specialists or special subjects teachers be involved in completing Checklists?

A Specialists can contribute a great deal to the richness and detail of the Checklist. The more information you have about students, the more accurate your assessment. Collaboration and dialogue among all of the adults who work with a child will enhance accuracy. The Guidelines should be shared with special subject and resource teachers so that they can channel appropriate information to you. Specialists can give the child's primary teacher observational records and/or work samples relevant to their subject areas, all of which can be used to inform the Work Sampling Checklist. Having conferences with special subject teachers can be a useful way to gather this information. An optional Special Subject Report form (described in Chapter 4) is available for use by specialists. (For further discussion of these issues, see Chapter 6.)

Q Why are Checklists filled out three times during the school year?

A Children grow and change at different rates. Their growth often occurs quite rapidly. As children change, you form new images of their achievements based on their current performance, and you may forget some of the details of their prior performances. Only by noting a child's specific performance at one point in time can you accurately assess the child's progress later. For this reason, we advocate a three-times-per-year framework for assessment so that the child's profile of skills and knowledge in one collection period can be compared with her profile in an earlier period. This facilitates assessment of progress and provides a chance to record change in performance.

Q What happens to the Checklist at the end of the year?

A We recommend that you include the Checklist in the child's school file at the end of the year so that it can be reviewed by the child's next teacher. At the beginning of the next year, the new teacher has the opportunity to scan the spring ratings on the Checklists and obtain a starting point for review and instruction. This is particularly helpful given that the Work Sampling System is continuous from one grade to the next.

Although parents have legal access to all information about their children, the Checklists are not intended to be sent home at the end of the year because they have been written with educators, rather than parents, in mind.

Q How long does it take to learn how to use the Guidelines and Checklists?

A After the first two collection periods, most teachers have internalized much of the information included in the Guidelines for the grade levels they teach. Although they may occasionally refer back to the Guidelines, they do it much less frequently than earlier in the school year.

The greatest difficulty teachers have in completing the Checklists is integrating the observing, recording, reviewing, and rating cycle into their daily schedules. This process is facilitated by the following:

♦ Observing and recording selectively, instead of trying to document everything all the time

♦ Planning when, how, and what will be observed each week

♦ Finding documentation strategies that feel comfortable

Q How long does it take to complete the Checklist?

A If you review and rate the Checklist in an ongoing way, scanning the Checklist takes less than five minutes, and reviewing all information collected in order to make final ratings takes about 15 minutes per child. If rating particular indicators is difficult or time consuming, you probably need more information about the child, and should continue to observe.

Q Which Checklist should I use for children above or below grade-level expectations?

A Development in children is rarely even. Many children who function above or below grade-level do not do so in all domains. Rather, they may be at grade-level for some domains while being above or below expectations in others. For example, a child who is very mature verbally may be less so socially. Because of this natural variability, we recommend that you use as a starting point the Checklist that corresponds to the child's age/grade level.

For those children who are functioning very differently from expectations, perhaps a child with a disability, information from the Omnibus Guidelines can be used to increase your understanding of the areas in which the child is above or below grade level. The examples in the Guidelines will help you to modify your instructional plans to reflect the child's skills and knowledge in all of the domains. The Summary Report should also be used to address the areas in which the child is performing above or below grade-level. Particularly for the child who is working below grade-level, it is important to describe what the child can do, not only the child's areas of difficulty. (Refer to Chapter 6 for more information on using Checklists with children with special needs.)

Q How can I possibly observe everything that is going on in the classroom?

A You cannot observe everything that happens in your classroom. To maximize the effectiveness of your observations, it is best that they be planned and focused. Reviewing the Guidelines in conjunction with weekly curriculum planning can help provide that focus. Devising a plan about whom and what to observe as part of weekly planning makes the task of observation more systematic. Some ideas include observing

♦ four or five pupils each day

♦ a group of students for the week

♦ one domain for several days

♦ a few components of one domain during a lesson

Becoming a skilled observer takes time and practice. Teachers usually find it beneficial to try out several methods of observation and recording, then talk them over with colleagues and revise their plans before they create a method that reflects their personal style. Above all, it is important to try to establish a routine in which you observe and document classroom activities on a regular and consistent basis.

Q Should I have a documented observation for every performance indicator on the Checklist?

A   Absolutely not. There are two reasons why documented observations for each performance indicator are unnecessary. First, each time you observe your students, you gain information that provides data for multiple performance indicators on the Checklist. For example, Ms. Stevens records two anecdotal notes about Raymond, a first grader, during one week in October (Examples 10 and 11). Each anecdote provided her with information about several performance indicators. To illustrate, we have listed the performance indicators that are informed by Ms. Stevens' observation below each anecdote.

EXAMPLE 10

1. 10/7 choose to wk w/manips at choice, many patterns, organized design, some symmetry

Related performance indicators:

I A 2—Shows initiative and self-direction.

I B 2—Uses materials purposefully and respectfully.

III C 2—Makes, copies, and extends patterns.

III D 2—Explores and solves spatial problems using manipulatives and drawings.

EXAMPLE 11

2. 10/9 during QR (quiet reading) brings me Zoobook on eagles: "This is amazing." We read a few pgs tog, listens intently to me, studies pictures, he reads 1 pg, uses picture cues, sounds out wds.

Related performance indicators:

I C 1—Shows eagerness and curiosity as a learner.

I C 2—Sustains attention to work over a period of time.

II B 1—Speaks clearly and conveys ideas effectively.

II C 5—Comprehends and interprets fiction and non-fiction text.

II C 1—Shows interest in books and reading.

II C 4—Uses strategies to construct meaning from print.

The second reason each performance indicator may not have a recorded observation is that you may have observed a child performing certain skills so frequently that you can rely on your memory.

Frequently Asked Questions About Guidelines and Checklists

Q How are the Guidelines and Checklists used in multi-age classrooms?

A Work Sampling fits well with multi-age classrooms because of the emphasis in these classrooms on the continuum of children's development. By examining all six levels of an indicator presented in the Omnibus Guidelines, you gain an understanding of what comes before and after each grade level indicator. Although the Omnibus Guidelines present several levels of development at once, the Checklists do not.

Teachers of multi-age groups use several different Checklists to reflect the developmental range their students represent. Thus, if you have a class of seven and eight year olds, you would complete second grade Checklists for the seven year olds, and the third grade Checklists for the eight year olds. Because of the consistency of the domains, components, and many of the indicators across grade levels, you do not have to learn entirely new information for each age represented in your classroom. The rationales and examples describe the differences from one grade level to another. The Omnibus Guidelines supports your instructional planning by enabling you to quickly identify similarities and differences among age levels and to move easily between grade levels (for further discussion see Chapter 6).

Q Can the Guidelines and Checklists be customized to meet the requirements of a particular state or district?

A The fourth edition of Work Sampling has been revised to conform to a wide range of local, state, and national standards, as well as to the standards and expectations of a variety of national curriculum groups and organizations. Nevertheless, some states, districts, and major educational providers (e.g., Head Start) have their own set of standards which do not correspond specifically to the Work Sampling components and indicators. In some cases, with the publisher's permission, it is possible to revise the Work Sampling materials so that they are more closely aligned with these standards. More information about customization is available from the publisher, Rebus Inc.

CHAPTER 3
Portfolios

Collecting, Selecting, and Evaluating Student Work

This chapter addresses the second element of the Work Sampling System—Portfolio collection. The chapter is divided into three sections:

PART I   Understanding Portfolio Collection

PART II   How to Use Portfolios

PART III   Frequently Asked Questions about Portfolio Collection

Overview of Portfolio Collection

What is it?

The Portfolio is a purposeful collection of student work

What are its purposes?

1 To show the quality of a student's work and thinking across the curriculum

2 To demonstrate progress and growth over time

3 To involve children in assessing their own work

4 To assist teachers with instructional planning

What are its features?

◆ It is structured around two types of items: Core Items and Individualized Items

◆ It contains work samples from three collection periods: fall, winter, and spring

◆ It is created jointly by students and teachers

How do I use the Work Sampling Portfolio?

Before the school year begins:

◆ Create individual portfolios and decide how and where to store them
◆ Devise procedures for collecting student work
◆ Consider methods to portray learning
◆ Plan for Core Item Collection

During each collection period:

◆ Plan curriculum with Portfolio collection in mind
◆ Teach students about Portfolios
◆ Talk with students about their work
◆ Collect work regularly
◆ Select work periodically
◆ Annotate work to enhance its meaning
◆ Keep track of selected work

Near the end of each collection period:

◆ Encourage student evaluation of Portfolios
◆ Evaluate the Portfolio for the Summary Report
◆ Share the Portfolio with the child's family

Related Materials

■ Portfolio Item Record self-stick notes

■ Reproducible Master of Core Item Collection Plan form

■ Reproducible Master of "Thoughts About My Portfolio" form

■ Portfolio Domain Labels

■ Reproducible Master of Portfolio Tally form

Part I   Understanding Portfolio Collection

Throughout each school day, students engage in classroom activities ranging from writing journal entries to making collages, from investigating scientific phenomena to constructing block structures, from solving math problems to creating poems. In the course of these activities, students' creations, language, and actions reveal their thinking and learning. Collecting examples of student work in portfolios is an effective method of documenting children's knowledge, skills, accomplishments, and approaches to learning.

When you communicate to students the purpose of learning activities and make your expectations for their work explicit, selecting samples of work for the Portfolio can be a joint endeavor. As children gain experience, they can take more responsibility for independently reviewing and evaluating their work. Through this process of reviewing and selecting work, children will come to understand your standards for evaluating work and will begin to develop their own personal standards.

As you learn about your students during the school year, the Portfolio and the Developmental Checklist give you two very different types of information. The Checklist provides a broad survey of a child's learning and focuses on whether or not a child can perform certain skills. In contrast, the Portfolio gives qualitative information about how a child learns and applies knowledge. The Work Sampling Portfolio creates a portrait of the child as a learner, shows the unique characteristics of an individual's work, and tells a story about the child's learning over time.

Purposes of Portfolio Collection

1   **To show the quality of children's work and thinking across the curriculum.** The primary purpose of Portfolio collection is to give qualitative information about children's thinking and learning. In order to understand children's thinking, you must examine their actions, language, and creations—that is, expressions of their thinking. Portfolios concretely portray children's understandings and offer the opportunity to study how children apply their learning in meaningful ways.

   Portfolios provide more descriptive and individualized information than the Developmental Checklists. Although two children might have identical Checklist ratings on a particular set of skills, it is unlikely that work showing their application of these skills would be identical. The portfolio provides qualitative information because it illustrates how children think in addition to illustrating what they know.

   Many approaches to portfolio collection focus solely on one domain (e.g., a writing portfolio). The Work Sampling System Portfolio documents children's performance and progress across the curriculum.

2   **To demonstrate children's progress and growth over time.** To determine if a child has progressed, you must have samples of similar work from different time periods. Work Sampling Portfolios contain examples of work that show the same type of learning across three collection periods. By comparing earlier and later work, you and your students can evaluate how their learning is progressing.

3   **To involve children in assessing their own work.** Studying the work in their portfolios gives children a concrete way to begin reflecting on their own learning. When children look at examples of past work and compare it to their current work, they are able to recognize their progress. Using Portfolios as a focal point, you can model reflective questions and comments and help children develop their own standards and goals for their learning. Only after teachers have prompted this type of analysis do children begin to internalize the standards for work that have been identified in school.

4   **To assist teachers with instructional planning.** Portfolios give you a picture of each student's strengths and weakness and an overall sense of how well the class is doing. You have information about the effectiveness of your teaching that will help to clarify your goals and determine next steps both for individuals and the group.

Structure and Organization of the Work Sampling Portfolio

Saving children's work is an activity familiar to most teachers. The Work Sampling Portfolio takes a new approach to this familiar activity by providing a structured framework to guide your decisions about which examples of student work to save. This structured approach will also create a portrait of the whole child without overloading the Portfolio with so many items that you become overwhelmed. The Work Sampling Portfolio is structured around two types of items: Core Items and Individualized Items.

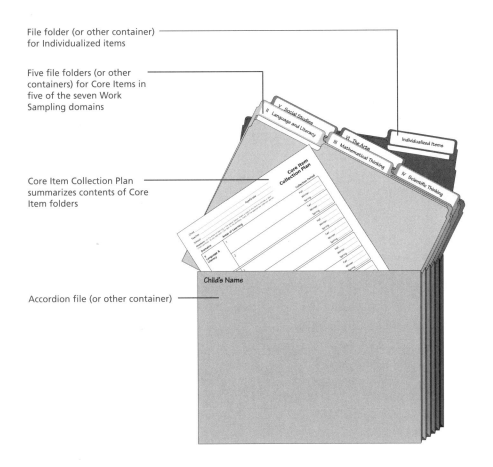

File folder (or other container) for Individualized items

Five file folders (or other containers) for Core Items in five of the seven Work Sampling domains

Core Item Collection Plan summarizes contents of Core Item folders

Accordion file (or other container)

Core Items

Definition

Core Items are representations (samples of work) of particular areas of learning collected within each of the following domains:

- Language and Literacy
- Mathematical Thinking
- Scientific Thinking
- Social Studies
- The Arts

These five domains lend themselves to concrete representations of student thinking. Most of our knowledge about children's status in Personal and Social Development and Physical Development and Health, on the other hand, is learned through direct observation rather than studying children's work. These last two domains, therefore, are more effectively documented on the Checklist than in the Portfolio.

The collection of Core Items in five domains ensures that the breadth of children's learning is represented and that the kinds of learning activities that have occurred in the classroom are documented. Although two areas of learning do not encompass an entire domain, if you select more than two, the Portfolio quickly becomes unmanageable because of the quantity of work being collected.

Areas of Learning

An ***area of learning*** is a strand of your curriculum (a part of a curriculum domain) that guides the collection of Core Items. Each domain encompasses many areas of learning. Careful selection of areas of learning results in Core Items that convey meaningful information about the quality of a child's thinking.

The responsibility for selecting areas of learning for Core Item collection rests with the teacher and school. First-hand knowledge of local curriculum and the student population is necessary to identify effective areas of learning. Some teachers prefer to define their own areas of learning; others choose from the examples offered in Appendixes A and B.

The teacher's selection of an area of learning reflects a particular understanding of how children learn. The Work Sampling System is based on the belief that children learn in an integrated way, combining many different skills and drawing on prior knowledge. This view presents a contrast to a mastery learning model in which children are expected to learn and demonstrate one skill at a time.

Effective areas of learning share the following five criteria. They:

- are important parts of the curriculum

- are specific enough to show student progress over time

- are relevant for all students

- reflect concepts or processes and are not dependent on particular content

- are most effectively documented in the Portfolio rather than on the Checklist

Further discussion about how to define areas of learning is found beginning on page 84.

Features of Core Items

ILLUSTRATE PROGRESS   The primary function of Core Items is to allow for the documentation of children's progress throughout the school year. Therefore, similar work must be collected over the three collection periods as the basis for comparison and for identifying progress.

For example, you may decide that "understanding and interpreting stories" is one area of learning that you want to highlight in the domain of Language and Literacy. As part of your Language and Literacy curriculum, you would incorporate many opportunities for children to engage in and practice the skills and concepts encompassed by this area of learning. You (and your students) would regularly collect examples of work that resulted from these activities. From your collection of several samples of work that represent this area of learning, you would select one sample for each collection period that was representative of the child's work during that time. These work samples are Core Items. By the end of the year, you would have three Core Items representing this area of learning in the Portfolio, one for each collection period. This enables you to compare the Core Items from each collection period to assess the child's progress.

Figures 1–3 show fall, winter, and spring samples representing the area of learning "writing to express ideas" from a kindergartner's journal. Mike's Core Items show that he made significant progress in writing over the year. In the fall, he expressed his ideas using drawing and writing. He used only initial consonants. In the spring, he composed two complete and related sentences, using beginning, middle, and ending sounds and some conventional spellings. The lines between words show his beginning understanding of how to separate words.

Understanding Portfolio Collection

FIGURE 1 (LEFT)
FIGURE 2 (RIGHT)
A kindergartner's fall and winter Core Items in Language and Literacy

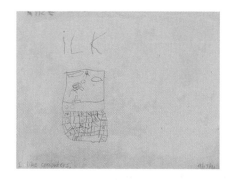

FIGURE 3
A kindergartner's spring Core Item in Language and Literacy

Figures 4 and 5 show a third grader's fall and spring Core Items for the area of learning "using patterns to organize information." Her progress from a rather simple symmetrical linear pattern in the fall to a more complex diagonal pattern in the spring is evident.

FIGURE 4 (LEFT)
FIGURE 5 (RIGHT)
A third grader represents her understanding of patterns differently at different times of the year (fall and spring)

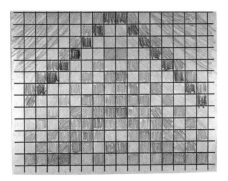

SHOW REPRESENTATIVE WORK IN FIVE DOMAINS Core Items are selected to show a child's usual or typical work in a particular area of learning. The Work Sampling Portfolio is not a "showcase" or "best work" portfolio. Selecting only a child's best work can inaccurately portray the child's performance. For example, consider the preschool child with a language disability who has learned to say fluently "How are you today?" If the child cannot generate and use other questions appropriately, then a representation of this practiced question should not be included as a Core Item to represent the area of learning "using questions to gather information." Or consider a first grade child who has spent a week working on a story with the help of a resource teacher. The final draft is a full page story, written in complete, well-organized sentences, and the words are all correctly spelled. Typically, this child's writing is two or three words written in invented spelling accompanying a drawing. If the full page story was selected as the Core Item for the area of learning "writing to express ideas," an inaccurate picture of the child's skills in this area would be portrayed in the Portfolio. In general, if a sample of work (or a representation of it) is much more advanced than a child's typical performance, it should not be selected as a Core Item.

PLANNED IN ADVANCE Before the school year begins, you and your colleagues choose two areas of learning that are central parts of your curriculum in each of five domains. The areas of learning you identify must be significant for all of your students because they will guide the collection of Core Items for the entire year. Planning in advance ensures that you will be able to evaluate progress in these important curriculum strands.

Areas of learning remain the same for the entire year. If you change them during the year, you will not be able to collect similar work over time and therefore will not be able to evaluate progress.

REFLECT THE SAME AREAS OF LEARNING FOR ALL STUDENTS The two areas of learning in each domain should be the same for all students in the classroom. Because areas of learning are central parts of the curriculum, they reflect important goals for all of your students.

Although areas of learning are the same for all students, the actual Core Items (samples of work) collected may be different for each student. For example, in a third grade classroom all the students are collecting Core Items for the area of learning "using strategies to solve number problems." In the fall, the Core Item selected for Deidre is a page from her math log in which she describes how she solved a problem about farm animals from the class math series. Charles' Core Item for the fall is a set of problems he solved related to his bridge building project. Roger's and Maria's Core Items are their descriptions of how they figured out how much money each student would have to contribute in order to make a pizza lunch for the entire third grade. Although each student's work is different, each work sample reflects the same area of learning.

Figures 6 and 7 illustrate two ways kindergarten children in the same classroom demonstrate their knowledge and understanding for the area of learning "using patterns to organize objects and information."

Understanding Portfolio Collection

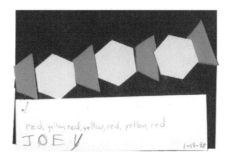

FIGURE 6 (LEFT)
FIGURE 7 (RIGHT)
Though different, these two Core Items both reflect the same area of learning, "using patterns to organize objects and information"

Individualized Items

Definition

Individualized Items are samples of student work that serve one of two functions: they either capture a child's individuality as a learner, and/or they illustrate how a child integrates learning from multiple domains. Unlike Core Items, Individualized Items are not planned in advance by the teacher, nor are they tied to specific domains. Instead, they represent a child's interests and talents, approach to learning, significant accomplishments, or application of learning from several domains. We recommend collecting a minimum of five Individualized Items during each collection period.

Features of Individualized Items

REFLECT SPECIAL INTERESTS AND TALENTS Work that illustrates the special interests each child has can be included in the Portfolio as Individualized Items. For example, the four year old who is intrigued by dinosaurs, can name each type and tell you where they lived and what they ate, should have several work samples reflecting this interest. Similarly, work that demonstrates a child's special talent as an artist or mathematician, can be saved as an Individualized Item.

ILLUSTRATE A CHILD'S APPROACH TO LEARNING Individualized Items might also represent each child's unique approach to learning. Is this a child who uses art as a primary means of expression? If so, there will be many work samples featuring artistic expression.

DOCUMENT SIGNIFICANT ACCOMPLISHMENTS Individualized Items provide a place to record children's important educational accomplishments and their best work. For one child, a representation of the first time he contributes a story to the class meeting might be included in the Portfolio. For another child, a record of the first chapter book she read independently may be included as an Individualized Item. Similarly, a record of a child's attainment of a developmental milestone (e.g., the first time a child skips) may be selected as an Individualized Item. Figure 8 shows an item selected by a first grader, with annotation from her teacher.

FIGURE 8
A first grader's Individualized Item (journal entry) that illustrates integrated learning and a specific accomplishment

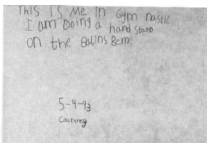

Individualized Item
• Personal and Social Development
• Language and Literacy
• The Arts
• Physical Development & Health

Courtney said, "I want this in my portfolio because I've been practicing and practicing doing a handstand like this, and this is the day after I finally did it."

A significant accomplishment, journal entry shows how she expresses ideas and emotions using drawing and writing.

SHOW INTEGRATION OF KNOWLEDGE In contrast to Core Items, which are linked to single domains, Individualized Items demonstrate how children integrate knowledge and skills across any combination of seven domains. You will probably find in your classroom that much of the work children do shows their skills, concepts, and knowledge from several domains at once.

When children are engaged in learning, it is unusual for them to learn in only one domain at a time. In fact, you may use an integrated or thematic curriculum approach because it fosters making connections between domains. For example, in a first grade class that is studying their neighborhood, the children are building a model that includes homes, the school, stores, and a playground. Their model reflects mathematical thinking, social studies knowledge and understanding, artistic skills, and their skills of planning and collaboration. An excellent example of an Individualized Item for a student in this class would be photographs of the model in process and completed, accompanied by the student's reflection about the process of the project. As an Individualized Item, this Portfolio piece conveys information about the student's learning in the domains of Social Studies, the Arts, Mathematical Thinking, and Personal and Social Development.

Figure 9 shows an Individualized Item from a fourth grade student's Portfolio. To create her "eco-mosaic" illustrating the ecology of the ocean, she applied skills, concepts, and knowledge from several domains including Personal and Social Development, Language and Literacy, Scientific Thinking, and the Arts. The teacher's comment on the work stated, "You worked hard and in an organized way on this project. You conducted thorough research, made and revised several drafts, and showed your understanding of ecosystems and the knowledge you gained about the ocean."

FIGURE 9
Fourth grade student's Individualized Item illustrating the integration of learning from several domains

Comparison of Major Functions of Core and Individualized Items

This table highlights the major differences between Core Items and Individualized Items.

	Core Items	Individualized Items
Major Functions	Progress	Child's unique charactistics
Relation to Domains	Work is linked directly to one of five Core Item domains	Work may represent multiple domains
Planning	Teacher plans in advance	Spontaneous
Collection Periods	Same areas of learning for each collection period for all children	Items vary across collection periods and children
Total Number	2 items x 5 domains x 3 collections = 30	5 items x 3 collections = 15

Total Number of Portfolio Items

By the end of the school year, a complete Work Sampling Portfolio contains 45 items.

	5	domains	
x	2	Core items per domain	(per collection period)
=	**10**	**Core Items**	(per collection period)
+	5	Individualized Items	(per collection period)
=	**15**	**Items per collection period**	
x	3	Collection periods per year	
=	**45**	**Items per year**	

Part II How to Use Portfolios

The completed Portfolio is a collection of work that illustrates a child's learning during one school year. Although the finished product tells much about the learner, the creation of the Portfolio—the process of Portfolio collection—is as important as the completed work. It is through the process of Portfolio collection that you and your students actively study their learning.

For you, the process of Portfolio collection can help you analyze your expectations for student learning, assess whether or not students are making progress, and reflect on the opportunities you offer children to apply their skills meaningfully and to represent their thinking in diverse ways.

For children, the process of Portfolio collection enables them to reflect on their learning. As they construct their Portfolios over the course of the year, they measure their work against classroom expectations, they internalize classroom standards for good work, they set personal goals, and they select work that illustrates progress and their unique characteristics as learners.

The process of Portfolio collection has several parts: collecting work regularly, selecting work periodically, and reflecting upon and annotating work to enhance its meaning. These stages of the process do not happen step-by-step, but occur in an ongoing and overlapping manner as described in Example 1.

EXAMPLE 1

The children in Ms. Romer's first grade classroom engage in a wide variety of classroom activities, some that result in products and others that are documented through photographs or anecdotal records. Ms. Romer and her students save samples of work daily in a collection bin. Every few weeks, Ms. Romer has a work review day in which her students go through the work in their collection bins and make choices or selections for their Portfolios.

Today Ms. Romer confers with Jackson. They review four different pieces of writing and decide which one illustrates Jackson's typical performance for the area of learning "writing to express ideas." Jackson selects a piece and says, "This is the best story I wrote this year." Together they discuss why and record their reflections on the back of the story. Ms. Romer encourages Jackson to put this piece in his Portfolio as an Individualized Item.

She selects another piece and explains to Jackson that this one is a good Core Item because it shows the skills he has as a writer. Ms.

Romer notes these skills on a Portfolio Item Record self-stick note, checks the box that says Core Item, and Jackson puts the piece into the Language and Literacy folder of his Portfolio.

It is this process of creating Portfolios—collecting, selecting, and reflecting upon work over the course of the year—that we will describe in detail after reviewing a timeline for Portfolio collection.

Portfolio Collection Timeline

The timeline below suggests an approximate time-frame for the activities associated with Portfolio Collection during a single collection period.

BEFORE THE START OF THE SCHOOL YEAR		COLLECTION PERIOD BEGINS								COLLECTION PERIOD ENDS	REPORTING PERIOD ENDS
		Week 1	Week 2	Week 3	Week 4	Week 5	Week 6	Week 7	Week 8	Week 9	Week 10	Week 11

Create and Store Individual Portfolios — Collect ... Collect ... Collect ... Collect ... Review and Evaluation of Portfolios

Devise Procedures for Collecting Work

Consider Methods to Portray Learning — Review & Select ... Review & Select ... Review & Select ... Review & Select — Share Portfolios with Families

Plan for Core Item Collection — Final Portfolio Selection

When learning to use Portfolios, the ultimate goal is that Portfolio collection become part of the culture of your classroom, fully integrated into your daily routines as illustrated in Example 1. To achieve this goal, it is necessary to understand certain concepts, plan particular classroom procedures, and perform practical tasks at different times of the school year. As you read the following section, keep in mind that you may only be collecting work in one or two domains when you first begin.

♦ **Before** the school year begins, your activities include planning and preparation. Planning means giving careful thought to the variety of ways you can help children represent their thinking and learning in Portfolios, devising procedures for ongoing work collection, and selecting areas of learning for Core Item collection. Practical tasks include assembling portfolios and collection bins, arranging for their storage, and completing Core Item Collection Plan forms.

♦ **During** each collection period, you should think about Portfolio collection regularly and incorporate several activities into your daily and weekly routines. These activities include conducting discussions with students about classroom work; collecting, selecting, and annotating samples of that work; and keeping track of and filing selected work. Performing these activities throughout the collection period rather than leaving them until the end will result in less stress for you and will allow you to use the information you learn from Portfolios to guide classroom instruction and student learning.

♦ **Near the end** of each collection period, you have to prepare for completing Summary Reports. This involves determining whether each student has a complete set of Core Items and Individualized Items, adding annotations to samples of work if needed, reviewing and evaluating Portfolios yourself, involving students in a Portfolio review and evaluation process, and deciding how Portfolios will be shared with children's families.

Before the School Year Begins

Give time and thought to these four tasks before the school year begins:

- Create individual Portfolios and decide how and where to store them.

- Devise procedures for collecting student work.

- Consider methods to portray learning.

- Plan for Core Item collection.

Create Individual Portfolios and Decide How and Where to Store Them

One of the first decisions you face is how to make your students' Portfolios. If you teach older students, they can take part in making their own Portfolios. Even young children can participate by decorating the covers of their Portfolios.

Although teachers use various methods for organizing individual Portfolios, two approaches are most common. The first is to use six file folders placed inside an accordion file for each student. Five of the folders contain work in the five domains represented by Core Items (Language and Literacy, Mathematical Thinking, Scientific Thinking, Social Studies, and The Arts). A sixth folder holds Individualized Items (Figure 10).

FIGURE 10
Individual Portfolio using accordion file and file folders

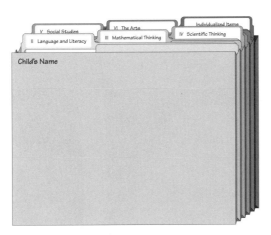

Figure 11 illustrates a second commonly used approach. Teachers use four pocket folders held together with a spiral binding. One of the pockets stores the Core Item Collection Plan, five pockets hold Core Items, and the remaining pockets store Individualized Items.

How to Use Portfolios

FIGURE 11
Individual Portfolio using pocket folders with spiral binding

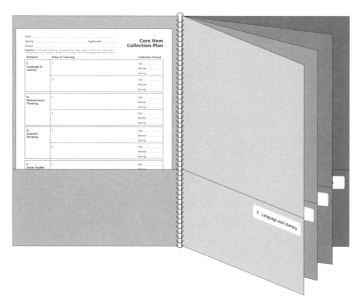

Using either method, teachers store Core Items together by domain, in chronological order (all work should be dated), to facilitate the evaluation of progress. Individualized Items are organized within the folder by collection period. Pre-printed **PORTFOLIO DOMAIN LABELS** are available to speed Portfolio setup.

Other methods for Portfolio construction include ring binders, large construction paper folded in half and stapled, hanging files, covered plastic tubs, and boxes.

After the Portfolio containers are created, decide how to store them in the classroom so they are accessible to children but protected. Milk crates (Figure 12), file cabinets or drawers, shelves, plastic or rubber tubs, and boxes can be used to store Portfolios. Some preschool teachers have made wall hangings with pockets for each child's Portfolio (Figure 13).

FIGURE 12 (LEFT)
A milk crate used to store Portfolios

FIGURE 13 (RIGHT)
A preschool teacher created a wall hanging with pockets to store Portfolios

If Portfolio collection is to become an integral part of the classroom, it is essential that you store Portfolios in a location that is both visible and accessible to children. Some teachers divide the class Portfolios and store them in two or more different locations around the room. In this way, children are less likely to crowd into a single location in the classroom when it is time to work with their Portfolios.

Devise Procedures for Collecting Student Work

After you have decided how to make Portfolio containers and where to store them, the next step for you to consider is how to collect work that may eventually become Portfolio items. As you begin to integrate Portfolios into your classroom, think about collecting work as one step in a process that starts with children participating in learning activities and completing assignments and ends with a completed Portfolio. Planning procedures in advance helps to ensure that work collection begins soon after school opens and proceeds smoothly.

As you develop procedures for collecting work, remember that the Portfolio is not a collection of all the work that students produce. Instead it includes a limited number of items. Some items show typical performance in particular areas of learning (Core Items) and others demonstrate the child's individuality as a learner and/or how the child integrates learning from multiple domains (Individualized Items). In order to make the best use of the Portfolio, it is important to select the most informative work for each child's Portfolio and, in the case of Core Items, to select work that is typical of each child's performance. To have a pool of items from which to make these selections, you must collect work regularly.

When you first begin to use the Work Sampling System Portfolio, you may feel pressured to fill the Portfolio with the correct number of Core and Individualized Items. In reaction to this pressure, teachers are often tempted to respond in one of two ways. The first is to put completed work directly into the Portfolio, eliminating the steps of collecting, reviewing, and selecting work. The problem with this shortcut is that you have no assurance that the work in the Portfolio is representative of the student's typical performance. For example, today John writes an article for the class newspaper. You put this article into his Portfolio as a Core Item representing the area of learning "writing to express ideas." Without the opportunity to compare it to work he finished last week or may complete next week, you cannot be sure that the newspaper article reflects his typical performance in this area of learning.

A second reaction to the pressure to have "complete" portfolios is to declare a specific day as Core Item day or Portfolio day in which all students' work from particular assignments goes into their Portfolios. Portfolios created in this way are less authentic because it is highly unlikely that a single activity on a particular day will result in work that is most typical or most informative for every child in your classroom. On "Core Item day" one child might be coming down with the flu, another may be anxious about something at home, and still others may not find that day's activities very motivating. Rather than compromising the quality of students' Portfolios in the interest of efficiency, we recommend that you resist the pressure to fill the Portfolio and instead, aim to have high quality pieces even if it also means having fewer items.

If you collect work in an ongoing way, you will have a large number of examples to review before making selections. After you have selected work, the remaining work in the collection bin or work folder can be sent home. Then students begin collecting work again. When you devise a plan for ongoing work collection, two issues are central: how much to collect and how to store collected work.

HOW MUCH TO COLLECT   Some teachers collect all the work children do; other teachers limit the work they collect. The degree to which teachers involve children in collecting their work and determining the work to be saved also varies from one teacher to another. Here are some procedures teachers have used for collecting work:

♦ Some teachers collect everything children do in a collection bin or work folder. Children put work in the bin or folder upon completion. Periodically teachers go through those collections to determine which work to keep and which work to send home.

♦ Some teachers tell children to save work that they might want to include in their Portfolios.

♦ Many teachers save work from all children from particular assignments and send the rest home daily or weekly. At the end of the day, they might tell their students to save their writing assignment from the morning and their science investigation reports.

You decide how to handle the process of ongoing work collection. You may be able to keep your current system intact, or to adapt it slightly to accommodate the Work Sampling System Portfolio collection process, or you may have to start from scratch by developing a new procedure.

HOW TO STORE COLLECTED WORK   Many teachers create "collection bins" or "work folders" as places for children's work to be saved. Regardless of their name, these storage areas should be easily accessible to students in the classroom. Think of these as temporary holding areas where work will be safe until it is reviewed and selected for the Portfolio. This stage of Portfolio collection is one in which all children, even the very youngest, can be involved easily. Putting a stamp pad and date stamp next to this bin or folder helps to ensure that every piece is dated before it is collected.

Here are some collection bins or work folders that teachers have made:

♦ a hanging file for each child stored in one or two milk crates

♦ a hanging file for each child stored in an accessible file drawer or file cart

♦ a mailbox for each child

♦ a folder or notebook in each child's desk or cubby

Consider Methods to Portray Learning

Having determined how to make Portfolio containers and decided upon a plan for collecting work, you are ready to begin thinking about methods to represent children's learning. Portfolios are filled with concrete representations of children's thinking and learning. As you gain experience using Portfolios, you soon realize that an important part of your job is to help children express their learning in concrete ways. Some activities that children participate in naturally result in tangible products. For example, when children write in journals or create stories, the actual work or a copy of it can become a Portfolio item. Not all learning activities, however, result in tangible products that can easily be put into Portfolios. For example, when a child takes part in a skit to show his understanding of the book he just read, the activity does not produce something to put in a portfolio. In this case, the teacher has to help children represent their learning concretely by videotaping the performance or writing an anecdote that can be put into the Portfolio.

One of the most significant challenges of Portfolio collection is to find ways to document thinking and learning—internal processes—in a tangible form. This is especially true for students in preschool, kindergarten, and first grade. At these ages, children's products do not necessarily reflect their thinking very accurately. Moreover, children engage in many activities that do not result in the creation of a product. In these situations, one part of the teacher's role is to find ways to represent children's learning. Consider the preschooler who counts the cups and plates in the dramatic play area thereby showing an understanding of one-to-one correspondence. To represent the child's understanding, a teacher could write an anecdotal note or "word picture" describing the event.

Even products children do produce often have to be translated into a form appropriate for a Portfolio. For example, if a child constructs a symmetrical design using pattern blocks, his teacher might sketch the child's symmetrical design, ask the child to reproduce it with paper pattern block shapes, or photograph the design for inclusion in the Portfolio.

Teachers have found many ways to represent, and help children represent, learning in a concrete form. Some techniques teachers have used include creating recording forms or worksheets; using photographs, videotapes, and audiotapes; documenting with sketches and diagrams; saving multiple drafts of a project; and writing word pictures. Each technique will be described below.

♦ **Recording forms or worksheets** Some teachers create worksheets that allow children to represent the result of their mathematical work with manipulatives (Figure 14). Others have prepared pre-cut shapes that replicate pattern blocks so that children can recreate their solutions to problems involving patterning, fractions, or symmetry (Figure 15).

FIGURE 14 (LEFT)
A second grade teacher's form to reproduce geoboard designs

FIGURE 15 (RIGHT)
A second grade teacher's form to recreate a child's understanding of fractions

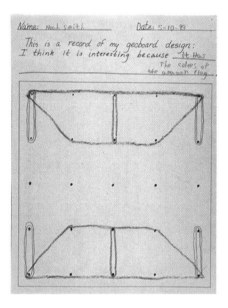

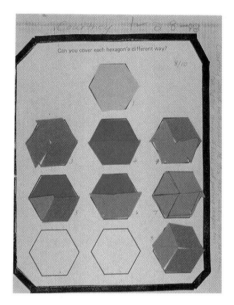

FIGURE 16
Form to record magnet exploration—first grade

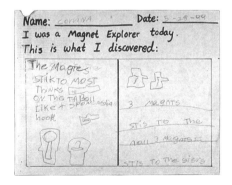

Figures 16 and 17 show two forms teachers have created to guide children in representing their scientific investigations.

FIGURE 17
Form to represent the investigation process (predicting, observing, and concluding)—third grade

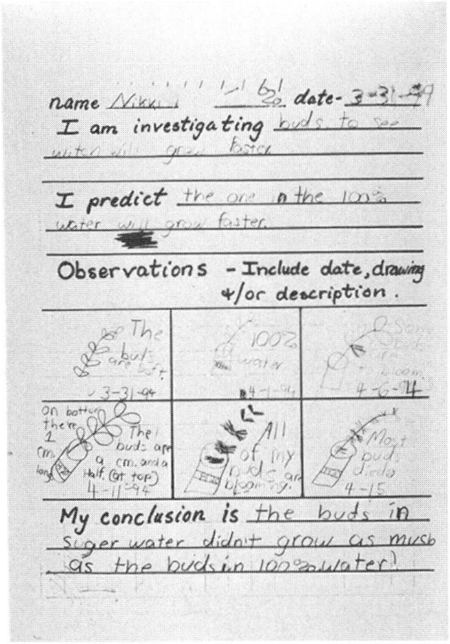

Still other teachers have arranged opportunities for children to represent their learning during play. During a study of hospitals, the dramatic play area in a kindergarten classroom became a hospital. Here is how one child "wrote" a prescription. Note how this child's spontaneous actions demonstrate her use of letter strings (Figure 18).

FIGURE 18
Representation of a child's emergent writing during dramatic play

♦ **Photographs, videos, and/or audio tapes** Photographs, videos, and audio tapes that capture children's thinking and knowledge enrich the Portfolio Collection. Their cost, however, can be an obstacle.

Many teachers use photographs in children's Portfolios. You may find it helpful to record the child's name, the date, and a comment about why you took each snapshot as you take photographs in your classroom.

After the film is processed, you can add this information to the photograph, making it a more informative item for the Portfolio. Figure 19 shows a teacher-made photograph form. Notice how the teacher's anecdotal note helps to increase the meaning of the photograph.

FIGURE 19
Teacher-created form for photographs and anecdotal records

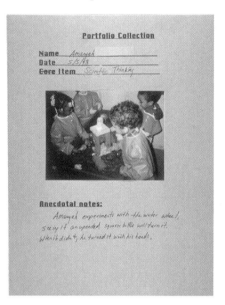

The **PHOTOGRAPHIC PORTFOLIO ITEM RECORD** form (Figure 20) is a variation of this form included in the booklet of Reproducible Masters.

FIGURE 20
Photographic Portfolio Item Record form

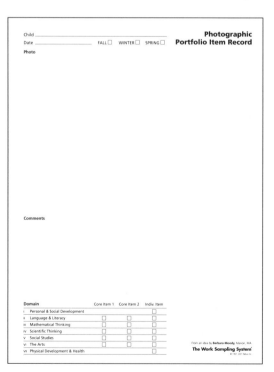

◆ **Multiple drafts or stages** Saving examples from different stages of a project rather than just the finished product is an effective way to illustrate the process of a child's learning. You might include a first draft, second draft, and final draft of a writing assignment or the planning sheet, completed project, and the child's reflection from a science or social studies assignment. If you teach very young children, you might photograph a painting or drawing at different stages of its creation.

Figures 21–24 show four stages in a castle project done by Chrystal, a fourth grade student, with her partner, Sara. Figure 21 shows Chrystal's initial homework assignment in which she identified what she already knew about castles and her questions for research. After some research, she drew a blueprint of a castle and wrote a report with Sara (Figures 22 and 23). Figure 24 is a photograph of the model they built and Figure 25 shows Chrystal's evaluation of her cooperative work on the project. The teacher's comments are noted on the Portfolio Item Record self-stick note (Figure 26).

FIGURE 21 (LEFT)
Chrystal's initial
homework assignment

FIGURE 22 (RIGHT)
Chrystal's castle blueprint

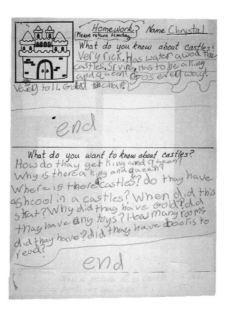

FIGURE 23 (LEFT)
Chrystal's report, written
in collaboration with Sara

FIGURE 24 (RIGHT)
A photo shows the
finished castle model

ABOUT A KEEP
by
Chrystal and Sara

The keep is the biggest and strongest point of the castle. The keep is home of the most important belongings. Some of the important people are: King, .Queen, Knight, Prince and Princess, servants Jester, Cook and Ladies in Waiting.

A dungeon is in the tower. Sometimes knights hide behind the parapets on a tower.

The curtain wall is built around a bailey. It is used so enemies can't get into the keep.

A portcullis is a gate, usually made of metal. The portcullis is used for keeping out enemies.

The drawbridge is a bridge which is made out of wood and goes u p and down.

The moat is a ditch filled with water. It was there so when enemies came to attact the castle it was difficult to get across the moat.

Our flag is from France.

FIGURE 25
Chrystal's evaluation

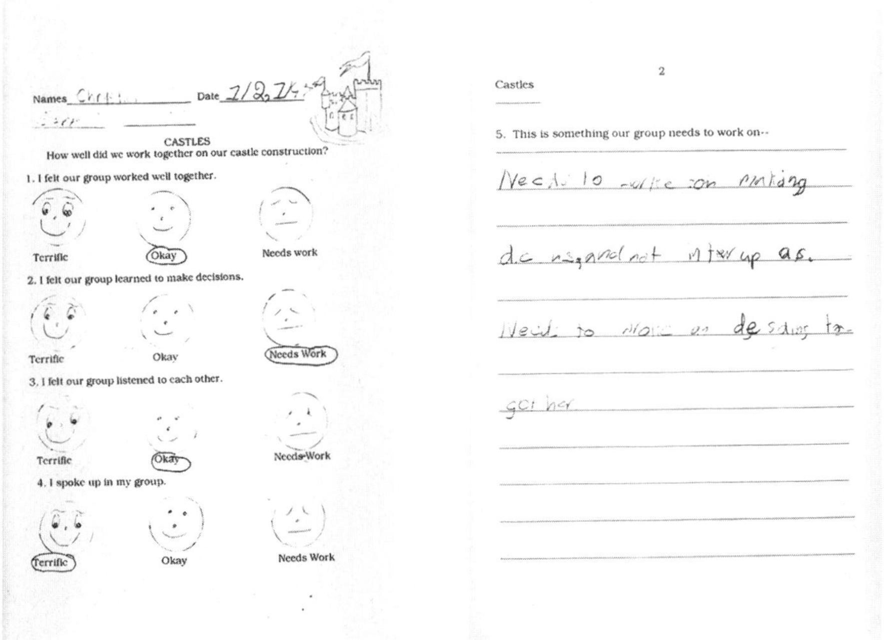

FIGURE 26
Chrystal's teacher's comments about her castle project, shown on a Portfolio Item Record self-stick note

Portfolio Item Record

Child **Chrystal (4th grade)**

Date **1/27**

FALL ☐ WINTER ☒ SPRING ☐

Domains	Core Item 1	Core Item 2	Indiv. Item
I Personal & Social Development			☒
II Language & Literacy	☐	☐	☒
III Mathematical Thinking	☐	☐	☐
IV Scientific Thinking	☐	☐	☐
V Social Studies	☐	☐	☒
VI The Arts	☐	☐	☒
VII Physical Development & Health			☐

Comments

This project shows Chrystal's ability to stick with a project from start to finish, as well as her ability to work well with a partner. She started with many questions and gradually focused her interest on the keep. Her blueprint for the castle model has some similarity to the finished model.

The Work Sampling System

♦ **Sketches and diagrams** You and your students can create sketches or diagrams that illustrate or describe a three-dimensional product. Figure 27 shows a teacher-made sketch of a child's block building.

FIGURE 27
A teacher's diagram of a child's block building

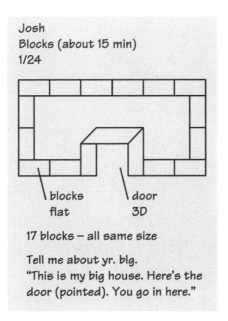

Josh
Blocks (about 15 min)
1/24

\\blocks   \\door
flat   3D

17 blocks – all same size

Tell me about yr. blg.
"This is my big house. Here's the door (pointed). You go in here."

Figure 28 shows a diagram drawn by a fourth grader. The diagram depicts the sombrero he made as part of his research about Mexico along with the teacher's comments.

FIGURE 28
A diagram depicting the result of a fourth grader's research, along with the teacher's annotations

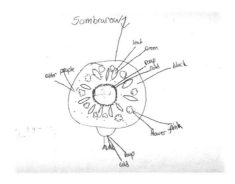

Individualized Item, Winter
• Personal and Social Development
• Social Studies
• The Arts

John's diagramatic drawing of the sombrero he made as part of his research about Mexico demonstrates his artistic talents and his attention to detail. He wore the hat proudly in the class performance of international music.

♦ **Word pictures** A teacher's anecdotal notes describing something a child has done or said is also an appropriate Portfolio item when it captures a moment in the same manner of a photograph. Example 2 shows a kindergarten teacher's anecdotal note. The description and the teacher's comment written on a Portfolio Item Record was placed in the Portfolio as a Core Item for the area of learning "predicting outcomes and formulating explanations."

EXAMPLE 2

October 19, 2000

A student brought a large shell to school. He asked us all to listen to it because he said that he could hear a toilet in it. We all laughed about it. Then I asked the children to think about why they could hear a sound in the shell. In response to the question, Mitchell said "Maybe some water stays in there. Sometimes little crabs could live in there."

Comments:

Mitchell always has an explanation for things. He thinks really hard about things and incorporates the ideas of others. He began the explanation on his own. After another child mentioned crabs, he added the second part to his explanation.

Undoubtedly, you will discover other ways to represent students' learning. Once you acquire the habit of asking yourself as you plan curriculum, "How might this learning be captured for the Portfolio?" you will find other creative ways of representing children's learning in tangible ways.

Plan for Core Item Collection

The last preparation task before school starts is planning for Core Item collection. This process involves understanding areas of learning, developing effective areas of learning, analyzing areas of learning in relation to teaching and learning, translating areas of learning into curriculum, and finally, managing the collection of Core Items. Although we will describe this process in detail in the section that follows, you may choose to select areas of learning from the examples in Appendixes A and B.

In a complete Work Sampling Portfolio, two areas of learning are identified in each of the five Core Item domains: Language and Literacy, Mathematical Thinking, Scientific Thinking, Social Studies, and The Arts. Before school begins, you will identify a total of ten areas of learning if you are implementing Core Item collection in five domains.

Understanding Areas of Learning

Remember some key ideas about areas of learning:

♦ An area of learning is a strand of the curriculum (a part of a curriculum domain) that guides the collection of Core Items.

♦ Each domain encompasses many areas of learning.

♦ Careful selection of areas of learning results in Core Items that convey meaningful information about the quality of a child's thinking and her progress over time.

♦ Effective areas of learning meet the following criteria:

   ♦ are important parts of the curriculum

   ♦ are specific enough to show progress over time

   ♦ are relevant for all students

- reflect concepts or processes and are not dependent on particular content

- are most effectively documented in the Portfolio rather than on the Checklist

A more thorough description and discussion of each of these five criteria follows.

IMPORTANT PARTS OF THE CURRICULUM To be effective for Core Item collection, areas of learning should:

- Reflect an integrated set of skills, rather than a single or isolated skill

- Permit the application of several skills in a meaningful context

- Provide opportunities for many different responses (in the form of Core Items) from children

- Invite child engagement on a daily or weekly basis

For example, "writing to express ideas" is an effective area of learning for Core Item collection in the domain Language and Literacy. It includes such skills as use of detail and descriptive language, use of conventions of print, and sequencing and organizing ideas. On the other hand, "punctuation" is not an effective area of learning. Although it is an important skill for primary children to acquire, punctuation becomes meaningful only in the context of writing. For this reason, "writing to express ideas" is a much more useful area of learning.

SPECIFIC ENOUGH TO SHOW PROGRESS OVER TIME To be effective, areas of learning should:

- Encompass a clearly identifiable progression of development

- Be defined specifically enough to ensure that comparable work is collected during each collection period

For example, if an area of learning in Mathematical Thinking is defined simply as "problem-solving," the work collected may reflect number concepts in the fall, spatial relationships in the winter, and the use of multiple strategies to solve a problem in the spring. Clearly, the work will be different from one collection period to the next. If you are to use it to evaluate progress, however, the work from each collection period must reflect the same area of learning. Therefore, "problem-solving" is too broad to be an effective area of learning for Mathematical Thinking Core Item collection. A more effective area of learning that would be specific enough to show progress over time is "using strategies to solve problems involving number concepts."

RELEVANT FOR ALL STUDENTS To be effective, areas of learning should:

♦ Apply to all students regardless of their place on the developmental continuum

♦ Define a wide range of performance, thus accommodating learning goals for all students in the classroom

For example, consider the preschool teacher who initially defines "the child's application of patterning in problem-solving" as an area of learning in Mathematical Thinking. As defined, this area of learning will not include those children who are just beginning to recognize attributes and to match and sort. In contrast, if the teacher defines the area of learning as "classifying, comparing, and ordering objects by attributes in order to organize them," children who are matching and sorting will be accommodated, as well as those who are recognizing and creating patterns.

REFLECT CONCEPTS OR PROCESSES To be effective, areas of learning should:

♦ Address concepts or processes that *underlie* or are *fundamental* to particular content

♦ Do not reflect specific content, because curriculum changes over the course of the school year

For example, an area of learning defined as "understanding how magnets work" is content-specific. In contrast, an area of learning defined as "observing and predicting to gather scientific information" is meaningful throughout the school year because it reflects the intellectual processes that underlie studies of content such as magnetism. If an area of learning relies on specific content, once children have learned that content, the area of learning may no longer be relevant.

BEST DOCUMENTED IN THE PORTFOLIO To be effective, areas of learning should include:

♦ Documentation of process (how children approach tasks or problems and the ways in which they represent their work) that is best shown through the Portfolio

♦ A different type of documentation than can be recorded on the Checklist (the Checklist focuses on whether a child can perform a specific skill or has acquired particular knowledge)

For example, "a child's ability to communicate through writing" requires documentation in a portfolio because it is the actual work that provides evidence of how the child is using writing to communicate. In contrast, if the area of learning had been identified as "uses letter-like shapes to depict words and ideas," the teacher is responding to specific skills that can be documented quite easily in the Checklist.

Developing Areas of Learning to Guide Core Item Collection

SELECTING EFFECTIVE AREAS OF LEARNING After you understand the criteria for developing effective areas of learning, you are ready to begin developing them for the school year. Teachers across the country evaluate their students on the same Developmental Checklist, but Portfolios incorporate local standards and expectations to ensure that they are also represented in assessment. Because an in-depth understanding of local curriculum and the local student population is necessary to decide on effective areas of learning, you and your colleagues share the responsibility for developing them.

Most often a group of teachers works together to identify areas of learning. In some schools, one of the two areas of learning in each domain is the same for all students in the school; the second area of learning varies from one grade level to the next. The first year that you use Work Sampling, you may decide to collect Core Items in fewer than five domains. For further discussion of how to modify Core Item collection in your first year, see Chapter 5.

When you meet with your colleagues to develop areas of learning, work in one domain at a time. Frequently teachers begin with Language and Literacy because most teachers have the greatest knowledge of this area. Once you have selected the domain, think about the goals you have for your students in that domain. What is most important for all of your students to learn? For example, you might identify the following goals or strands of your curriculum in the domain of Language and Literacy: communicating orally, using symbols to communicate ideas, writing to express ideas, comprehending and interpreting text, showing interest in reading. As you can see, a domain encompasses many potential areas of learning.

Once you have a list of three or four possible areas of learning for Language and Literacy, evaluate each one against the five criteria described beginning on page 84. Ask yourself whether the proposed area of learning is an important part of your curriculum, whether it is specific enough to show progress over time, is relevant for all students, reflects concepts or processes and is not dependent on particular content, and is most effectively documented in the Portfolio rather than on the Checklist. If it meets all five criteria, it is a good choice.

Eliminate the potential areas of learning that do not meet all five criteria. If you have several that meet all the criteria, select two from the list to use this year. If all of your potential areas of learning have been eliminated, brainstorm a new list of possiblities and repeat the evaluation process.

Appendixes A and B list recommended areas of learning. They also describe potential Core Items for preschool and elementary classrooms.

After deciding on an area of learning, you are ready to analyze it. This analytic process will help you and your colleagues develop a rich and shared understanding of the area of learning which in turn will help you as you plan curriculum, talk with children about their work, and evaluate work near the end of each collection period.

SKILLS AND CONCEPTS As a first step in this process, talk with colleagues about the skills and/or concepts encompassed by the area of learning. This conversation can include teachers of different grade levels with each teacher contributing information relevant to the grade level she teaches. Included in the Reproducible Masters booklet is a chart formatted to facilitate this process. As you examine each area of learning, think about the skills, knowledge, and concepts that are part of it.

A group of first grade teachers analyzed the area of learning "using patterns to understand relationships and organize information" in the domain of Mathematical Thinking. They generated the following list of skills and concepts:

- exploring different types of patterns (pictures, words, movement, rhythm, number, shape)

- creating original patterns

- extending and translating patterns by identifying the rule that generated the pattern

- representing and describing patterns

- using calculators to explore patterns

- making generalizations based on observed patterns

- connecting patterns to other disciplines (e.g., in Scientific Thinking, looking for patterns in nature; in Language and Literacy, recognizing patterns in stories)

- solving mathematical problems using patterns

Knowing the skills, concepts, and knowledge encompassed by an area of learning will provide you with a basis for selecting and evaluating student work in that area.

EXPECTATIONS FOR CHILDREN'S PROGRESS The second step of this analytic process is to spend some time discussing how children's performance in this area of learning changes during the school year. Our first grade teachers above began to chart their expectations for children's progress using some of the skills and concepts they had identified.

FALL	WINTER	SPRING
perceive simple patterns and extend them	recognize different patterns (AB, AAB, ABC)	recognize 2- and 3-D patterns
create simple patterns	create more complex patterns	make patterns in more than one direction (forward, backward, in a circle)
	begin to observe and extend patterns with numbers	make number patterns using one and rule
describe pattern rule with simple patterns	describe patterns in daily life	make predictions based on patterns
	begin to observe patterns across the curriculum (e.g., in stories, in science investigations)	make generalizations based on observations of patterns

Their chart shows that they expect children to complete more complex patterns over the school year and to make patterns in more than one direction. It also shows that they do not expect children to have much awareness of number patterns at the beginning of the year, but would expect this by the end of the year. These expectations reflect the curriculum standards of the local district. Teachers from another school district might have slightly different expectations for children's progress in this area of learning.

HOW INSTRUCTION CHANGES OVER TIME As a next step, these teachers discussed how they would change instruction to support children's progress. Over the course of the year, they would take these steps:

♦ increase the number and variety of materials available to children for exploring and creating patterns

♦ teach increasingly complex patterns

♦ create opportunities to discuss patterns across the disciplines

♦ teach a variety of ways to name, record, and describe patterns

♦ teach children to use calculators to extend patterns

Some groups of teachers chart their expectations as these first grade teachers did. Others make a graph or simply draw a horizontal line to represent the school year and list on it how they expect children's performance and their teaching to change over the course of the year.

This analytic process will help you anticipate the progress that you hope to see during the school year, which in turn will enable you to plan curriculum and instruction to promote that progress.

The process of analyzing an area of learning can be especially valuable when it crosses grade levels. For example, a group of teachers spanning preschool through grade two discussed the area of learning "writing to express ideas" in Language and Literacy. They created charts of how they expected children's writing to change over the years. Teachers of older children could see the foundation of their students' skills beginning in preschool, and teachers of young children recognized how the rudimentary skills their students possess change over time. We recommend that you consider doing this activity with your colleagues.

After you have analyzed areas of learning from a theoretical perspective, it is time to think about the practical aspects of collecting Core Items. Using an area of learning that you have identified, think about how children's participation in curriculum activities will produce concrete representations of this area of learning that can be included in their Portfolios.

CLASSROOM ACTIVITIES We suggest that you brainstorm a list of curriculum activities related to each area of learning. Consider group projects, independent work, and materials that children can use in the classroom that engage them in the relevant area of learning. Write them in the left column under "Classroom Activities." Here is the list from our first grade teachers.

CLASSROOM ACTIVITIES
Creating block patterns
Working with Unifix cubes, beads, pegboards, or other manipulative materials
Block building
Drawing and painting
Weaving
Rhythm activities of clapping games

CORE ITEMS Once you have a list of activities, ask yourself how each activity can be represented in the Portfolio. Keep in mind that because different children express themselves in different ways, each activity may be represented in several ways in the Portfolio. Write these ideas in the right column headed "Child's Work/Core Items," as shown in the table below.

CLASSROOM ACTIVITIES	CHILD'S WORK/CORE ITEMS
Creating block patterns	Drawings, photographs, and written or dictated descriptions
Working with Unifix cubes, beads, pegboards, or other manipulative materials	Tracings, cut-out pictures, drawings, photographs, each with descriptions (written or dictated)
Block building	Photograph with description
Drawing and painting	Drawings, paintings, written or dictated descriptions
Weaving	Weaving with written or dictated descriptions
Rhythm activities or clapping games	Video or audio tapes, or anecdotal descriptions

This process of analysis — listing skills and concepts, sketching the continuum of progress, identifying related curriculum activities, and considering how each activity can be reflected in the Portfolio — is repeated for each area of learning. If you keep records of your work, you will begin the school year with a list of areas of learning, related curriculum activities, and ideas about how each can be included in the Portfolio. This process simplifies ongoing curriculum planning during the year.

The **CORE ITEM PLANNING WORKSHEET** form (Figure 29) is available in the booklet of Reproducible Masters to help keep track of your ideas. Figures 30 and 31 show the outcome of work done by third grade teachers for the area of learning "observing and recording scientific phenomena" in Scientific Thinking, using different charting methods.

FIGURE 29
Core Item Planning Worksheet

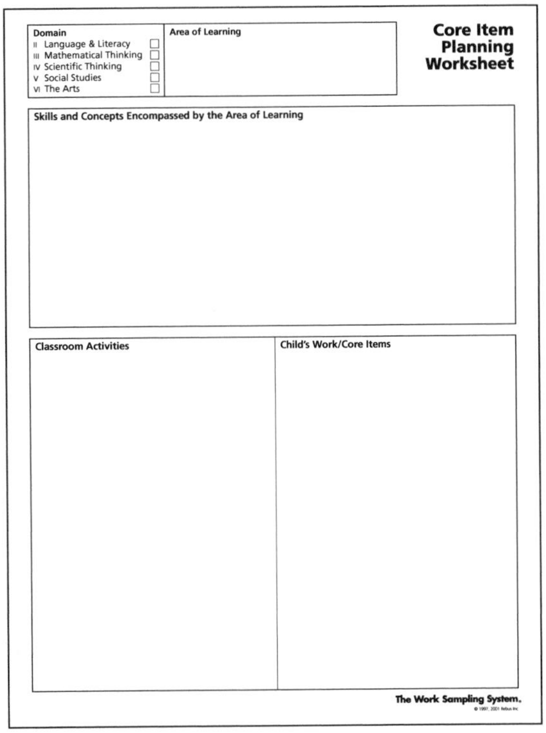
Domain
II Language & Literacy ☐
III Mathematical Thinking ☐
IV Scientific Thinking ☐
V Social Studies ☐
VI The Arts ☐

Area of Learning

Core Item Planning Worksheet

Skills and Concepts Encompassed by the Area of Learning

Classroom Activities	Child's Work/Core Items

The Work Sampling System.

FIGURE 30

A completed Core Item Planning Worksheet for Scientific Thinking in third grade

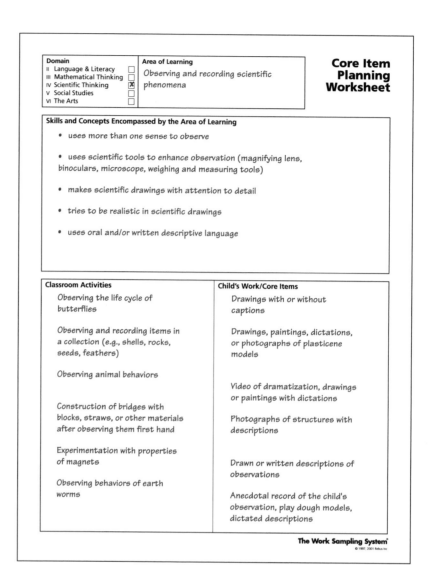

FIGURE 31

The chart used by the third grade teachers to identify expectations for children's progress in Scientific Thinking over the school year and related changes to instruction

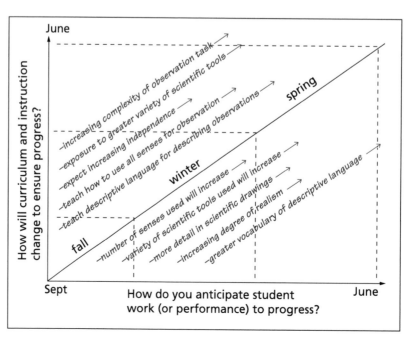

Managing Core Item Collection

The **CORE ITEM COLLECTION PLAN** form (Figure 32) that is available in the booklet of Reproducible Masters serves as a table of contents for each Portfolio. After you have decided upon areas of learning, list them on this form and make copies for all of your students. Add each child's name to the top of a copy and place it in the front of the child's Portfolio. As work is selected, check off the appropriate collection period on the right side of the form.

FIGURE 32
Core Item Collection Plan
form

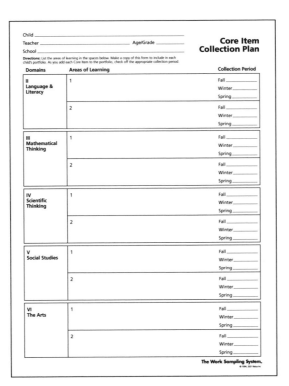

Figures 33 and 34 show two examples of completed Core Item Collection Plan forms, one from a kindergarten teacher and the other from a third grade teacher.

FIGURE 33
Core Item Collection Plan form with areas of learning completed for a Kindergarten classroom

Child _____

Teacher _____ Age/Grade _____

School _____

Core Item Collection Plan

Directions: List the areas of learning in the spaces below. Make a copy of this form to include in each child's portfolio. As you add each Core Item to the portfolio, check off the appropriate collection period.

Domains	Areas of Learning	Collection Period
II Language & Literacy	1 Understanding and interpreting literature	Fall _____ Winter_____ Spring_____
	2 Using letters and symbols to represent words or ideas	Fall _____ Winter_____ Spring_____
III Mathematical Thinking	1 Applying the concepts of patterns and relationships to problem-solving	Fall _____ Winter_____ Spring_____
	2 Using strategies to solve number problems	Fall _____ Winter_____ Spring_____
IV Scientific Thinking	1 Observing and describing scientific phenomena	Fall _____ Winter_____ Spring_____
	2 Questioning, predicting, and explaining in a scientific investigation	Fall _____ Winter_____ Spring_____
V Social Studies	1 Collecting and understanding information about self and family	Fall _____ Winter_____ Spring_____
	2 Recognizing similarities and differences between self and others	Fall _____ Winter_____ Spring_____
VI The Arts	1 Using an artistic medium to express ideas and emotions	Fall _____ Winter_____ Spring_____
	2 Exploring a variety of artistic media	Fall _____ Winter_____ Spring_____

The Work Sampling System.
© 1994, 2001 Rebus Inc

FIGURE 34
Core Item Collection Plan form with areas of learning completed for a third grade classroom

Child _____

Teacher _____ Age/Grade _____

School _____

Core Item Collection Plan

Directions: List the areas of learning in the spaces below. Make a copy of this form to include in each child's portfolio. As you add each Core Item to the portfolio, check off the appropriate collection period.

Domains	Areas of Learning	Collection Period
II Language & Literacy	1 Writing for a variety of purposes	Fall _____ Winter_____ Spring_____
	2 Reading for meaning	Fall _____ Winter_____ Spring_____
III Mathematical Thinking	1 Applying correct operations to solve problems and explaining solutions	Fall _____ Winter_____ Spring_____
	2 Using a variety strategies to solve mathematical problems	Fall _____ Winter_____ Spring_____
IV Scientific Thinking	1 Observing and recording scientific phenomena	Fall _____ Winter_____ Spring_____
	2 Planning and conducting an experiment to test a hypothesis	Fall _____ Winter_____ Spring_____
V Social Studies	1 Creating maps and other geographic representations	Fall _____ Winter_____ Spring_____
	2 Collecting, understanding, and interpreting information about the relationship between people and their environment	Fall _____ Winter_____ Spring_____
VI The Arts	1 Using artistic media to express ideas or emotions	Fall _____ Winter_____ Spring_____
	2 Interpreting, analyzing, and responding personally to artistic pieces and experiences	Fall _____ Winter_____ Spring_____

The Work Sampling System.
© 1994, 2001 Rebus Inc

Once you have developed areas of learning, devised procedures for collecting work, and have made plans for making and storing Portfolios, you are ready for the ongoing work collection that begins when students start school.

During Each Collection Period

In the previous section we have described how you set up Portfolio collection. In this section we describe Portfolio collection in action. During each collection period, several activities can be incorporated into your daily and weekly routines to make Portfolio collection a more valuable and a more manageable experience for you and your students. These activities can be organized under four headings:

- Plan curriculum with Portfolio collection in mind.

- Involve students in Portfolio collection.

- Collect, select, and annotate work.

- Manage the selection process.

As you read through this section, you may feel that it is difficult to add any more activities to your already busy schedule. Keep in mind that teachers report that Portfolio collection is easier once it becomes integrated into their ongoing classroom routine. As you gain comfort with the Portfolio process, you can add these tasks one at a time in a way that is manageable.

Planning Curriculum with Portfolio Collection in Mind

Portfolio collection becomes an integral part of the classroom only when teachers plan curriculum with assessment in mind. Often, when teachers begin to use Portfolios, they plan curriculum and create Portfolios as two separate activities, and consequently feel burdened by the dual demands of assessment and teaching. We view instruction and assessment, however, as interdependent aspects of teaching: assessment provides the information that can make teaching more responsive to students' needs. By connecting Portfolio collection to your daily and weekly curriculum planning, you can make Portfolios a natural part of your classroom routine.

Link Areas of Learning to Classroom Activities

As you plan your weekly schedule, keep in mind the areas of learning that you have identified for Core Item collection. By including activities that relate to your identified areas of learning, you ensure that your students will have an ample number of work samples from which to select Core Items. This makes it more likely that work selected for the Portfolio accurately represents students' typical performances. Several areas of learning will be included in your plans each week, since areas of learning have been chosen because they are important parts of the curriculum.

Consider Ways to Concretely Represent Children's Learning

As we discussed earlier in this chapter, a major challenge of Portfolio collection is to represent children's learning tangibly. Many of the activities you plan for children enable them to express their learning in ways that result in such concrete products as a drawing, a journal entry, or a written solution to a math problem. But much of the important thinking and learning that children do in the classroom do not naturally result in a concrete product that can be easily placed in a Portfolio.

For this reason, you can facilitate Portfolio collection in your classroom by planning for Portfolio items as you do your daily and weekly planning. Refer to the discussion beginning on page 77 for a description of some methods teachers have used to translate children's thinking and learning into tangible Portfolio products.

Provide Many Ways for Children to Express their Learning

You will help to ensure authentic and valid Portfolios if you offer a variety of ways for children to express their learning.

One of the assumptions of the Work Sampling System is that because individual children express their knowledge in different ways, an effective assessment must provide children with many different ways to express their learning. Many children prefer or are most comfortable with particular avenues of expression, such as drawing, dramatizing, writing, model making, speaking, or playing a musical instrument. Each child's Portfolio will include multiple examples of his preferred means of expression. Although we recognize that it is not possible to give children different ways to express themselves for every activity, try to give children some choices in how they represent their learning over the course of the week.

Children also need to develop a range of ways to communicate their learning. Some methods are conventional—we want all children to have a certain level of competence and confidence in oral and written expression. At the same time, however, we want children to stretch themselves and to experiment with less familiar ways to convey their understandings, such as dramatizing or sculpting. By providing children with many ways to communicate their learning, you are supporting their individual approach to learning while encouraging them to acquire skills in using conventional means of expression.

Clarify Learning Goals and Expectations

As you plan activities, ask yourself two questions: What do I want children to learn? What are my expectations for their work? You will be better able to give students specific and helpful feedback on their work when you have clarified your own expectations. Students are more likely to be successful when they have a clear understanding of the purpose and expectations of a task.

Some teachers find it useful to record the goal of the learning activity directly on the assignment or worksheet at the time they create it. Others also include a brief statement about the expectations for the assignment. This type of annotation on assignments provides excellent documentation for Portfolio items. Even if the work is sent home rather than becoming part of the Portfolio, your efforts are not wasted because parents will also find the information useful (See page 105 for a detailed discussion about annotating Portfolio work).

Involve Students in Portfolio Collection

We believe that creating Portfolios should be a collaborative effort between students and teachers. At the beginning of the year, you introduce Portfolios and explain the procedures for collecting and selecting work. Throughout the year, you and your students talk about their work. These teacher-student conversations are fundamental to good teaching and provide the most significant vehicle to help students take responsibility for their own learning.

Teach Students about Portfolios

If portfolios are new to your classroom, your first conversation with children is likely to be similar to other conversations about new materials, procedures, or activities in the classroom. You can introduce this discussion by asking students to describe what they already know about portfolios, and building on their ideas, explain what portfolios are and why they are kept. Some teachers link Portfolios to scrapbooks or photo albums. Talk with children about professionals who keep portfolios and the reasons they use them in their work. If family members are artists, architects, photographers, or journalists, consider inviting them to share their portfolios with your class. The nature and extent of this conversation will vary depending on the age of your students.

After an introductory discussion, you can describe your role and the students' roles in Portfolio collection. Students can participate by decorating their Portfolios or helping you decide which method to use to create their

Portfolios. When you are ready to start collecting work, you can teach them the routines and procedures for managing the Portfolio collection process. Communicate the plan you devised before the school year began for ongoing work collection and teach children how to date and add comments to their work before filing it in the collection bin.

Eventually you will engage students in more sophisticated discussions related to their Portfolio work. These discussions may touch on how their work shows progress, expectations for work, their reflection on and evaluation of their work, and setting personal goals for improving their work.

Talk with Students about their Work

The daily conversations you have with students about their work will influence the success of Portfolio collection in your classroom. Your conversations with students should focus on four topics.

PURPOSES OF ACTIVITIES AND PROJECTS When children understand why they are doing something they are more motivated to work productively and do their best. Sometimes the purpose of the activity is conveyed through informal conversation. For example, a preschool teacher might say, "Playing at the water table lets you try out your ideas about how objects move in water." Other times, a teacher makes the purpose of the activity explicit by writing a purpose statement on the assignment sheet or by stating the purpose during a meeting. A teacher might write or say, "Drawing and writing about our trip helps you remember details about the apple orchard."

Once the purpose of an activity has been clearly stated, the teacher and the student can discuss and evaluate the student's work in relation to that purpose. This is an important first step in teaching students how to evaluate their own work. When students understand the goal of the assignment, and can evaluate whether or not their work has fulfilled that purpose, they can make effective selections for their portfolios.

EXPECTATIONS Discuss your expectations for performance with your students. By doing this you increase the likelihood that students will actually demonstrate the skills and behaviors that you want to assess. To help students take responsibility for their learning, let them know how they are expected to go about the task and when relevant, the characteristics of a good finished product. When teachers do not make expectations clear to students, children do not understand whether they have or have not met the expectations. Nor do they know how to improve their work. Establishing a purpose for assignments and defining expectations help students become reflective about their learning and begin to evaluate their own work.

CONSTRUCTIVE FEEDBACK Clear, age-appropriate feedback will let your students know how their work compares to the stated expectations. A comment such as "good work" or a grade of "B" doesn't tell the student what he has learned from the assignment, what he did well, what he could have done differently, or how he could improve. However, a comment such as "Your story includes many funny details. Let's discuss the ending; it doesn't connect to the rest of the story" is more informative and gives the student direction in how to proceed. Moreover, when specific feedback accompanies the work, it also provides excellent annotation for the Portfolio. Constructive and specific feedback is an integral part of classroom life as students engage in and complete tasks.

EVALUATION Feedback and evaluation are often one and the same. Your evaluation of work, whether it is a grade, a score, or a comment, should be directly linked to the expectations you have defined for the task. Some teachers establish rubrics or other scoring systems based on clearly defined criteria. Evaluation of student work can include your evaluation and the student's self-evaluation. Questions that can guide a student's self evaluation include: How did I do in relation to the expectations? and What did I learn from doing this project?

Talking with students about their work is an essential part of the teaching and learning process and central to students' active involvement in the Portfolio process. Students can only begin to make meaningful selections for their Portfolios and reflect on their own learning when they know what is expected of them and understand how they are performing in relation to those expectations.

Collecting, Selecting, and Annotating Work

As children work every day in your classroom, you (and they) will collect work regularly, periodically select work for the Portfolio, reflect upon the work, and when necessary, add annotations to enhance the meaning of the work.

Collect Work Regularly

As part of the classroom routine during each collection period, you and your students will use the procedures you devised before school started to collect work on an ongoing basis. If the system you devised does not work smoothly, we strongly recommend that you revise it. As part of the ongoing collection routine, remember these three ideas:

♦ **Review procedures** with your students from time to time. Children are likely to need reminders to use the established collection procedures especially at the beginning of the year.

♦ **Date all work.** Dating work is essential in order to assess progress. The date is the single most important piece of annotation to add to Portfolio work. It is helpful to put a date stamp next to the collection bin and encourage children to use it. When date stamps are first introduced, young children may spend more time dating their work than they did completing it. After the novelty wears off, however, even young children can easily assume this responsibility.

♦ **Add comments** or annotations about work at the time it is placed in the collection bin. You or your students can quickly jot down some notes about a piece of work prior to putting it into the collection bin. When a child decides to save a piece of work, encourage him to record the reason for saving it. If you decide it should go into the collection bin, record your reason for saving the piece.

Select Work Periodically

Selecting work means going through a collection of work from time to time and choosing pieces to put into the Portfolio. Here are four issues to consider when thinking about the selection process: choosing Core Items, selecting Individualized Items, establishing procedures, and involving children in the process.

CHOOSING CORE ITEMS As discussed earlier, work is selected as a Core Item because it represents the child's typical application of the skills and concepts encompassed by an area of learning. You will recall that although the area of learning is the same for all children, the actual Core Items for each child in your classroom are likely to be different.

Beginning in third grade, students are increasingly able to understand the structure and purposes of the Portfolio. With the benefit of ongoing discussions and conversations, along with repeated experiences of examining and reflecting on their work, students can become quite skilled and independent in choosing appropriate items. Selecting Core Items requires knowing the skills and ideas that are included in each area of learning. Teachers, in conjunction with students, have developed a variety of forms that guide students' selections. Figure 35 shows one such form developed by a fourth grade teacher.

How to Use Portfolios

FIGURE 35

A fourth grade teacher's form to help students select their own Core Items

> Winter Collection Period
>
> SELECTING A CORE ITEM FOR: "Writing to communicate ideas"
>
> Look through your collection of Language and Literacy work and look for a piece that shows how you use the skills and ideas we've been learning:
>
> • Clear topic focus and flow of ideas
>
> • Interesting beginning
>
> • Complete middle (details, dialogue, explanations)
>
> • Use of new vocabulary words
>
> • Ending that closes the piece of writing
>
> • Paragraphs
>
> • Appropriate punctuation
>
> • Proper use of capital letters
>
> • Correct spelling
>
> • Effective use of time and cooperative learning

Students at this age can distinguish between "best work" and typical work; they can understand that the work they select should show what they can do at a given point in time. Beginning with the second collection period, some teachers ask students to look at the Core Item from the previous collection period and compare it to the selection they are currently making to look for evidence of progress.

SELECTING INDIVIDUALIZED ITEMS Work is selected as an Individualized Item because it reflects the child's unique characteristics as a learner or the child's application of learning from several domains. A minimum of five Individualized Items are included during each collection period. For Individualized Items, children can learn to select pieces that reflect some unique quality they possess or pieces that show their learning across domains.

ESTABLISHING PROCEDURES Teachers use different timetables and methods for selecting work. In some classrooms teachers and children review work in the collection bin weekly, selecting a few pieces for the Portfolio and sending other work home. You may find that weekly selection is too frequent and choose instead to do it every few weeks or on a monthly basis. Regardless of the frequency of selection, it is always possible to replace earlier selections with newer ones that are more appropriate or more representative of the child's current performance. Once a collection period has ended, however, the selections made during that time remain a part of the child's Portfolio.

Some teachers select work during individual conferences while other teachers work with small groups to select work. Below we list a few ideas that teachers have used successfully. Adopt and adapt these in ways that work for you.

♦ Children select work individually and discuss their selections with the teacher.

♦ Children select Individualized Items and teachers select Core Items.

♦ Children review their work in pairs, in small groups, or in individual conferences with the teacher.

♦ After children learn the domains, they find, for example, all the math work from the collection bin and work together to find pieces that match the area of learning.

INVOLVING CHILDREN Making selections of work for the Portfolio can be done by you, by you with your students, or by students working alone with occasional guidance from you.

Teachers begin involving children in studying their own work and making Portfolio selections in different ways. Some find it helpful to give children specific guidance for reviewing their collected work. Here are some of the things they may ask children to look for:

♦ something that was enjoyable to do

♦ something that shows how much they are learning

♦ work that was difficult

♦ a piece of writing that shows their use of descriptive language

♦ work that shows at least two strategies they used to solve a math problem

♦ something they wrote that describes an important observation they made

The decision about how to involve children in the selection process rests with individual teachers. Some child involvement in this process is invaluable, though, because it gives children the opportunity to reflect on their learning and progress, and to set goals for future learning. Engaging students in discussions of their own thinking and learning pushes them to higher and more abstract levels of thinking.

Children's involvement in work selection looks different at different ages. Preschool children's involvement may be limited to occasionally requesting that a favorite drawing or photograph become part of the Portfolio.

Older children will be able to review their work in light of their own goals and expectations and make informed selections more independently.

With young children it is most effective to select work weekly. They tend to need more guidance in making selections. Older children can select work every few weeks or once a month.

PRESCHOOL As children grow, their role in the design and selection of the Portfolio grows with them. Three year olds should not be expected to make meaningful choices of work for their Portfolio. Frequently, items in the Portfolio may be teacher notes or "word pictures" that are not meaningful to preschoolers. Occasionally, teachers may provide opportunities for older preschool children to make choices. These children will only be asked to select one item from a group of three or four. For example, the teacher may say to a child, "I see you made three paintings with finger paint this week. Which one of these would you like to put in your Portfolio?" The teacher may also ask children why they chose the one they did and talk with them about their choice. At this age children's comments about why they made their choice and what they like about it may not be deeply reflective or informative.

KINDERGARTEN Learning to make choices can be a focused activity of Portfolio review in kindergarten. Within clearly defined limits, kindergarten children can begin to make choices about the work they want included in their Portfolio. Teachers may provide criteria for making choices, such as deciding between hard and easy tasks, or selecting something they will work on again or have tried for the first time. More open-ended choices may be possible from a small collection of work, such as choosing something that shows how the child writes or draws and saying why, choosing the painting the child likes most, or selecting the patterns the child finds most interesting. Topics of informal conversation in the classroom might address why children made certain choices, why some work was fun to create, what else they would like to learn, and so on.

PRIMARY GRADES In second and third grade, children are continuing to learn to review their work and to choose which items to include in the Portfolio. A prompt that can be introduced after initial experience with Portfolio review and selection may be, "Choose the journal entry that shows the most about the way you write." Or, you may pose a question more specifically to address an area of learning: "Which item would you choose to show how you solve mathematical problems?"

By third grade, many students will be able to understand the structure and purposes of the Portfolio. Given clear sets of criteria for Core Items and Individualized Items, they will be able to select work that fits each category. For Core Items, they will be able to understand what the areas of learning mean and to choose pieces of work that represent their current level of skill, knowledge, and understanding. For Individualized Items, they will be able to choose pieces that truly reflect some unique quality they possess or pieces that show their learning across domains. As students mature and gain experience with the selection process, they will become increasingly independent in selecting appropriate work for the Portfolio.

Annotate Work to Enhance Its Meaning

WHY ANNOTATE? The audience for the Portfolio includes you, the student, the student's family, and other teachers or administrators in the school community. Portfolio pieces have greater meaning to all reviewers when annotation summarizing the reflection process has been added. For you, comments that describe either the child's approach to the assignment or the learning reflected in the work will help you clarify your thinking about what the learner knows and does not know. Your annotations will be useful when you complete the Summary Report. They will help you evaluate the Portfolio, provide evidence for the evaluations you make, and may provide you with language for the narrative portion of the report.

For children, notes attached to work make a strong statement about the importance of the work and the process of reflecting on learning. In addition, the process of creating these annotations can become a valuable and integral part of classroom life. When you and your students participate in regular, serious reflection and commentary on the learning that occurs each day, the classroom becomes a true community of learners.

For those outside of the classroom community, annotation makes the learning embedded in the work explicit. Because the Portfolio is part of a learning process and not simply an interesting collection of children's work, it is crucial that other people have access to the same background information about the work that you do.

Annotation may be a quickly written note on the back of the work or it may be recorded on a **PORTFOLIO ITEM RECORD SELF-STICK NOTE** (Figure 36). The Portfolio Item Record saves time by allowing you simply to check off whether the work is a Core Item or Individualized Item and which domain or domains the work reflects. Space is also provided for you to write comments. A variation for your students to use, called "**MY PORTFOLIO ITEM RECORD**" form (Figure 37), is available in the booklet of Reproducible Masters.

FIGURE 36
Portfolio Item Record
self-stick note

Portfolio Item Record

Child _____

Date _____

FALL ☐ WINTER ☐ SPRING ☐

Domains	Core Item 1	2	Indiv. Item
I Personal & Social Development			☐
II Language & Literacy	☐	☐	☐
III Mathematical Thinking	☐	☐	☐
IV Scientific Thinking	☐	☐	☐
V Social Studies	☐	☐	☐
VI The Arts	☐	☐	☐
VII Physical Development & Health			☐

Comments

The Work Sampling System
32411 (3/97) © 1994, 2001 Rebus Inc

FIGURE 37
"My Portfolio Item
Record" form is designed
for students to use

My Portfolio Item Record

My Name _____

Date _____ FALL ☐ WINTER ☐ SPRING ☐

Comments

The Work Sampling System
© 1997, 2001 Rebus Inc

HOW TO ANNOTATE Annotation of Portfolio pieces can take many forms and can occur at many times. The time of annotation suggests the type of information that might be added to the work. This section includes some ideas about Portfolio annotation, both when you might add it and what it might include.

♦ **Annotating during planning or at time of assignment** Develop an assignment description that includes what the child is being asked to do, the learning goals, and the expectations for the assignment. Descriptions may be built into the teacher-created recording form or written on a separate sheet, duplicated, and attached to the child's work (Figures 38 and 39).

FIGURE 38

A kindergarten teacher's annotation describing a math problem based on a story

The kindergarten class listened to Rooster's Off to See the World, by Eric Carle. In the story, Rooster gets two cats, three frogs, four turtles, and five fish to go off with him on a journey. The children were asked to figure out how many animals went along on the trip in all.

What to look for:

• Whether or not the child understood the problem

• Whether or not the child finished the problem

• How the child represented the animals: with drawings? objects? letters? symbolic marks? numbers?

• The accuracy of the numbers of each type of animal

• The accuracy of the total number of animals

FIGURE 39

A third grade teacher described this assignment with families in mind

_____ wrote a story in his/her "sloppy copy" writing book, and then conferenced with a friend and/or the teacher about it.

Next, editing and revisions were done, also in the sloppy copy book.

Then he/she typed the story up on the word processor (copy #1), and made other last changes (copy #2).

Last of all, the teacher made final corrections on the computer and made the final draft printout.

♦ **Annotating at time of work completion** Summarize the feedback conversation you had with the student or ask the student to reflect on the work. Information you might note includes: what the child did, the child's approach to the task, whether or not the child met the expectations for the assignment, and the skills and knowledge evident in the work (Figures 40 and 41).

Core Item, Fall
• Mathematical Thinking

Area of learning:
"Use of different strategies to create and solve mathematical problems"

Christopher used numbers, pictures. and words to represent addition problem with trading. Grouped children in picture.

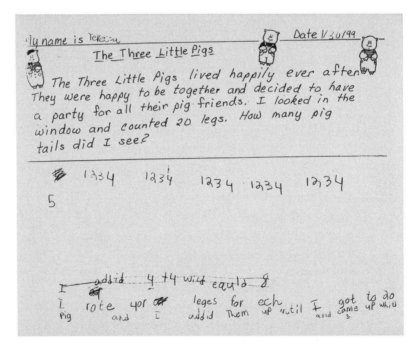

Core Item, Winter
• Mathematical Thinking

Area of learning:
"Using strategies to solve numerical problems"

Teressa fulfilled expectations for this assignment. Found a visual way to solve the problem and explained her solution in words. Used numbers to represent pig legs and counted groups of 4 to solve the problem.

♦ **Annotating at time of collection** Describe the context for the work or the details about the circumstances in which the work was created that you might later forget (e.g., child- or teacher-initiated, the child's familiarity with the task, independent or teacher-assisted) (Figures 42 and 43).

FIGURE 42
Jenny's teacher added these comments at the time of collection to explain how this Individualized Item shows integrated learning in four domains

Individualized Item, Fall
• Personal and Social Development
• Mathematical Thinking
• Scientific Thinking
• Physical Development & Health

Jenny loves the block area and works by herself for 20–30 minutes at a time. She is persistent and methodical in her approach, combining her knowledge of shapes and structures to create simple buildings. At first she tried to build this structure:

When it wouldn't stand, she added center support as seen in the photo.

FIGURE 43
Hafka's teacher added comments at the time of collection to explain how this Core Item represented the specified area of learning

Core Item, Winter
• The Arts

Area of learning:
"Responding to artistic experiences"

We've had ongoing discussions about art and emotions—how artists express feelings and how audiences have feelings when they see painting, sculptures, or dances or when they hear music or poetry. After listening to some string quartet music, Hafka painted this picture and dictated, "The music made me feel sad. It made me think about how my grandpa died." Hafka has made a clear connection between the arts and emotions.

♦ **Annotating at time of selection** Explain why the work was selected as a Core or Individualized Item and who selected it (Figure 44).

FIGURE 44

Emily's teacher selected this as an Individualized Item because it shows Emily's unique approach to solving a problem she set for herself

Individualized Item, Winter
• Mathematical Thinking
• The Arts
• Physical Development & Health

In making her chain of girls, Emily decided to dress them all the same. How would she do it? Instead of using one color and doing them all at the same time, she finished the first one, then copied it one after the other. (Notice the black lines of the foreheads.)

Figures 45–48 show the work of a kindergarten child named Marybeth that has been annotated by her teacher in several ways. At the time when the assignment was planned, Marybeth's teacher created an assignment sheet that was later attached to the back of the work (Figure 45).

FIGURE 45

The teacher's assignment sheet was later attached to Marybeth's Core Item to provide additional information about the context of the work

Family Graph

Based on a list of your family members, create a graph showing the number of boys and girls in your family. Here are the steps to follow:

1. Make a list of the people in your family.

2. Use stick figure people to show your family members on your graph. Cut them out of the paper.

3. Label your graph.

   Boys

   Girls

4. What does your graph show?

   Are there more boys than girls?

   Are there more girls than boys?

   Are boys and girls equal?

Marybeth produced the item shown in Figure 46. At the time of collection, the teacher described Marybeth's approach to the task on the back of the work (Figure 47). At the time of selection, the teacher noted the learning evident in the work in relation to the area of learning, using the Portfolio Item Record self-stick note (Figure 48).

FIGURE 46
Following the assignment sheet, Marybeth produced this Core Item in Mathematical Thinking for the area of learning "understanding of concepts of number and quantity"

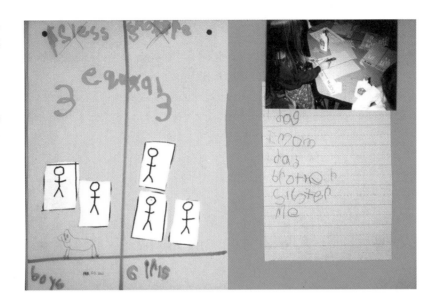

FIGURE 47
Marybeth's teacher added this description at the time of collection of the work

Marybeth counted and labeled the girls' side as "more" and the boys' side as "less." When she consulted her list, she realized that the dog had been left out. She did not want to use a person to represent the dog. So she drew the dog herself. She found a card that had a picture of a dog to help her draw the picture. She wrote on the picture "3 equal 3."

FIGURE 48
Marybeth's teacher used the Portfolio Item Record self-stick note to indicate the learning evident in the work, at the time it was selected to be a Core Item

Portfolio Item Record

Child __**Marybeth**__

Date __**10/12**__

FALL ☒ WINTER ☐ SPRING ☐

Domains	Core Item 1 2	Indiv. Item
I Personal & Social Development		☐
II Language & Literacy	☐ ☐	☐
III Mathematical Thinking	☒ ☐	☐
IV Scientific Thinking	☐ ☐	☐
V Social Studies	☐ ☐	☐
VI The Arts	☐ ☐	☐
VII Physical Development & Health		☐

Comments

Marybeth did this task almost completely on her own. Her slow deliberate working style helped her self-correct. She uses one-to-one correspondence to count accurately the number of people on her list and her graph. Correctly used mathematical words to describe her work.

The Work Sampling System
32411 (3/97) © 1994, 2001 Rebus Inc

Although we have listed four occasions when you might annotate student work, you are not expected to annotate every piece of work at each of these times. Instead, your goal is to add to the work the particular type of annotation that makes the meaning of the work clear, as illustrated by Marybeth's teacher.

Managing the Selection Process

Before the school year begins, you will have completed a Core Item Collection Plan form, filling in the areas of learning for each domain. We recommend that you store these in the front of each Portfolio to serve as a table of contents for the Portfolio and as a record-keeping tool for you. As Core Items are selected, you (or your students) can check off the appropriate collection period on the form. At a glance, you will be able to see what is and is not in each child's Portfolio.

Many teachers find it helpful to use the **PORTFOLIO COLLECTION TALLY** form (Figure 49), available in the booklet of Reproducible Masters, to keep track of the Core Items that have been selected for the entire class. The form is designed so that you see at a glance whether or not a student's Portfolio includes two Core Items for each of five domains and five Individualized Items. As you and your students select Portfolio items, you make a check or write the date in the appropriate box. Before the school year begins you can record students' names on the form so that you will be ready to keep track of selected Portfolio items.

FIGURE 49
Portfolio Collection Tally form

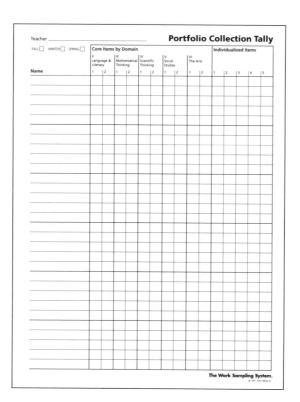

Near the End of Each Collection Period

At this point, you have a clear idea of how to set up Portfolio collection before school starts and the ongoing routines related to Portfolios that occur during each collection period. Near the end of each collection period, you will prepare to write Summary Reports and to conduct conferences with families. This stage of the process involves three tasks:

- Student review and evaluation of the Portfolio.

- Teacher review and evaluation of the Portfolio for the Summary Report.

- Preparation for sharing Portfolios with families.

Student Review and Evaluation of the Portfolio

Portfolios enable students, even very young children, to examine their work over time and make comments about their performance and progress. In the previous section we described ways that you might talk to students about their work. When students have had the benefit of these conversations, their review and evaluation of work in the Portfolio at the end of a collection period is apt to be more thoughtful and perceptive.

For students, reviewing work provides an opportunity to reflect on what has been occurring in the classroom and what they have been doing and learning. Looking at work reminds them of the experiences that led to the creation of the work. Reviewing their work helps children see the changes they have made since the beginning of the year and how much they have grown. Review is also an opportunity for them to notice where their work is weak, and to become motivated to revise.

PRESCHOOL Self-evaluation is a learned skill, a capability developed through experience and guidance. Preschoolers are generally not very reflective. For them the physical act of reviewing the Portfolio will likely be the most relevant. They can be introduced to the idea of having a collection of their work and can feel great satisfaction in reviewing their work and seeing their growth.

KINDERGARTEN In addition to reviewing the work and remembering experiences, kindergarten children can begin to make more focused comments about their work. They might identify aspects of the work that were especially hard or easy. They may be able to describe what a piece of work tells about their learning: "This painting shows that I am a good painter and that I know about thunder and lightning." Reviewing the

Portfolio near the end of each collection period helps focus kindergartners on what they have learned and what they need to learn in the future.

FIRST AND SECOND GRADE   As children become older, they begin to evaluate their work more carefully. First and second graders begin to talk about what constitutes good work. Some questions that will help students evaluate individual samples of work are:

♦ What did you learn from this work?

♦ What do you want to know more about in this area?

♦ Where do you feel you have shown the most progress?

THIRD THROUGH FIFTH GRADE   Children this age begin to set goals for their learning and can review their progress toward these goals. They can answer specific questions about their Portfolios:

♦ How did you choose the work in the Portfolio?

♦ What does your work show about you as a learner?

♦ What are some things you can do well, and what are some things you still want to work on?

Or you may ask them to comment on individual items by responding to such questions as:

♦ Why did you select this piece?

♦ What do you see as the strengths of this item?

♦ What was especially important to you when you were working on this?

♦ What did you struggle with?

♦ If you could work on this more, what would you do?

♦ How is this the same as or different from your other work?

♦ What does this work show about you as a writer, scientist, mathematician, or artist?

As children become more capable of reflection, evaluation, and setting goals and working toward them, their role in the Portfolio process expands. However, it is also important not to overdo this aspect of classroom life. Most learning is important for its own sake and not for the purpose of documentation. Teachers tell us that when students are asked to respond to every activity formally, by writing, drawing, or other means of expression, they can grow tired of the demand and lose their enthusiasm for the work itself.

The "**THOUGHTS ABOUT MY PORTFOLIO**" form included in the booklet of Reproducible Masters allows students to reflect on the work in their Portfolios. It provides a place for the student's name and room for the student to write or dictate comments (Figure 50). One copy of the form can be used for each collection period.

FIGURE 50
"Thoughts About My Portfolio" form

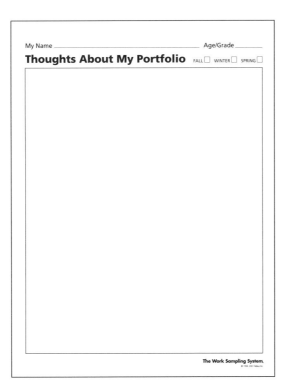

My Name _____   Age/Grade _____

Thoughts About My Portfolio   FALL ☐ WINTER ☐ SPRING ☐

The Work Sampling System.

Some teachers use this form, or one similar to it, as an opportunity to confer with students about their work at the end of each collection period. These conferences provide opportunities for students to set goals for themselves, to make plans with the teacher for working toward new goals, and to evaluate their progress. Figures 51–53 show children's evaluations of their own Portfolios.

FIGURE 51 (LEFT)
FIGURE 52 (RIGHT)

Children's evaluations of
their own work and
Portfolios—first grade
and third grade

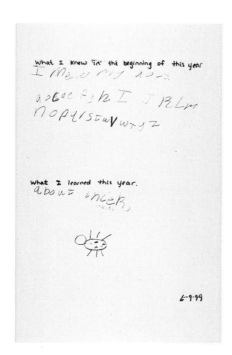

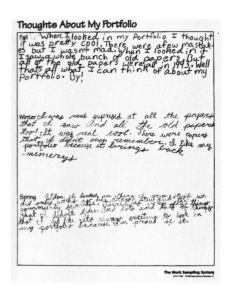

FIGURE 53

A fourth grader's self-
evaluation

Teacher Review and Evaluation of the Portfolio for the Summary Report

Near the end of each collection period, you will review each child's Portfolio and evaluate the work based on your delineated classroom or grade-level expectations. These standards come from three sources:

◆ Your knowledge of child development helps you understand what can be reasonably expected from children of a given age. You can use the

Developmental Guidelines as a good source of information about child development.

♦ Your experience with children of a given age or at a certain grade level is another important source of reasonable expectations. Work Sampling encourages you to work with your grade level colleagues to articulate clear expectations for different types of work.

♦ Local curriculum expectations are the third source of guidance in establishing expectations for your students. There are bound to be local and regional variations in what teachers are required to teach at each grade level. These requirements should be taken into consideration when evaluating your students' Portfolio work.

Working with a set of clear standards for each type of work in the Portfolio, you will examine a student's work and compare it to those standards. As you go through this thought process, you might attach additional written comments to the work to help family members interpret the work accurately. Some relevant considerations include the following:

♦ How does the work meet these expectations?

♦ Where specifically does it fall short of these expectations?

♦ Which specific features of the work show emerging skill?

♦ What kind of work would be considered advanced for children of this age?

♦ Which areas need continued observation?

Different Evaluation Standards for Core Items and Individualized Items

Work selected as Core Items is evaluated only for the specified area of learning in the specified domain. For example, a Social Studies Core Item should be evaluated only for the knowledge of the Social Studies concepts defined in the given area of learning, even if the Item also reveals the child's fine-motor abilities or talents in artistic expression.

When you examine Individualized Items, you should be looking for additional evidence to inform your evaluation of the child's domain-related learning and for information that will help you individualize classroom instruction.

Evaluation of the Portfolio is also a critical part of completing the Summary Report. This topic will be discussed in greater detail in the next chapter.

Preparation for Sharing Portfolios with Families

As Portfolio collection becomes central to the classroom, it also becomes an important vehicle for sharing classroom life with families. Teachers have developed many different ideas about how to share the Portfolio with families. We encourage you and your colleagues to be creative when considering how to introduce Portfolios. Here are some questions that may guide your decision-making process:

♦ What vehicle will I use to share the Portfolio?

♦ How often will it be shared with families?

♦ Who will participate in the conference?

♦ Will the entire contents of the Portfolio be shared? If not, which pieces will be shared?

CONFERENCES For many teachers, the Portfolio provides the central focus for the family-teacher conference. Teachers may illustrate their comments on the Summary Report with work from the child's Portfolio. They may also share the child's reasons for including items in the Portfolios.

Children can also be involved in family-teacher conferences, using their Portfolio as the basis to illustrate their efforts, progress, and achievements. This enables parents and teachers to support children by recognizing well-done work and by helping to plan goals for children. Some teachers conduct Portfolio conferences with children before the family-teacher conferences and share with the child the information they will be discussing with the family.

It is usually overly ambitious to attempt to share the Portfolio in its entirety at a conference. You may find it helpful to identify a few pieces of work that illustrate the main points you want to communicate to family members. You might flag these with Post-it notes on which you have written a few notes to remind you why you are sharing those particular pieces. Alternately, you could rotate the Portfolio pieces so that the work in question juts out of the Portfolio as a way to remind you to share these pieces.

PORTFOLIO NIGHT Some schools sponsor "Portfolio Nights," when parents are invited to school with their child to review the Portfolio. In other schools, family members are invited to come in at their convenience and look through the Portfolio with their child.

Students can brainstorm to come up with questions family members may ask about their Portfolios. Then, working with a partner, they can role-play a Portfolio sharing session. With adequate preparation, even young children can take responsibility for presenting and explaining the contents of their Portfolios to family members.

In schools with two conferences a year but three or more reporting periods, teachers have used Portfolio Nights to communicate with families during one of the reporting periods that is not scheduled to have a conference.

Part III Frequently Asked Questions About Portfolios

Q What do I need to begin Portfolio collection?

A To ensure a smooth start to Portfolio collection, it is important that you have supplies ready before the beginning of the school year. This includes the materials to create a Portfolio for each child, storage bins, and work folders.

Next you should plan areas of learning for Core Item collection. This entails deciding on two areas of learning for each of the five Core Item domains. Each area of learning should be written on the Core Item Collection Plan Sheet. This sheet should be copied and included in each child's Portfolio. You are now ready to begin collecting children's work. Alternatively, you can select areas of learning from the lists in the Appendix.

Q I prefer to create my students' Portfolios in a different way. Is it okay to use a method different from those described in this chapter?

A Yes. The suggestions included in this chapter are not intended to prescribe the definitive way to create Portfolios or collect work. Rather, they are proposed as suggestions and jumping-off points from which teachers can develop their own methods. Because you know best the resources available to you, you are in the best position to make decisions about how to create Portfolios, how to prepare work folders, and how often to make Portfolio selections. What is essential is the systematic collection of two kinds of work: Core Items and Individualized Items.

Q Should all work go into work folders?

A At the beginning of the year, it is probably a good idea for most work to be saved in work folders or collection bins. As you and your students become more familiar with Portfolio collection, you may decide that some kinds of work can go home immediately while other work gets saved in ongoing collection folders. In general, it is important to save the work that is most informative about the child's learning.

Q What makes a Portfolio item informative?

A Work samples are informative when they reveal how children integrate multiple skills in a meaningful context. For example, journal entries provide information about how the child espresses ideas, organizes written text, applies conventions of print (spacing, capitalization, and punctuation), spells, and uses vocabulary. They also provide a window into the child's personal and social development by revealing the child's interests, motivations, daily life, style of thinking, and attitudes. In contrast, a work sheet that requires the child to read a passage of text and to apply rules of capitalization sheds light only on the child's ability to capitalize correctly. Classroom activities should be broad rather than narrow and designed in such a way that they place few limits on what may be learned.

Q How can I find time to file the children's work?

A Many teachers find it most efficient to use class time with students for reviewing, selecting, and filing student work. This will help you avoid large piles of work that need to be filed at the end of the collection period. Some teachers rely on parent volunteers to help with the filing and general management tasks associated with Portfolio collection. Older children can assume many of the management tasks themselves.

Q Should I keep my notes about students in their Portfolio?

A No. Portfolios are intended to contain only the children's work. This is not the place to keep Checklists, your observation notes, or notes to and from home. For each child, you should have another file in which you keep your memos and notes, Checklists, and copies of Summary Reports. These Teacher Files can be stored in a file cabinet because they are not expected to be made available to children (Teacher Files are described in detail in Chapter 2).

Sometimes, however, anecdotal notes or "word pictures" become Portfolio Items. You may write a note to record some work a child did in the classroom that cannot be otherwise documented for the Portfolio. For example, you may observe a child working at the water table, posing questions to the other children and suggesting ways they could find the answer to the questions by setting up experiments using the water table equipment. This anecdotal note might become a Core Item to represent the area of learning in Scientific Thinking, "using questioning, predicting, and experimenting in scientific investigations."

Q Should work that is included in the Portfolio be graded?

A Although student work should be evaluated, grades are not the most meaningful way to give feedback to students. Your comments on student's work are most valuable when they help students reflect on their skills and progress. When work in the Portfolio is graded in conventional ways (for example, with a number or letter grade), the grade rather than the work becomes the focus.

Q As a preschool teacher, I feel that it is very important to document growth in Personal & Social Development and Physical Development & Health. Why aren't they included as domains for the collection of Core Items?

A These two domains have not been designated as Core Item domains because children's work in these two areas does not lend itself to the creation of products that can be easily included in the Portfolio. For example, products do not generally result from gross-motor activities or from dramatic play. Assessment of these domains requires anecdotal note-taking and greater teacher involvement.

Personal & Social Development and Physical Development & Health are extremely important domains. In order to keep the workload manageable, however, they are documented solely through teacher observations recorded as ratings on the Developmental Checklists. Remember too that Individualized Items may reveal aspects of a child's development in these two domains.

If you decide that you want to collect Core Items in these domains and are willing to spend the additional time, you should do so. Such Portfolios will contain a higher proportion of anecdotal notes for these domains than for the other domains.

Q If the entire class has the same areas of learning in each domain, won't all the portfolios contain children's responses to the same projects or assignments?

A Children's Portfolios will not contain representations of all the same projects or assignments because Portfolio items are collected in an ongoing way during the course of each collection period and because they are based on learning that occurs on more than one occasion in the classroom.

Consider a second grade class collecting Core Items for the Scientific Thinking area of learning "observing and describing scientific phenomena." Activities in this class for the fall may include:

- Collecting, observing, drawing, and describing leaves
- Observing and recording the habits of the class pet
- Observing and charting the foods eaten by the class pet
- Observing and drawing the growth of seeds

Children in this class have many opportunities to observe and describe natural phenomena. The sample selected for each child will depend on the child's interest in the activity and the quality of her work. Because there have been many opportunities for children to observe and describe, this area of learning will be represented in different ways in different children's portfolios.

Q How do I integrate Portfolio collection into my existing curriculum and classroom schedule?

A To ensure the best fit between Portfolio collection and your classroom, think about Portfolio collection as you plan each week. Some teachers list their areas of learning in their plan book. As you review your curriculum plans, consider purposeful activities and the types of representations children might create, such as writings, drawings, maps, models, dictations, charts, and graphs.

Many teachers do not realize that what they already do is appropriate for Portfolio collection. Usually you do not need to plan special or different learning activities for children; you only need to plan them and collect work from them differently. Because you choose areas of learning based on important curriculum goals, Core Items are generated from ongoing classroom activities.

Q How will Portfolio assessment influence my curriculum and instruction?

A Reviewing children's work will provide an opportunity for you to monitor individual students' work. As you carefully study children's work, you will learn more about your students as learners and as people—their work habits, personal styles, thought processes, accomplishments, strengths, and difficulties. After reviewing a Portfolio, for example, you may notice that one student consistently makes elaborate drawings, sketches, and paintings. With this knowledge, you can begin to consider ways to involve this student in learning through art, to reinforce his strengths, and to show him the connection between the visual arts and other domains of learning. Or you may observe that a child comprehends story structure but has difficulty representing this understanding because of weak fine motor skills. You may suggest that the child recite the story into a tape recorder. In this way she will experience success, and you will gain a more accurate representation of her understanding of story structure. By studying children's work over time, you can observe their strengths and the kinds of tasks that cause difficulty.

Frequently Asked Questions About Portfolios

You will also gain more information about how your students are responding to instructional activities. You may notice, for example, that a graphing activity was too complicated for children and that most children understand less about graphing than you expected. As a result, you may decide to engage children in additional, less-complex graphing experiences. Or you may see that students' work folders are full of examples of Social Studies topics but less often include Scientific Thinking. This may indicate that students have had limited opportunities for scientific investigation in the classroom.

For many teachers, using the Work Sampling Portfolio brings an increased sense of purpose and focus to their curriculum planning. Identifying and analyzing areas of learning for Core Item collection helps teachers to clarify the skills and concepts they want children to learn, thus improving how they design activities, evaluate student work, and give students feedback. Part of their curriculum planning is focused on questions such as these: What is the logical next step for this group of students to grapple with in writing? What strategy for numerical problem-solving should I introduce next? What level of scientific experimentation are my students ready for? Portfolio collection, when done well, can guide your curriculum planning by providing you with comprehensive information about the teaching and learning in your classroom.

Q How can I involve specialists in the Portfolio process?

A Portfolio collection can be greatly enriched when classroom teachers and specialists collaborate. Specialists provide many opportunities for children to create products that document learning. In addition, specialists and resource teachers can support classroom themes and units by planning related activities in the special subject area. Collaboration between classroom teachers and specialists broadens the range of materials and media that children may include in their Portfolios (For further discussion of these issues, see Chapter 5).

Q What happens to Portfolios at the end of the year?

A We recommend that individual schools or districts make this decision. An important factor to remember is that Portfolios are collections of children's work and belong to the children and their families. Therefore, most of the work eventually goes home with the student at the end of the year or at the beginning of the next year.

Some schools have developed their own year-end strategies. Some create a cumulative school Portfolio for each child by keeping one Core Item from one or two domains from the final collection period each year.

Sometimes, teachers also decide to keep several items from the fall collection during the child's first year of school to illustrate the child's entering performance. After items are selected for the next year's teacher or for a cumulative school Portfolio, the major part of the Portfolio is sent home with children.

Q Should I show the Portfolio to the child's new teacher before sending it home?

A The Portfolio collection process can help children and teachers make the transition from one grade to the next. Part of the transition process involves reflecting on the year's learning. At the end of the school year, you can ask students to review their entire Portfolio. Through reviewing their Portfolio with your guidance, children will be able to observe their own growth and development.

A second part of the transition process is getting acquainted with the new teacher. The Portfolio can be used as an interactive way for teachers to get to know their new students. After reviewing the year's work, you might suggest that children select two or three items to keep at school to show their new teacher in the fall. With the aid of the Portfolios, either in whole or in part, children can introduce themselves to their new teacher, showing their work and expressing their own reflections and observations. The new teacher will have an opportunity to begin the dialogue with individual children about important learning experiences to anticipate during the coming year. After the Portfolio conference in the fall, the child may take his Portfolio home.

CHAPTER 4
Summary Reports

Summarizing Performance and Progress

This chapter addresses the third element of the Work Sampling System—the Summary Report. The chapter is divided into three sections as follows:

PART I   Understanding the Summary Report

PART II   Completing the Summary Report

PART III   Frequently Asked Questions about the Summary Report

Overview of the Summary Report

What is it?   The Summary Report is a form used to provide information about student performance and progress to families and administrators; it replaces conventional report cards

What are its purposes?

1   To profile student strengths and difficulties across seven domains

2   To give families information about student performance and progress

3   To guide instructional planning

4   To provide information to administrators about student achievement

What are its features?

♦ Completed by the teacher three times during the school year

♦ Distributed to the child's family, cumulative school file, and teacher

♦ Available as a 3-part carbonless paper form or as Summary Report Manager software for Macintosh or Windows computers

♦ Two types: standard and narrative-only. Separate forms are available for each, both are available in the Summary Report Manager

♦ The Standard Summary Report includes ratings of performance and progress and space for commentary, and identifying information

♦ The Narrative Summary Report includes space for commentary only

♦ All versions are available in Spanish

How do I complete the Work Sampling Summary Report?

Before the school year begins determine which type to use (standard or narrative-only), decide which version to use (paper or software), and complete identifying information

During each collection flag observations and work samples to share with families

Near the end of each collection period:

♦ Review the information collected for each student
♦ Evaluate and rate student performance and progress
♦ Write a narrative for each student that profiles the child's strengths and your areas of concern
♦ Share the Summary Report with the child's family

Related Materials

■ Summary Report Manager software

■ Special Subject Report form

■ Reproducible Master of Summary Report: Student and Family Comments form

Part I Understanding the Summary Report

Assessment involves two complementary processes: documentation and evaluation. In Work Sampling, teachers gather evidence that illustrates student performance in each of the seven Work Sampling System domains. Throughout each collection period, teachers observe students during classroom learning activities and document their observations. They also review student work as they help students make selections for inclusion in the Portfolio. These ongoing processes of documentation are fundamental to the Work Sampling System.

In addition to documentation, assessment involves evaluation and decision-making. At the end of each collection period, teachers integrate what they have learned from the Developmental Checklists and the Portfolio Collection Process with their own knowledge of child development in order to make evaluative decisions about the student's performance and progress in each of the seven domains. They summarize their knowledge of the child as they make ratings and write a commentary describing the child's strengths and areas of concern. These evaluative decisions are recorded on the Summary Report.

Purposes of the Summary Report

1   **To profile student strengths and difficulties across the domains.** The primary purpose of the Summary Report is to serve as an individualized profile of a student's achievement in the seven Work Sampling domains. Teachers combine information from their observations, the Checklist, and the Portfolio to make evaluative decisions about a student's performance and progress. This profile replaces report cards.

2   **To give families information about student performance and progress.** The second purpose of the Summary Report is to provide information about the current level of the student's accomplishments (performance) and about the student's growth over time (progress). Because family members are the primary audience for this report, your goal is to synthesize what you know about a student's learning so that the information is meaningful to families.

3   **To guide instructional planning.** The process of synthesizing and summarizing knowledge about their students helps teachers plan curriculum and instruction. As you review your observations, Checklist ratings, and Portfolios, you will gain insight that can help you to individualize instruction. At the end of a collection period, after you have written reports for your entire class, you will have a new perspective on whether you are meeting the needs of all of your students and whether you have addressed all aspects of the curriculum.

4   **To provide information to administrators about student achievement.** The information summarized on the Summary Report is useful for administrators who want to know how students in a particular classroom or school are achieving. Methods have been devised to aggregate ratings on the Summary Reports from a class, grade level, or school to give administrators an overall profile of student achievement.

Organization and Structure of the Summary Report

This section describes the Standard and Narrative Summary Report forms and explains several important concepts related to the Summary Report: evaluation, performance, progress, and standards for the ratings.

Structure of the Standard Summary Report

Child's identifying information and attendance record

Current collection period (fall, winter, or year-end)

List of domains and components

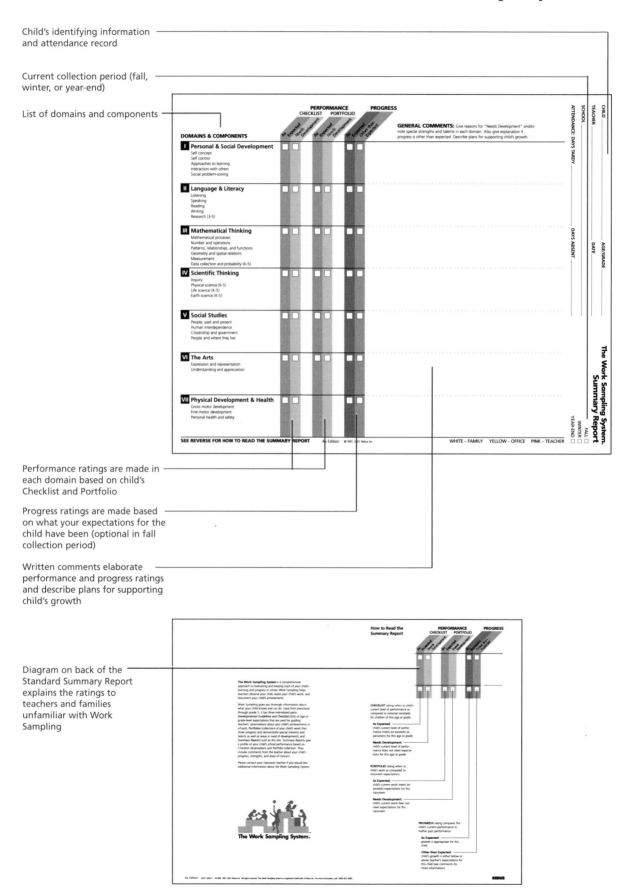

Performance ratings are made in each domain based on child's Checklist and Portfolio

Progress ratings are made based on what your expectations for the child have been (optional in fall collection period)

Written comments elaborate performance and progress ratings and describe plans for supporting child's growth

Diagram on back of the Standard Summary Report explains the ratings to teachers and families unfamiliar with Work Sampling

Structure of the Standard Summary Report

Current collection period
(fall, winter, or year-end)

Child's identifying
information and attendance
record

List of domains and
components

The narrative space has faint
lines between the seven
domains, but you may also
divide the space according to
your needs

CHILD _____ AGE/GRADE _____	**The Work Sampling System.**
TEACHER _____ DATE _____	**Narrative Summary Report**
SCHOOL/PROGRAM _____	FALL ☐
	WINTER ☐
ATTENDANCE: DAYS TARDY _____ DAYS ABSENT _____	YEAR-END ☐

DOMAINS & COMPONENTS | **CHILD'S DEVELOPMENT:** Child's growth, special strengths and talents, and areas of difficulty. Plans for supporting child's development.

I Personal & Social Development
Self concept
Self control
Approaches to learning
Interaction with others
Social problem-solving

II Language & Literacy
Listening
Speaking
Reading
Writing
Research (3-5)

III Mathematical Thinking
Mathematical processes
Number and operations
Patterns, relationships, and functions
Geometry and spatial relations
Measurement
Data collection and probability (K-5)

IV Scientific Thinking
Inquiry
Physical science (K-5)
Life science (K-5)
Earth science (K-5)

V Social Studies
People, past and present
Human interdependence
Citizenship and government
People and where they live

VI The Arts
Expression and representation
Understanding and appreciation

VII Physical Development & Health
Gross motor development
Fine motor development
Personal health and safety

4th Edition   20313 (6/01)   ©1994, 1997, 2001 Rebus Inc. All rights reserved. The Work Sampling System is a registered trademark of Rebus Inc.   WHITE – FAMILY   YELLOW – OFFICE   PINK – TEACHER

Evaluation

Evaluation is the process of judging how closely something compares to a standard. In Work Sampling, the Summary Report allows you to summarize what you know about each student in order to evaluate his **performance** and **progress** against different standards at the end of each collection period.

This element of Work Sampling inspires strong feelings and raises many issues. Our own experience of being evaluated often influences how we think about evaluating our students. Sometimes you may feel uneasy about making judgments and decisions about your students' learning. Because of the uneven path of young children's development and their potential for rapid growth, you may be reluctant to make evaluative statements that may be true only for a short time. Moreover, because all children do not start school with the same advantages, it may seem unfair to evaluate them using the same standards. Evaluation is complex. It means different things to different people. It has personal meaning as well as myriad professional connotations.

The Summary Report couples the complexity inherent in evaluation with the public nature of report cards. The Summary Report reaches outside of the classroom to administrators, families, and the community. You may worry that communicating information about learning problems will be difficult because you will have to deal with parents' feelings about their child's struggles. In addition, the act of formally evaluating students' performance and progress brings the teacher's role as decision maker, and the accuracy of her judgments, under public scrutiny.

Teachers make informal evaluative decisions daily, however, as they form different small groups of children for particular activities, assign work geared to students' skill levels, and select materials for different students based on the students' knowledge of particular topics. Families appreciate formal evaluations because they want assurance that their children's educational program is preparing them to compete with children across the nation. So formal evaluation is part of classroom life and an important part of the Work Sampling System. As you read this chapter, you will see that evaluative information can be accurate, presented fairly, and leave families and children informed and optimistic about future learning.

Performance

The performance rating describes the level of a child's behavior, skills, and accomplishments at a particular point in time. When you evaluate a child's performance, you are examining the student's skills within a collection period and comparing them to a standard of performance for children of that age.

The Summary Report has two separate ratings of performance. One addresses performance as shown on the Checklist; the other addresses performance as displayed in the Portfolio.

Progress

Progress refers to growth or change over time. When you evaluate a child's progress, you are comparing the child's current performance with his past performance, rather than comparing his current performance to an external standard.

The progress rating on the Summary Report incorporates information from the Checklist and the Portfolio across collection periods.

Standards of Comparison

The Summary Report uses three different standards of comparison. Each rating that you make involves a different comparison. When you evaluate a student's performance based on the Checklist, you compare the student's performance to national standards or expectations for children of a particular age or grade. These age- or grade-related expectations are described in the Developmental Guidelines.

When you evaluate a student's performance as displayed in the Portfolio, you compare the student's performance to classroom expectations for performance. These expectations are based on local curriculum standards, your professional experience, and your knowledge of child development.

When you evaluate a student's progress you use information from the Checklist and Portfolio to compare the student's present performance to the student's past performance. In this case the standard of comparison is internal, the child's own performance.

Another way to understand the three different standards of comparison is to think of the first column on the Standard Summary Report as comparing the child's performance to expectations for all children, the second column as comparing the child's performance to expectations for the children in this classroom, and the progress column as comparing this child today to this child at an earlier time. This information is summarized in the table below.

	LOOK AT	**COMPARED TO**
Performance – Checklist	Observation notes and Checklist ratings	National standards for children of this age or grade
Performance – Portfolio	Child's work	Classroom expectations
Progress	Current performance on Checklist and Portfolio	Child's own past performance

Part II   Completing the Summary Report

Unlike the other two elements of Work Sampling, most of the work associated with the Summary Report takes place near the end of each collection period.

You will find the job more manageable, though, if you address a few tasks before the school year begins and if you collect illustrative observations and work samples during each collection period.

Summary Report Timeline

The timeline depicts the schedule for activities associated with the Summary Report for a single collection period.

BEFORE THE START OF THE SCHOOL YEAR		COLLECTION PERIOD BEGINS									COLLECTION PERIOD ENDS	REPORTING PERIOD ENDS
		Week 1	Week 2	Week 3	Week 4	Week 5	Week 6	Week 7	Week 8	Week 9	Week 10	Week 11
Choose Summary Report Type **Choose Paper Form or Software** **Enter Identifying Information**		**Identify Observational Records and Portfolio Items Useful for Completing Summary Report**									**Review Collected Information** **Rate Performance and Progress** **Write Narrative Comments** **Share with Student and Family**	

Before the School Year Begins

Before school opens, there are two decisions to make and one task to complete. First, your school or district must decide which form of the Summary Report to use: the Standard Summary Report form that includes ratings and a narrative, or the Narrative Summary Report that omits the ratings and is entirely narrative. Both forms require an evaluation of student performance and progress.

Second, you must decide whether you will hand write or word process the reports. The Summary Report is available as a three-part carbonless paper form or as software—the Summary Report Manager.

The only task you need to complete before the school year begins is to enter each student's identifying information on the reports for the year. This information includes the child's name and age or grade level, the teacher's name, the date, the school, and identification of the appropriate collection period.

During Each Collection Period

During each collection period, your ongoing observation, documentation, collection, selection, and filing of Portfolio work will prepare you for completing Summary Reports. We recommend that as you move through the collection period you mark specific examples from your observational notes that you may want to refer to in the Summary Reports. In addition, you can flag pieces of Portfolio work that you may want to share with the child's family at their conference.

Near the End of Each Collection Period

Most of the work related to Summary Reports occurs near the end of each collection period. It is important that before you begin working on Summary Reports, you (and your students) have organized all observational data, made final Checklist ratings for the collection period, and filed all selected work in Portfolios. If you wait and organize your documentation at the same time you begin to write your Reports, you will find the process much more time consuming and burdensome. After you have collected and organized the information, complete the following four steps:

- Review the information collected for each student.

- Evaluate and rate student performance and progress.

- Write a narrative for each student that describes a profile of the child's strengths and your areas of concern.

- Share the Summary Report with the child's family.

Review the Information Collected for Each Student

Before beginning work on a student's Summary Report, collect and review all the information you have about that child. This should consist of the following:

- observation notes
- Developmental Checklist
- Portfolio
- information from the child's family
- information from specialists
- previous Summary Reports

When you are well prepared to begin the rating and writing process, Summary Report completion flows more smoothly.

Evaluate and Rate Student Performance and Progress

For each domain, you will rate three aspects of student achievement: performance based on the Developmental Checklist, performance as displayed in the Portfolio, and progress. We describe these three ratings tasks in the next sections. Figure 1 shows the rating categories.

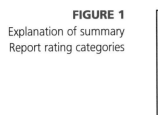

FIGURE 1
Explanation of summary
Report rating categories

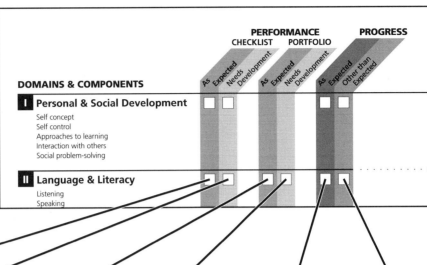

As Expected
The child's current level of performance meets (or exceeds) expectations for this age or grade. Work is in the "Proficient" and "In Process" categories with very few items marked "Not Yet."

Needs Development
The child's current level of performance does not meet expectations for this age or grade. The child's work is primarily in the "Not Yet" category with some "In Process" and very few "Proficient" ratings.

As Expected
Core and Individualized Items provide evidence of appropriate or greater than expected skills, knowledge, behavior, and accomplishments, as compared to classroom expectations.

Needs Development
Core and Individualized Items provide evidence that the child has not yet developed skills, knowledge, or behaviors expected for this classroom.

As Expected
Growth and development in skills, behavior, and knowledge since entering the classroom are appropriate for this child.

Other than Expected
Growth and development in skills, behavior, and knowledge since entering the classroom are either below or above expectations for this child.

Rating Checklist Performance

The first task is to determine the student's performance rating according to information from the Developmental Checklist. Ask yourself, "How does this child's current level of performance compare to expectations for children of this age or grade?

Within each domain, determine whether the child's performance is *"As Expected"* or *"Needs Development."* "As Expected" signifies that the child's performance meets or exceeds the expectations identified in the Developmental Guidelines for children at this grade level. "Needs Development" means that the child's performance does not meet these expectations.

Begin by reviewing the ratings you made on the Checklist indicators for the current collection period. Remember that if you are rating performance in the winter, you review only the winter ratings on the Checklist.

To summarize the Checklist ratings, examine the pattern of ratings within each domain. When most of the child's ratings are in the "Proficient" and "In Process" categories, with very few items marked "Not Yet," rate the child's performance as "As Expected" (Figure 2).

Completing the Summary Report

FIGURE 2
"As Expected"

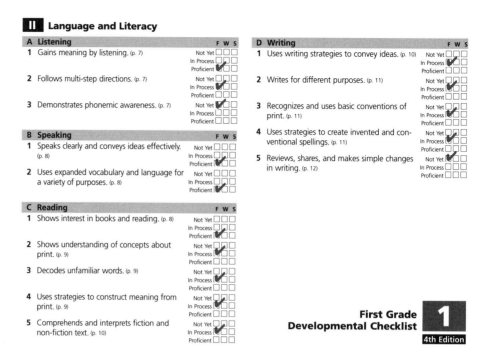

However, when the Checklist indicators are primarily rated "Not Yet," with some "In Process" ratings and very few indicators marked "Proficient," rate performance as "Needs Development" (Figure 3).

FIGURE 3
"Needs Development"

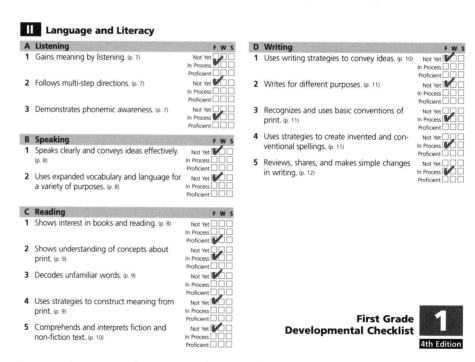

In most instances, this approach to evaluation provides a good estimate of overall performance according to the Checklist. You may find, though, that some children's ratings are evenly distributed across the three Checklist categories, while other children have all of their ratings in the "In Process" category. In either of these cases, you must take into account two other factors: your level of concern about the child's performance, and where you are in the school year.

Consider the next example (Figure 4). A child showing this pattern of ratings is evaluated as "As Expected" on the Summary Report in the fall because her teacher knows she had difficulty adjusting to the new classroom. When this pattern persists after the winter collection period, however, the teacher decides to evaluate the child's performance as "Needs

FIGURE 4

"As Expected" in the fall, but if pattern persists into winter, the rating changes to "Needs Development"

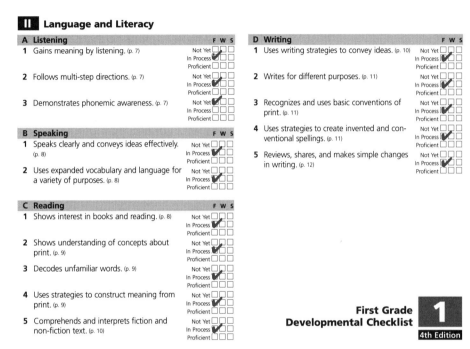

Development." The child has now adjusted to the new classroom and teacher and has had many opportunities to develop new skills and behaviors. But she has mastered very few skills, and as a result the teacher evaluates the child's performance in this domain as "Needs Development."

Remember that when you evaluate performance on the Checklist, you are comparing each student's performance to expectations for all children as identified in the Developmental Guidelines.

Rating Portfolio Performance

Evaluating a child's performance as displayed in the Portfolio requires a different approach from evaluating performance on the Checklist. Of the three Work Sampling elements, the Portfolio is most influenced by local standards and curricular expectations.

Although teachers across the country evaluate their students on the same Developmental Checklist, teachers in different locations select their own areas of learning and provide different learning opportunities for their students. Work in each student's Portfolio will be different, reflecting the student's unique interests, accomplishments, and work styles. School districts have differing expectations for student learning and for what teach-

Completing the Summary Report

ers are required to teach at each grade level. Because of state and local variations, it is difficult to have predetermined standards for Portfolio evaluation. Therefore, when you evaluate a child's performance on the Portfolio, you must compare his work to local expectations for children at this age or grade level.

Classroom expectations for Portfolio evaluation arise from at least three sources:

LOCAL CURRICULUM EXPECTATIONS You know your curriculum, the learning experiences you offered children during the collection period, and your district's standards for children's performance in different grades. We encourage you to work with your grade level colleagues to articulate clear expectations for different types of work.

KNOWLEDGE OF CHILD DEVELOPMENT You may refer to the Guidelines, as well as other sources of information about child development, for descriptions of what children of different ages are able to do and how they represent their learning.

EXPERIENCE WITH CHILDREN AT THIS AGE OR GRADE LEVEL Through your own professional experience, you have learned how children of different ages respond to different assignments and learning activities. After using Work Sampling for some time, the ongoing processes of reviewing and selecting work for Portfolio will also provide you with a store of knowledge concerning how students express their learning through various classroom activities.

As with the Checklists, performance on the Portfolio is rated using the categories "As Expected" or "Needs Development." Once again, "As Expected" means that the child's performance as demonstrated in the Portfolio meets or exceeds the expectations described below. A rating of "Needs Development" indicates that the child's work does not meet your expectations. Near the end of each collection period, you review each child's Portfolio and evaluate the work based on your classroom or grade-level expectations. Ask yourself, "How does the work compare to classroom expectations for children at this age or grade level?"

The following review process will help you evaluate Portfolio performance within a domain. Consider the following example of rating Mathematical Thinking for the winter collection period:

1 First, find the Mathematical Thinking Core Item folder and remove items from the winter collection period.

2 Find the Individualized Items that provide information about Mathematical Thinking by looking at the boxes you have checked in the Individualized Item column of the Portfolio Item Record self-stick notes. Remove those items.

3 Now, review the Core Items and Individualized Items you have just removed. When reviewing Core Items, focus on the specific area of learning that the item represents. Ignore other characteristics such as neatness, fine-motor control, language facility, or artistic features.

4 Consider how well the student's work meets expectations for students at this age or grade level and at this time of year, given the learning opportunities you have provided. Then assign an evaluative rating for the student's performance in Mathematical Thinking for the collection period.

Rating Progress

The third rating task is to evaluate each child's progress. For the progress rating, you need to review information from the Checklist and Portfolio and compare current performance to performance at an earlier point in time. Because children do not develop at the same rate, the standard for rating progress must be different for each child. Ask yourself, "Compared to her earlier performance, has this child made expected progress?"

Within each domain, you must evaluate whether a student's progress is ***"As Expected"*** or ***"Other than Expected."*** Use the Checklist ratings and the Portfolio work as evidence to compare the student's performance across collection periods. In other words, compare the child's current performance with her earlier performance. Because children within the same early childhood classroom may differ from one another developmentally by as much as two years, it is not possible to establish definitive standards for rating progress. You must use your teaching experience and your knowledge of child development as guides when considering whether a child has shown sufficient growth since your previous evaluation.

The "Other than Expected" rating is used whenever a child's progress is not typical. A child who displays progress beyond expectations and a child who shows less progress than expected will both be rated "Other than Expected." It is therefore essential that you add comments to the report to describe the abundance or the lack of progress reflected by the rating.

For example, when preparing the winter Summary Report, a teacher reviews the winter Checklist ratings and compares them with the fall Checklist ratings. She also reviews Portfolio work from the winter and compares it with the fall work samples. If the child has made appropriate growth, then the child's progress is rated "As Expected." If, however, the child's performance has not changed since the previous collection period, or if it has shown growth beyond expectations, then the child's progress is rated as "Other than Expected." Whenever you rate a child's progress as "Other than Expected," it is necessary to explain the reasons for this rating in the commentary section of the Summary Report.

After completing the performance and progress ratings for each domain, it is time to begin planning the narrative.

Write a Narrative for Each Student

After you make the ratings, your next task is to write a narrative for each student that profiles the child's strengths and your areas of concern. Teachers frequently communicate information about students in writing. They send notes home to families, they write questions and thoughts about individual students, and they note observations of students throughout the day. The commentary on the Summary Report, however, calls for a different type of writing. Unlike the spontaneous jotting of an anecdotal record, the commentary on the Summary Report is a product of thoughtful reflection based on accumulated evidence from multiple sources.

The audience for the Summary Report influences the type of information that should be included. Your knowledge of a child's family will help determine the specific content and form of the report. Consider the following questions:

♦ Is the family particularly interested in a specific aspect of the child's learning?

♦ Is the child's family familiar with the school's assessment practices?

♦ Is a family member highly critical of the child?

♦ Is the family distrustful of teachers and schools?

Your writing should take into account what you know about the family and their relationship with the student.

The narrative explains the performance and progress ratings, and emphasizes important and unique aspects of each student. As you plan your narratives, you will make decisions about content and organization. These decisions will touch on such issues as what to write, what language to use, how much to write, how to organize the narrative, and how to get started writing narratives.

What to Write

The goal of the narrative section of the Summary Report is to provide an individualized profile of a student's strengths and areas of difficulty across the seven domains. These comments allow you to highlight the unique learning characteristics, interests, and accomplishments of each child. You should address the quality of a student's work, as well as level of performance. The narrative gives you space to elaborate on a "Needs Development" rating by stating specific information about learning goals. In the winter and at the end of the year, you should also comment on student progress, especially when progress is rated "Other than Expected."

ADDRESS STRENGTHS AND AREAS OF CONCERN If you structure your comments by domain, you may want to organize them within each domain according to the functional components. By addressing components that represent a child's strengths before you comment on the components that are difficult for the child, you can convey a positive tone that emphasizes the child's current level of competence (Example 1).

EXAMPLE 1
Personal and Social
Development

PERFORMANCE	PROGRESS
Checklist	
As Expected	**As Expected**

COMMENTS

Debra's actions in the classroom show that she feels good about herself. She interacts well with peers. She handles classroom materials with respect and purpose. She shows eagerness and curiousity as a learner. Debra has difficulty remaining with a task until it is completed, but already has shown some improvement in this area.

ADDRESS PERFORMANCE AND PROGRESS Comments should address children's current levels of achievement, as well as their growth over time. Especially for a child who is struggling in a particular domain, it is important to describe the child's progress, even if his performance does not meet expectations for children of his age or grade (Example 2).

EXAMPLE 2
Mathematical Thinking

PERFORMANCE	PROGRESS
Checklist	
Needs Development	**Other than Expected**
Portfolio	
Needs Development	

COMMENTS

Tonya is beginning to show an interest in solving mathematical problems. She recognizes patterns, but has difficulty reproducing them with concrete materials. She struggles with math and has made little progress. We're working together on this at school and it would be helpful if you help her to notice and copy patterns at home.

EXPLAIN THE RATINGS Another function of the commentary on the Summary Report is to explain performance and progress ratings. The Summary Report allows you to describe and explain any apparent discrepancies. In this way, the narrative supports the ratings, and at the same time provides

Completing the Summary Report

detail and explanation about an individual student's learning (Example 3).

EXAMPLE 3 Mathematical Thinking	

PERFORMANCE	PROGRESS
Checklist	
Needs Development	**As Expected**
Portfolio	
Needs Development	

COMMENTS

George's math skills are gradually developing. He benefits from practice counting objects and working with number symbols. He has difficulty using comparative mathematical language (more than, less than, greatest, largest, etc.).

Several combinations of ratings may elicit confusion or questions from a student's family. Within a domain, the Checklist and Portfolio ratings may differ, or the Performance and Progress ratings may differ (Example 4). At first glance, these combinations may not make sense. But these combinations can be valid, accurately reflecting the child's learning and performance in the classroom. For more information, see "Frequently Asked Questions" at the end of this chapter.

EXAMPLE 4 Language and Literacy	

PERFORMANCE	PROGRESS
Checklist	
As Expected	**As Expected**
Portfolio	
Needs Development	

COMMENTS

Tyrell follows 2-to-3 step directions and speaks clearly when conveying his ideas and thoughts. He listens with interest to stories read aloud and can tell or draw events very well. He is slowly gaining confidence as a writer and uses invented spelling to write simple sentences, although this is only beginning to be reflected in his Portfolio.

ADDITIONAL CONTENT FOR THE NARRATIVE As you become comfortable writing narrative reports, you may begin to include other types of information including suggestions for the family and descriptions of the child's long-term progress.

Many families want to participate in their child's learning. Suggestions for concrete ways that the family can work with the child at home to further his educational goals may also be included in the Summary Report (Example 5). Asking families to help students acquire particular concepts shows that you value their involvement.

EXAMPLE 5
Mathematical Thinking

PERFORMANCE	PROGRESS
Checklist	
Needs Development	**As Expected**
Portfolio	
Needs Development	

COMMENTS

Sam shows beginning understanding of addition. He needs more practice counting by 1s, 2s, and 5s, and solving problems. He is having some difficulty recognizing and labeling coins, so it would be helpful to him to work some of this vocabulary into discussions at home.

Progress is an important focus of the Summary Report. To ensure that the child's current performance is portrayed in the context of the entire school year, refer to previous reports before beginning to write the current report. It is helpful for parents, especially parents of children who are experiencing difficulties in school, to see that the teacher acknowledges the progress that their child has made. The comment in Example 6 exemplifies this point.

EXAMPLE 6
Personal and Social
Development

PERFORMANCE	PROGRESS
Checklist	
Needs Development	**As Expected**

COMMENTS

After reviewing her fall report, I see that Susan has made progress in Personal and Social development. Overall, she is more comfortable in the classroom. However, her social skills vary from day to day. Some days she can take responsibility for completing her work; other days she needs my support. She can work and play with a few children in the class—often she needs my help to work with peers. Offering little, frequent reminders before activities is effective for Susan. Perhaps you could try this at home.

Language of the Narrative

The writing on the Summary Report should support the document's major goal: to communicate constructive and clear information about a child's performance and progress in easily understood language. Comments should be specific, include examples, and avoid the use of educational jargon. The report should be positive in tone and should respect the child's efforts and achievements. Moreover, the report should be grammatically correct and free of spelling errors.

BE SPECIFIC AND DESCRIPTIVE Comments are most meaningful to families when they are specific and descriptive, rather than abstract and vague. Below are three descriptions of a kindergartner's Personal and Social Development (Examples 7–9). Consider which example provides a sense of the individual child. Which gives the most descriptive information? If you were the parent of a kindergarten-age child, which of these comments would you most like to receive?

<table>
<tr><td rowspan="3">EXAMPLE 7
Personal and Social
Development</td><td>PERFORMANCE</td><td>PROGRESS</td></tr>
<tr><td>Checklist</td><td></td></tr>
<tr><td>As Expected</td><td>As Expected</td></tr>
</table>

COMMENTS

Ann continues to be an enthusiastic learner. She is interested in a variety of activities but tends to choose reading and writing during Choice Time. Her self confidence has grown significantly, reflected by her ability to take risks in new areas. Last week she was the first volunteer to pet the naturalist's snake. She plays well with other children and has one special friend.

<table>
<tr><td rowspan="3">EXAMPLE 8
Personal and Social
Development</td><td>PERFORMANCE</td><td>PROGRESS</td></tr>
<tr><td>Checklist</td><td></td></tr>
<tr><td>As Expected</td><td>As Expected</td></tr>
</table>

COMMENTS

Candy enjoys selecting a variety of Choice Time activities. She works and plays alongside others and is beginning to interact more easily with children and adults in large group situations.

<table>
<tr><td rowspan="3">EXAMPLE 9
Personal and Social
Development</td><td>PERFORMANCE</td><td>PROGRESS</td></tr>
<tr><td>Checklist</td><td></td></tr>
<tr><td>As Expected</td><td>As Expected</td></tr>
</table>

COMMENTS

Roderick's confidence in himself as well as his work is improving.

Example 7 provides both general and specific information. The reader can see that Ann's teacher knows her quite well. Examples 8 and 9 give very general information and do not provide individualized pictures of how these two children learn and work.

USE LANGUAGE FROM THE DEVELOPMENTAL GUIDELINES You may find it helpful to use language from the Guidelines, as Glen's teacher does (Example 10). If you incorporate language from the Guidelines, it is important that you add specific examples unique to the child so that the report retains a sense of the child's individuality.

EXAMPLE 10
Language and Literacy

PERFORMANCE	PROGRESS
Checklist	
As Expected	**As Expected**
Portfolio	
As Expected	

COMMENTS

Glen usually follows directions but sometimes has difficulty staying on task. He speaks clearly when sharing his ideas and thoughts. He shows interest in reading-related activities and can retell information from a story. He often tells the class about books he has read at home. He is beginning to use invented spelling but needs more confidence and practice.

INDIVIDUALIZE THE NARRATIVE Note how a first grade teacher describes Trey's performance in Scientific Thinking (Example 11). Using the child's own words personalizes this comment in a striking way.

EXAMPLE 11
Scientific Thinking

PERFORMANCE	PROGRESS
Checklist	
As Expected	**As Expected**
Portfolio	
As Expected	

COMMENTS

Trey applied scientific processes when he studied foxes. He continued with this study for several weeks, always thinking up new questions to investigate. Toward the end of the study, he announced to me one day, "I want to study foxes until I'm in 3rd grade." He has learned and retained a great deal of information about foxes.

BE POSITIVE The tone of the Summary Report should be positive. Try to begin and end with a positive comment and to state what a child can do, not only what she is unable to do. Talk with your colleagues about how to write in positive ways about what a child is not yet capable of doing without being misleading about the level of the child's performance. Examples 12 and 13 show how a negative comment can be rewritten with a more positive tone.

EXAMPLE 12
Personal and Social
Development

PERFORMANCE	PROGRESS
Checklist	
Needs Development	**Other than Expected**

COMMENTS

Because Steven is a very quiet child, it is hard to determine his thoughts. He interacts well with others and is respectful of their belongings. However, he doesn't show any eagerness to learn, lacks participation within a group, and daydreams instead of seeking help.

Completing the Summary Report

EXAMPLE 13
Personal and Social
Development

PERFORMANCE	PROGRESS
Checklist	
Needs Development	**Other than Expected**

COMMENTS

Steven interacts well with one or two children at a time and is respectful of their belongings. Because he is a very quiet child, it is hard to know what he is thinking, how he feels about classroom activities, and when he needs help from teachers. In the next few months, I hope to see greater interest and participation in classroom activities. We will work together on learning when it is appropriate for him to ask for help with his work.

Below is another example of a comment with a negative tone (Example 14). Think about how to state it more positively. Remember that it is best to begin and end with a positive comment.

EXAMPLE 14
Personal and Social
Development

PERFORMANCE	PROGRESS
Checklist	
Needs Development	**Other than Expected**

COMMENTS

Courtney has shown little growth in this domain. She rarely makes independent decisions or assumes independent responsibility for completing her work. She has difficulty following class rules. Courtney has many friends, but needs to learn to interact more comfortably with adults.

For a student who is struggling in specific areas, first state what she can do, and then discuss the skills you will concentrate on improving in the future (Examples 15–17). Another approach is to comment on current capabilities and then set goals or project the skills you hope the child will attain by the end of the year (Examples 18 and 19).

EXAMPLE 15
Mathematical Thinking

PERFORMANCE	PROGRESS
Checklist	
Needs Development	**As Expected**
Portfolio	
As Expected	

COMMENTS

Sally has mastered addition of two-digit numbers. During the next few weeks, we will be focusing on subtraction.

EXAMPLE 16 Language and Literacy	PERFORMANCE	PROGRESS
	Checklist **Needs Development**	**As Expected**
	Portfolio **Needs Development**	

COMMENTS

Ted's interest in language and reading can be seen by his eagerness to listen to stories read aloud and willingness to draw pictures in his journal. He is not yet writing words to accompany his pictures and seems reluctant to speak up during class discussions. In the next few months, I will focus attention on and support his growth in these areas.

EXAMPLE 17 Personal and Social Development	PERFORMANCE	PROGRESS
	Checklist **Needs Development**	**Other than Expected**

COMMENTS

Although Jerome continues to make progress in all academic areas, his overall attitude has not been as positive this past marking period. He seems more impatient with others and is easily frustrated. He's working on solving conflicts appropriately and also on getting assignments done in a reasonable period of time.

EXAMPLE 18 Mathematical Thinking	PERFORMANCE	PROGRESS
	Checklist **As Expected**	**As Expected**
	Portfolio **As Expected**	

COMMENTS

Pat's exploration of classroom materials show her enjoyment of math as well as her growing skills. She recognizes, extends, and creates patterns, understands the concept of number and quantity (0–10), instantly recognizes the number of dots on a die (1–6), and has a beginning sense of geometry, measurement, graphing, and math vocabulary. A goal for Pat is to develop strategies for adding quantitities.

EXAMPLE 19 Personal and Social Development	PERFORMANCE
	Checklist **Needs Development**

COMMENTS

Matt enjoys coming to the morning meeting. He continues to need individual guidance and support from me to participate in group discussions. My goal for Matt in the next few months is for him to develop greater independence in this area.

Completing the Summary Report

When teachers pay close attention to the tone of their comments, families can read Summary Reports and feel hopeful and confident about their child's development. Summary Reports should never convey a negative or angry tone.

Now, take a moment to compare Examples 20 and 21. Which is more positive?

EXAMPLE 20
Language and Literacy

PERFORMANCE	PROGRESS
Checklist	
Needs Development	**As Expected**
Portfolio	
Needs Development	

COMMENTS

Mary usually needs to be given directions more than once. She does not contribute enough to class discussion and needs to write more in her journal. She is very familiar with sentence structure and is able to use upper- and lowercase letters efficiently.

EXAMPLE 21
Language and Literacy

PERFORMANCE	PROGRESS
Checklist	
Needs Development	**As Expected**
Portfolio	
Needs Development	

COMMENTS

Mary is very familiar with sentence structure and is able to use upper- and lowercase letters efficiently in her writing. She usually needs to hear directions more than once in order to be able to follow them. During the next collection period, we will concentrate on helping Mary to contribute more frequently to class discussions, and to write more in her journal.

A comment takes on a more positive tone when the teacher states what the child can do before presenting areas of concern. A report that is positive in tone does not mislead the family about the student's performance or gloss over areas of difficulty, but leaves families hopeful about their child's future accomplishments.

BE RESPECTFUL Finally, the language in a Summary Report should demonstrate respect for children, for their approaches to learning, and for their accomplishments. Be careful about word choice and avoid the use of colloquialisms or slang that may be misinterpreted. The teacher in Example 22 uses strong, provocative language ("bossy, sulky, and stubborn") that may be interpreted differently by different readers. Example 23 shows how this comment could be rewritten.

EXAMPLE 22
Personal and Social
Development

PERFORMANCE	PROGRESS
Checklist	
Needs Development	**Other than Expected**

COMMENTS

Rashawna seems a bit more confident in herself as a learner and becomes involved in her work if she is working alone. Although she is preoccupied with maintaining friendships, she is overly bossy, stubborn, and sulky, causing many friendship problems. Her focus in large groups is not good and she distracts others.

EXAMPLE 23
Personal and Social
Development

PERFORMANCE	PROGRESS
Checklist	
Needs Development	**Other than Expected**

COMMENTS

Rashawna shows a bit more confidence in herself as a learner; she can remain attentive to her work when she works alone. She is very concerned about maintaining friendships, yet she tries to tell her friends what to do and has difficulty compromising. Goals for the next collection period include helping Rashawna interact more cooperatively with peers and helping her to focus in large groups without distracting others.

How Much to Write

Teachers often wonder whether they have to write about every component and every indicator for each child. This is not necessary, nor is it recommended. One of the main goals of the Summary Report is to summarize information about a child. It is more effective, therefore, not to describe all that you know about a child, but to integrate, condense, and summarize your knowledge into a form that is understandable to families and in an amount that does not overwhelm them. Although you may not comment on every indicator, or even each component, you should address every domain. The question of how much to write is best answered by asking yourself whether you have conveyed the essential information about this child's learning. If the answer is yes, then you have written enough. Consider Examples 24–26 from the domain of Personal and Social Development.

EXAMPLE 24
Personal and Social
Development

PERFORMANCE	PROGRESS
Checklist	
As Expected	**As Expected**

COMMENTS

Sasha is an enthusiastic learner who helps others.

Completing the Summary Report

EXAMPLE 25
Personal and Social
Development

PERFORMANCE	PROGRESS
Checklist	
Needs Development	**Other than Expected**
COMMENTS	

Terry has made little progress in this domain and continues to have many conflicts with other children.

EXAMPLE 26
Personal and Social
Development

PERFORMANCE	PROGRESS
Checklist	
As Expected	**As Expected**
COMMENTS	

Bob shows a great deal of comfort and confidence in himself. He enters group play with other children confident that he will be accepted. Bob is very self-directed. He finds materials for his art projects from many different centers in the classroom. Bob follows classroom rules and routines, and handles materials respectfully. He manages changes in routine easily, such as when we have a substitute teacher. Bob is a very eager and curious learner who chooses a variety of classroom activities.

How much to write is influenced by the type of information you want the family to have. The brevity of Example 24 is permissible, given the positive tone of the message. In the case of Example 25, the nature of the message warrants a lengthier response. When a child is having difficulty in a particular domain, you should write longer, more detailed and descriptive comments. Example 25 does not communicate how Terry becomes involved in conflicts or how his teacher is going to help him learn to interact more cooperatively with peers. Negative comments require support; otherwise they are not very useful. Having specific details and examples during the conference will be helpful for both you and family members. It is unnecessary and overly time-consuming to address every indicator, as in Example 26, for a child who is succeeding in a domain. Being clear and providing specifics, however, is always beneficial.

How much contact you have had with the family will also influence the writing of the narrative. The first report to a family that you do not know may be more formal in tone and comprehensive than subsequent reports. A report to a parent who regularly visits the school and volunteers in the classroom may be shorter than reports to parents who are unfamiliar with the classroom, the curriculum, and the scope of activities. If the family frequently communicates with you, your report may reflect the concerns they have expressed in previous conversations. Whether you will give the Summary Report to the family at a conference will also influence how you write it.

The final issue to consider when determining how much to write is whether you have depicted a child's individuality rather than simply listed his skills and knowlege. Although two children may have identical ratings on a Summary Report, it is unlikely that they have acquired exactly the same skills in the same way. An effective Summary Report communicates each child's personality and approach to learning. The report should give the reader a feel for or a sense of the child. Adding specific examples of behavior and language, drawn from your observation records, will help the reader understand the child.

How to Organize the Narrative

Here are several approaches you can use to structure and organize your comments: 1) write a paragraph for each domain; 2) write an integrated report that allots different amounts of space for each domain; or 3) identify the most important information about the child and write comments about those major points only.

♦ **Domain paragraphs** Many teachers write a paragraph for each domain that highlights the child's strengths and areas of difficulty and includes instructional plans. These teachers incorporate performance and progress information into each paragraph.

♦ **Integrated reports** Teachers who feel constrained by writing only one paragraph per domain can write an integrated report about the child. Such a report covers all domains, but some domains have more detail than others. This method permits you to allot space according to the importance of each domain to a child's learning.

♦ **Highlight reports** Some teachers select several major points about the child that are most important to communicate to the family. They then write comments constructed around these points.

Make your own choices about the organization you will use, and about whether to write phrases or full sentences. Although the commentary section of the Summary Report form is divided with faint lines between domains, you can decide how much space to allot for each domain.

How to Get Started Writing Narratives

Sometimes teachers find it difficult to begin writing narratives. If you have not been required to write reports in the past, it will take some time to develop a style that is both efficient for you and informative for the family. To help you determine the most important points to include, you may want to follow the following process:

Completing the Summary Report

1   As you review your data about a child, jot down phrases that describe the child's strengths and areas of difficulty in each domain.

2   Underline or highlight the information that is most important to communicate to the child and family.

3   Review your phrases for one domain.

4   Organize these phrases to fit into categories. Your categories may correspond to functional components, but do not have to.

5   Synthesize groups of phrases into a few sentences.

6   For each domain, include a) a statement that describes the child's strengths, b) a statement that identifies an area that needs development or is of concern (if any), and c) a statement that describes a goal.

7   To individualize the child's report, use the phrase "for example" or "as shown by" followed by a reference to an observational note or a piece of work. It is not necessary to have an example for each point or for each domain.

The following are examples of formats for composing narrative statements for one domain.

EXAMPLE 27   Tim does _____, _____, and _____ well. He is not doing _____ yet. For example, _____. My goal during the next few months is to help Tim develop _____. It would help if he worked on _____ at home.

EXAMPLE 28   Lynn's strengths are _____ and _____ as shown by [specific example from observational data].

Although she does _____, she is not yet able to _____. During the next few months we will work on _____ to help her with this.

EXAMPLE 29   Dwight is performing as expected in [component 1], [component 2], and [component 3]. We are working together to improve his skills in [component 4] and [component 5]. You and Dwight together can work on [specific skills to practice].

Appendix D includes two examples of completed Summary Reports.

Share the Summary Report with the Child and Family

The Summary Report is designed to be discussed with the family at a conference, rather than being sent home without personal contact. This will make you more confident that parents understand the report, and parents will have the opportunity to ask questions, contribute information, and share their concerns. Some teachers send the Summary Report home and then ask parents to bring it with them to the conference. This allows the family time to read the report and to formulate questions privately before coming in for the conference. Family members with limited reading skills will need the report read to them during the family-teacher conference.

Although ideally each Summary Report should be discussed at a conference, we realize that this is not a realistic expectation in most schools. It is critical that the first Summary Report of the school year be shared at a conference. This gives you an opportunity to explain the Summary Report format to family members and to establish personal contact. If there are two conference times, we recommend sharing the first two reports at conferences and sending the final report home without a conference.

Some teachers have found it helpful to describe their classroom curriculum in a statement attached to each Summary Report (see Appendix C). This is especially important if you will not be holding a family conference.

Conferences are most successful when teachers are prepared and families actively participate in the conference. Because conferences are generally quite brief, you will have to prepare in advance to make the most of the short time you have together. After you complete the Summary Report, identify the most important points to communicate in a face-to-face situation. Some teachers create a structure by focusing on strengths, concerns, and plans. They may make brief notes about points to highlight.

Portfolio work is an effective form of documentation to share with families. Some teachers select work in advance to discuss at the conference. They flag the pieces they want to use to illustrate their points.

At the beginning of the conference, elicit information from the family to acknowledge the unique knowledge and perspective they bring to the conference. Some questions that you might want to ask include:

♦ What does the child like to do?
♦ How does the family perceive the child's personality and strengths?
♦ What special interests has the child shown at home?
♦ What is the child saying about school?
♦ What are the family's goals for the child to work on this year?

Many teachers find it helpful to send questions home in advance so that parents can feel prepared and participate fully in the conference. You can ask questions to elicit information from the family, but the family should also be given ample opportunity to ask questions they may have about their child's educational program and performance at school.

Completing the Summary Report

Involving Students in Evaluation

As much as possible, the student should participate in the Summary Report process. Involving students will help make assessment less mysterious and anxiety-provoking for them. Rather than viewing evaluation as something external, the student can begin to see evaluation as part of the learning process and as something over which she has some control.

In previous chapters, we described student roles in the Checklist and Portfolio collection processes. As with the varying levels of student involvement in reviewing and selecting Portfolio items, student involvement with Summary Reports takes many different forms. It is critical that evaluation become a part of the learning process, and that students not feel that evaluation is a secret or is only of concern to parents and teachers. Consider the following possibilities for student involvement.

♦ **Student review and reflection on work** As the end of a collection period nears, you may ask students to review the work they have done during the past 8 to 12 weeks. Students may select particular items that they want you to share with their family, or they may write a paragraph about their progress and the learning goals they have set for themselves for the next collection period. You can use the "Thoughts about My Portfolio" form to elicit students' comments about the growth shown in their Portfolios.

♦ **Meetings with students before family-teacher conferences** Some teachers hold a conference with every student before the family-teacher conference. The teacher reviews the Summary Report with the student and asks her if there is any information she wants the teacher to communicate to the family. You may want to ask your students to complete the student part of the SUMMARY REPORT: STUDENT AND FAMILY COMMENTS form (Figure 5) available in the Reproducible Masters booklet.

FIGURE 5
Summary Report:
Student and Family
Comments form

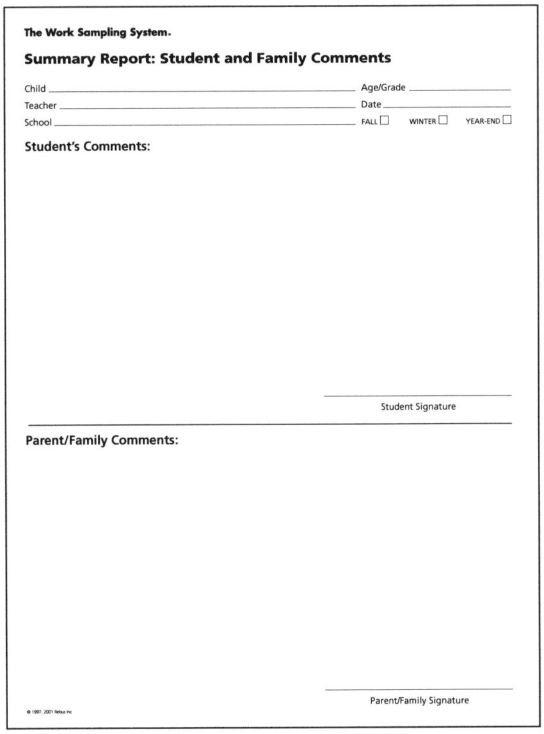

The Work Sampling System.

Summary Report: Student and Family Comments

Child _____ Age/Grade _____
Teacher _____ Date _____
School _____ FALL ☐   WINTER ☐   YEAR-END ☐

Student's Comments:

_____
Student Signature

Parent/Family Comments:

_____
Parent/Family Signature

© 1997, 2001 Pelion Inc.

♦ **Student participation in conferences** You may invite students to participate in family-teacher conferences. One advantage of this approach is that students will not feel that the content of the conference is only for adults. By participating in conferences, they will be able to see how important their education is to their family and to you.

♦ **Student-led conferences** This represents the highest degree of student participation in the family-teacher conference. It requires advance work by both you and the student to prepare the student for his role in the conference. You may discuss the student's work and progress with him and arrive at a consensus regarding information that is important enough to be shared. The student can then select work that illustrates his learning.

At the conference, the student will introduce his family to you. Conferences may be scheduled to allow time for the student to give his family a tour of the classroom or school. When the conference begins, the student shows his work. After the child has had an opportunity to talk about the work, the teacher also adds comments. The conference ends with the teacher, student, and family setting learning goals for the next collection period.

Part III Frequently Asked Questions About the Summary Report

Q When should I start completing Summary Reports?

> **A** You should begin to work on Summary Reports about two to three weeks before the end of the collection period or the start of parent conferences. It is important that your Checklist ratings are all complete and that the Portfolios are in order before you begin writing Summary Reports.

Q I'm ready to start completing Summary Reports. I'm surrounded by piles of Checklists, Portfolios, observational notes, and other materials. What should I do first?

> **A** Teachers organize their work on Summary Reports in several different ways. Some teachers begin by making their Checklist and Portfolio performance ratings for every student in their class in every domain. Other teachers gather all the information they have on a particular child and complete that child's entire Summary Report. Still other teachers evaluate the entire class for one domain before going on to the next domain.
>
> Regardless of method, the process begins with a review of documentation and evidence. For example, if you decide to organize your work by domain, you might start with Language and Literacy. Begin by reviewing the Checklist in the Language and Literacy domain, and make a determination about performance (this is one of the reasons that it is so important to complete students' Checklists before beginning Summary Reports). Next, review the Core and Individualized Items in the Portfolio and rate performance. Finally, review all available information from the Checklists and Portfolios and rate the child's progress since the beginning of the school year. After making all the ratings, write comments about the domain of Language and Literacy.

Q How does performance differ from progress?

> **A** Performance and progress have two very different meanings. Performance refers to the level of a student's behavior, skills, and accomplishments at a particular point in time. In the Work Sampling System, the student's current level of performance is documented in two ways: by the teacher's observations as recorded on the Checklist, and by the child's work as represented in the Portfolio. Performance is evaluated on the

Summary Report near the end of each collection period. The ratings describe whether the child's performance within a particular domain is "As Expected" or "Needs Development" as compared with expectations for children of that grade level.

In contrast, the progress rating focuses on growth or change over time. The child's current performance is compared with her previous performance. The progress rating does not compare a student's progress with an external measure of progress. Instead, progress is evaluated solely within the context of an individual child's work; the child is compared with herself alone. You are asked to determine whether the child's progress within each domain is "As Expected" or "Other than Expected." Rapid or exceptional progress as well as slow progress should be noted and accompanied by explanatory comments in the narrative.

Q Should I evaluate progress in the fall?

A At the end of the fall collection period, the progress rating is optional. Sometimes, however, teachers have observed enough growth from the beginning of school to the end of the fall collection period that they feel comfortable making a progress rating. This decision is left to the individual teacher and may vary from child to child within a classroom.

Q Should performance and progress ratings always agree?

A Performance and progress ratings will not always agree. Children may perform up to expectations and still not show growth. Or the opposite may be true. The performance of a student with special needs, for example, may be delayed in several domains. But, this child may show excellent progress when his current performance is compared with his previous performance within a particular domain (Examples 30 and 31). Similarly, a second-grader who is unable to identify letters in September but who is sounding out words in March may have her Checklist and Portfolio performance in Language and Literacy rated as "Needs Development," but her progress would be rated "As Expected." These different ratings make sense when the differences between the standard for progress and the standards for performance for each component of the Work Sampling System are kept in mind.

Frequently Asked Questions About the Summary Report

EXAMPLE 30
Language and Literacy

PERFORMANCE	PROGRESS
Checklist	
Needs Development	**Other than Expected**
Portfolio	
Needs Development	

COMMENTS

At the beginning of the year, Latoya was unable to communicate with children or adults in the classroom. Now she is regularly communicating with us using facial expressions, gestures, and single words. She understands a great deal more than she can currently express. Her progress in this area has been exceptional.

EXAMPLE 31
Language and Literacy

PERFORMANCE	PROGRESS
Checklist	
Needs Development	**As Expected**
Portfolio	
Needs Development	

COMMENTS

Allison continues to receive speech/language and reading services. Her vocabulary and expressive skills have grown rapidly. Just recently, she has begun to ask questions of her peers during group settings. This is exciting! Books hold Allison's interest. Although her recall of details is improving, predicting and interpreting information is still difficult. During group discussions, Allison can attend for only a few minutes. To support her in this, I will tell her the topic of the discussion and ask her some questions to aid her thinking.

Q Should performance ratings be the same for the Checklist and Portfolio?

A Not necessarily. Sometimes a student's performance is rated as "As Expected" on the Checklist and as "Needs Development" on the Portfolio. In the case below, a teacher's observations and Checklist ratings show that Matthew's accomplishments and skills in Language and Literacy are "As Expected" when compared with national expectations. His work in the Portfolio, however, does not meet the teacher's standards. One reason for this combination of ratings is the difference in scope of the Checklist and the Portfolio. It may be that the student has difficulty understanding the areas of learning sampled by the Core Items of the Portfolio.

For example, Matthew may be quite competent overall in Language and Literacy. He listens attentively, engages in group discussions, and is beginning to learn to read. However, he has not begun to write. If the areas of learning in Language and Literacy are "writing to communicate ideas" and "understanding and interpreting text," Matthew's Portfolio performance rating will be "Needs Development," while the Checklist rating for Language and Literacy may be "As Expected." In this case, the teacher might write the comments shown in Example 32.

EXAMPLE 32
Language and Literacy

PERFORMANCE	PROGRESS
Checklist	
As Expected	**As Expected**
Portfolio	
Needs Development	

COMMENTS

Matthew listens attentively in group discussions and actively participates, offering information and his own ideas appropriately. He is interested in books and is beginning to read books with many pictures and 2-3 sentences per page. However, Matthew does not yet use writing. To express himself, he will draw pictures and describe them verbally, but is reluctant to do any written work. My goal for Mattthew is for him to begin to write captions and simple sentences to accompany his illustrations.

A different example is a child who is rated "As Expected" for the Portfolio and "Needs Development" for the Checklist. Within the domain of Mathematical Thinking, the specified areas of learning may be "geometry and spatial relations" on the one hand, and "patterns and relationships" on the other. The child may be doing excellent work in these two areas, but may have difficulty understanding number concepts and operations, probability and statistics, and measurement. In this case, the Checklist performance rating would be "Needs Development." The Portfolio work, however, may show that the child is performing "As Expected" in "geometry and spatial relations and patterns and relationships" (Example 33)

EXAMPLE 33
Mathematical Thinking

PERFORMANCE	PROGRESS
Checklist	
Needs Development	**As Expected**
Portfolio	
As Expected	

COMMENTS

Rosa has shown improvement in mathematics. She understands spatial relationships as shown through her block buildings and drawings. She creates and duplicates complicated patterns, as seen in her Portfolio work. However, she is having difficulty understanding number and measurement concepts, so we will focus on these during the next few months.

Frequently Asked Questions About the Summary Report

Q Why is it necessary to make a judgment, rather than just describe a child's current performance?

> A Some teachers feel that having external standards and evaluating students according to those standards may not be equitable. Because all children do not start school with the same advantages, it may seem unfair to evaluate them with the same yardstick. With Work Sampling, children are evaluated against several different standards.
>
> ◆ The Developmental Guidelines and Checklists describe reasonable expectations for children at different grade levels based on *state and national standards.*
>
> ◆ Portfolio work is evaluated within the context of *local (classroom and school) standards.*
>
> ◆ Children's progress is evaluated in terms of the *individual child.*
>
> Having standards for learning ensures that we regularly take stock of children's performance and progress, so that we may better adapt our teaching to their needs.
>
> It is important to acknowledge that we make informal evaluative decisions everyday. As we observe our students in the classroom, we evaluate their participation in classroom activities, and we develop and adjust our instructional plans. When teachers review work samples for inclusion in the Portfolio, they internally monitor whether the work meets their expectations, expectations that are set both by interacting with other professionals and through numerous "portfolio conferences" held with students. These daily assessment decisions help to create subsequent learning plans.
>
> When you engage in the process of completing the Summary Reports, you make similar evaluative decisions, but in a more formalized way. The Summary Report allows you to summarize your knowledge of the student's work and behavior over a longer period of time. Evaluative decisions are based on the accumulated evidence from many sources of information gathered during the collection period.

Q How do you know you are maintaining standards?

> A Work Sampling's Developmental Guidelines and Checklists are based on state and national standards for curriculum. It is essential that you follow the Guidelines and apply them when making evaluations. Portfolios do not have similar national standards, but instead emerge from the teacher's own classroom or community. By regularly observing students and reviewing Portfolio contents with students and colleagues, you clar-

ify your own standards of assessment and transmit these standards to your students.

It is essential that you clarify your own standards for Portfolios and communicate those standards to your students. This involves establishing content criteria—making the skills and concepts encompassed by each area of learning explicit so you and your students have a clear sense of what is being evaluated. It is also important to set explicit performance criteria—clearly described levels of expectation so that judgments made about work are predictable and consistent. Many teachers, in conjunction with their students, are developing rubrics to help with the process of evaluation. Rubrics help make both content and performance criteria very explicit. In addition, it is critical that teachers within a school district communicate with one another to ensure that similar standards for Portfolio work are being applied from one classroom to another.

Many teachers plan regular meeting times during the school year to discuss the standards for each part of the Work Sampling System. Groups of teachers discuss the meaning of each performance indicator and describe detailed expectations for it. Moreover, they begin to articulate what performance looks like when a student is rated "Not Yet," "In Process," or "Proficient." In the middle of the year, teachers return to their selected areas of learning, taking the lists of skills and concepts and the descriptions of progress they developed before school started, and they elaborate upon them to articulate specific standards for Portfolio work. Similarly, teachers discuss how to make progress ratings in systematic ways.

Q How do I know I am making objective and fair decisions on the Summary Report?

A Because your ratings and comments on the Summary Report are based on extensive evidence and documentation of the child's work and behavior collected over time, your evaluation is less likely to be influenced by whether the student was having a good or bad day on the day you write the report. We advise you to make final Checklist ratings based on data from multiple observations before you begin writing Summary Reports. Similarly, the extensive evidence you accumulate on each student's performance helps ensure that your stress level—or the performance of the student whose report you have most recently completed—will not influence your evaluation. The process of evaluation requires that you step back, review your knowledge of a child (supported by observations, Checklist ratings, and work in the Portfolio), and reflect on the overall picture before synthesizing these sources of information into a portrait of the child. Bias has no place in assessment, and the information described above is intended to neutralize its potential impact.

It is for this reason that Checklist ratings are informed by multiple observations and completed prior to writing Summary Reports.

Q **Why include comments?**

A First, teacher comments describe and explain the performance and progress ratings. Although two children may have identical ratings, it is unlikely that they have acquired the same skills and knowledge. For example, two first grade children are rated "As Expected" in Mathematical Thinking. However, one of them is very strong in creating patterns and understanding spatial relationships but has difficulty with simple addition and subtraction. The other understands number concepts and operations and performs computations accurately, but has great difficulty perceiving patterns and understanding the relationship between shapes. The commentary allows you to describe each child's performance in a more specific and detailed way.

The second reason for including comments on the Summary Report is to individualize and personalize the report. Although two children may have fairly similar skills, it is unlikely that they will demonstrate their skills and knowledge in the same fashion. For example, three third graders, all rated "As Expected" in Language and Literacy, use strategies to extract meaning from print equally well. However, one child reads voraciously and uses books to find information about topics of personal interest, another reads for pleasure and escape, and the third reads efficiently but finds enjoyment in writing fantasy stories. The commentary allows you to describe not only skills the child has acquired, but also how the child demonstrates those skills. Just as student work in the Portfolio elaborates on what can be learned from the Checklist ratings, the commentary on the Summary Report enriches the information provided by the performance and progress ratings.

Q **How long does it take to complete a Summary Report?**

A Because teachers have different ways of working, it is difficult to answer this question simply. A teacher who rapidly finds a comfortable way to gather and review Checklists and Portfolios, and who writes with ease, will require much less time to complete a Summary Report than a teacher who is overwhelmed with the amount of information and is uncomfortable writing comments. It is important to realize that completing Summary Reports the first time may take twice as long as the second time. The more often you complete Summary Reports, the more natural it will be to describe children in these terms.

Q How should Summary Reports be used at conference time?

A Work Sampling System conferences rely on the same techniques for establishing rapport and positive working relationships with families as those used with other reporting systems. Work Sampling enriches family-teacher relationships by offering extensive documentation to share with families. Most teachers structure the conference around the Summary Report and use examples from the Portfolio to illustrate important points. Although the Checklist is primarily designed for use by the teacher, it may be shown to parents to help clarify a student's performance within a particular domain.

Q How can specialists be involved in Summary Reports?

A Because expectations for special subject teachers (Art, Music, Physical Education, etc.) vary among districts, each district must decide whether and how special subject teachers will be involved in Work Sampling. This decision should be based in part on the extent of contact that specialists have with students (how frequently they see students and for how long), the specialists' caseloads, and whether specialists had responsibility for student evaluation before the Work Sampling System was adopted. Because of individual policies within school districts, determining the role of specialists in Work Sampling must be addressed on an individual basis, district by district, after consideration of how specialists function and how district and contractual realities constrain the specialist's role. (For further discussion of these issues, see Chapter 6.)

Student evaluation is most accurate and comprehensive when teachers and specialists collaborate. Incorporating a specialist's expertise into a Summary Report enriches the evaluation. Having two views of a child's development within a particular domain provides a more comprehensive, and therefore more reliable, assessment of the child.

The **SPECIAL SUBJECT REPORT** form (Figure 6) has been created for specialists who have independent responsibility for evaluating students or for those who want to make comments about students. The Special Subject Report form includes four carbonless copies (family, teacher, specialist, and school file) and is designed to help special subject teachers transmit information to the child's primary teacher and to the child's family. Special subject teachers check the domain(s) that they will address. Some districts require special subject teachers to comment on every student.

Others ask teachers to comment only if a child's performance or progress does not meet the teacher's expectations. This is an optional form that may assist special subject teachers in districts where they are responsible for student evaluation.

FIGURE 6
Special Subject Report form

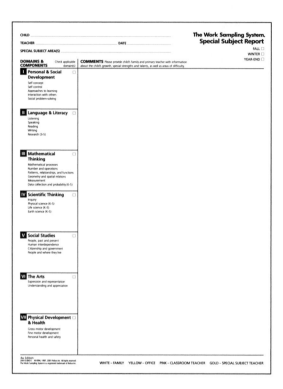

Q Should Summary Reports be written differently at different times of the year?

A Although the Summary Report accomplishes the same functions at each collection period, each period's Summary Report also differs slightly in perspective. The fall Summary Report will reflect your initial understanding of a child. Most teachers at this time of the year have a general sense of what students know in each of the domains and about how students express their knowledge. This first Summary Report provides a baseline measure of the child's skills at the start of the year. Because the child still has many months to acquire the skills and knowledge expected for her grade level, and because you are only beginning to know her, ratings made in the fall are often best described as preliminary.

The Summary Report completed at the end of the winter collection period describes what children have learned as well as what they still need to accomplish. By this time, you know the student quite well and are able to use your knowledge to modify instruction to best meet her needs. Moreover, with two-thirds of the school year completed, you are fairly confident in your understanding of the child and the ratings you have made.

The year-end report summarizes the child's performance and progress over the course of the year. Here you have the opportunity not only to review the child's performance for the entire school year, but also to discuss progress from the beginning of the year to the end. As teachers become familiar with this method of summarizing a child's learning and reporting to parents, their reports begin to show continuity from one reporting period to another.

CHAPTER 5
Getting Started with Work Sampling

Having read this manual, you may be thinking, "How do I begin using Work Sampling?" This chapter addresses four issues related to getting started:

■ Tips for You as You Learn Work Sampling

■ Gradual Implementation of Work Sampling

■ Enlisting the Support of Colleagues

■ Informing the Community about Work Sampling

Tips for You as You Learn Work Sampling

Many teachers have embarked on the process of learning to use Work Sampling. Most of them have benefited from the advice offered by a veteran Texas teacher at one of our very early workshops. She said to her colleagues, "Be patient, be flexible, have faith, and be willing to take risks." Learning anything new is hard and can cause discomfort. As you begin using Work Sampling, we invite you to listen to the wisdom of our colleague above. In addition, consider the following:

♦ It is not possible to do everything at once.

♦ It is not possible to become knowledgeable about something new without going through a period of learning.

♦ Learning includes trial and error, making mistakes, and growth.

♦ Learning may be uncomfortable and requires patience and time.

♦ Learning happens best when there is "hands-on" experience and time for "messing about."

It is likely that you keep these ideas in mind when thinking about the learning environment you set up for students. Allow yourself the same optimal learning conditions when embarking on the implementation of the Work Sampling System.

The first year of learning Work Sampling can feel daunting. It is important to be flexible and to allow yourself time to become familiar with the system (see the next section about gradual implementation). Remember that Work Sampling is designed to work for you and with you. Try to use it in a way that fits your classroom life, your curriculum, and your personal approach to learning and teaching.

Gradual Implementation of Work Sampling

We believe, and teachers have confirmed, that using performance assessment, and specifically the Work Sampling System, can enrich your work as a teacher by giving you the in-depth knowledge about each of your students that will help you to support them as learners. However, learning to use Work Sampling, as with learning anything new, takes time and patience. To support your learning process, we strongly advocate gradual implementation—using parts of the system rather than all of it when you begin in order to gain comfort and familiarity with this method of assessing children.

We know that you will be learning to use Work Sampling while you are managing your everyday responsibilities in the classroom, an already challenging task. Your school may even be involved in implementing several other new initiatives at the same time. Beginning to use Work Sampling gradually will permit you to achieve some mastery and control over a part of the system and will reduce the likelihood of your feeling overwhelmed.

Most decisions about gradual implementation are made at a school or district level. In general, gradual implementation plans specify how much of the system (the number of domains or elements) teachers will use initially and when they will add additional domains or elements. Some programs begin by using all three elements in fewer than seven domains. Others use only one element for a specified period of time before adding others.

Gradually Adding Domains

In this plan, you start the year using all three elements: the Guidelines and Checklists, the Portfolio, and the Summary Report. You would focus, however, on only two or three domains at a time. For example, teachers collect work during the first collection period in the first three domains only, add two additional domains during the second collection period, and add the final two during the third collection period.

There are many variations. Some teachers spend the entire first year focused on only three domains, adding one at each collection period. They add the other four domains during their second year. Other teachers begin the first collection period using only one domain. This way they can concentrate on learning to observe children, setting up organizational strategies, and involving their students. Once they have these strategies in place, they add the additional domains during the second and third collection periods. The amount of time it takes you to implement the entire

Getting Started with Work Sampling

System depends on how much of Work Sampling is new to you and how many new skills and routines you need to develop.

If you choose this implementation plan you will begin Portfolio collection in two domains only because Portfolio items are not collected in the third domain—Personal and Social Development. To further decrease the initial work load, you can decide to select one area of learning, rather than two, in the domains of Language and Literacy and Mathematical Thinking. During the second collection period, you can add a second area of learning to each of the initial domains and select only one area of learning in each of the new domains you are adding. We strongly encourage you to collect Individualized Items from the start because they provide an excellent way to involve students in selecting Portfolio items.

The advantage of adding domains gradually is that it gives you time to see how the three elements of Work Sampling work together and complement each other. The disadvantage of this approach will become evident when you begin to think about Summary Reports. During the first collection period, you will complete the ratings and narratives on the Summary Report only for the three domains you are currently addressing. But, the domains that you have not yet addressed must also be evaluated: families will require a report about their child's learning in these domains.

Programs have solved this problem in at least two different ways:

♦ Some programs use the Summary Report to report only on the domains that they have addressed with Work Sampling. They use their traditional report card to report on the other areas of the curriculum.

♦ Other programs use the Summary Report as their sole method of reporting to families. They complete the Report fully for three domains, making ratings and writing comments. For the other domains, they comment on the child's learning in the narrative portion of the report, but do not make ratings. The narrative comments will be more general than the narratives describing the child's learning in the three Work Sampling domains, but all domains will be addressed and reported using one form.

We do not advocate the first approach. Teachers report that the logistics of dealing with two very different reporting formats are difficult. Moreover, if the traditional reporting format is very different from the Summary Report, families may have difficulty reconciling the two methods of evaluation.

We recommend the second approach. For this approach to be effective, however, the community must be informed that teachers are taking a year to become proficient using a new method of assessment, that to help them learn this new method teachers will focus on three domains only at the beginning of the school year, and that although teachers are still teaching in all areas of the curriculum, the information on the latter half of the Summary Report will not be quite as detailed as that in the first three domains. Our experience has been that most communities are able to understand this explanation and appreciate the more detailed information they receive as their teachers gradually add domains throughout the school year.

The following are steps for getting started with all three elements using the first three domains (Personal and Social Development, Language and Literacy, and Mathematical Thinking).

1 Read and become familiar with the Developmental Guidelines for these three domains.

2 Set up your Portfolio collection system for these domains.

   ♦ Devise collection procedures and set up work folders

   ♦ Create and label individual portfolios (for Language and Literacy, Mathematical Thinking, and Individualized Items)

   ♦ Determine how and where to store Portfolios

3 Working with other teachers in your building or district, plan one or two areas of learning for Core Item collection in Language and Literacy and Mathematical Thinking.

4 Set up an organizational system for observation and Checklist review. Create a teacher file to store:

   ♦ the Checklist

   ♦ notes and reminders about activities to observe or plan

   ♦ observation notes

   ♦ correspondence with the family

   ♦ any other materials about the child that will help you to make evaluations

5 Decide on the methods and tools you will use for documenting observations of children in the three domains.

   ♦ Select any of the Checklist Process Notes that seem useful to you

   ♦ Make enough copies of your process note sheets to use during the first weeks of school

- If you think of other ways to record your observations, design a master

- Fill in the children's names as appropriate

6 Develop a plan for ongoing observation of student learning in three domains. Plan how, when, and what you will observe during the first days and weeks of school.

7 Consider how to involve children in the assessment process.

- Decide how to introduce Portfolios and work folders to children

- Think about whether you are ready to involve students in work collection and review. If so, decide how will you introduce these activities to your students

- Consider ways to let students know how and why you observe them

8 Decide whether you will use the paper Summary Report forms or the Summary Report Manager software.

- Install the Summary Report Manager software

- Put names on Summary Reports

One Element at a Time

Some schools decide to implement the Work Sampling System one element at a time, starting with Developmental Checklists in the fall, adding Portfolios in the winter, and completing Summary Reports in the spring. A variation of this plan is to use only Checklists and Portfolios in the first year. During the second year some schools begin using the Summary Report. This plan necessitates the use of an interim reporting method during the first year. In several settings teachers have continued to use standard graded report cards. In other places, teachers have developed an interim report card that helps families make the transition from a graded report card to the Summary Report.

When you begin using Portfolios, we recommend that you begin gradually, selecting and analyzing one or two areas of learning in one or two domains. Once you understand areas of learning and the logistics of Portfolio collection, it will be easier to add additional areas of learning in the other domains. You can begin collecting Individualized Items immediately because it is an ideal way to foster student involvement.

The advantage of this method is that it gives you time to learn how to use each element well. If you have not used formal observation and recording with Checklists in your classroom, and you have not previously used

Portfolios, you may find this plan beneficial. The disadvantage of this plan is that teachers sometimes feel frustrated during the first year by their reliance on traditional reporting methods after having collected such extensive Work Sampling data on their students.

The following are steps for getting started with the Guidelines and Checklists.

1   Read and become familiar with the Developmental Guidelines.

2   Set up an organizational system for observation and Checklist review. Create a teacher file to store:

   ◆ the Checklist

   ◆ notes and reminders about activities to observe or plan

   ◆ observation notes

   ◆ correspondence with the family

   ◆ any other materials about children that will help you with their evaluations

3   Decide on the methods and tools you will use for documenting your observations of children.

   ◆ Select any of the Checklist Process Notes that seem useful to you

   ◆ Make enough copies of your process note sheets to use during the first weeks of school

   ◆ If you think of other ways to record your observations, design a master

   ◆ Fill in the children's names as appropriate

4   Develop a plan for ongoing observation. Plan how, when, and what you will observe during the first days and weeks of school.

5   Consider how to involve children in the assessment process. Talk with them about how and why you observe them.

Exploration Followed by Gradual Implementation

A third method of learning to use Work Sampling is to spend the first year "messing about"—reading the Guidelines, observing students, collecting student work in folders, experimenting with organizational techniques. During this exploration year you can also introduce the community to new methods of assessment and tackle some of the school and district policy issues we will discuss later in this chapter. During the second year, you can begin using Work Sampling by implementing all three elements in a few domains or by implementing one element at a time.

Getting Started with Work Sampling

The three plans we have described are the most commonly used. We encourage you, though, to devise a method that is uniquely suited to conditions in your school, program, or district.

Establishing and Using Timelines

Regardless of the gradual implementation plan you devise, we strongly encourage you to establish a time frame showing when you will add domains, when you will add new elements, and when you will use the entire system. Teachers have found it helpful to have clear goals for implementation and to monitor their progress so that plans can be changed if necessary.

To help manage implementation, the chapters related to the three Work Sampling elements are organized according to chronology: tasks you complete before school begins, those you repeat throughout each collection period, and tasks you accomplish near the end of each collection period. This organization assists teachers with management and helps them avoid feeling overwhelmed at the end of each collection period.

The beginning of Part II in each element chapter includes a timeline designed to help you manage the work related to that element. Once you have implemented the entire system, use the timeline below to help you manage the three elements concurrently during each collection period.

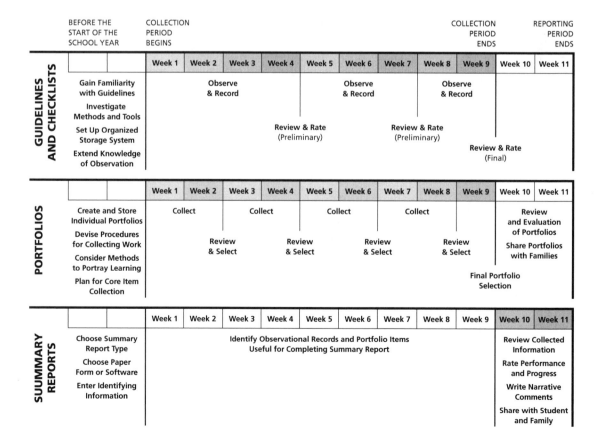

Enlisting the Support of Colleagues

The first year of using Work Sampling is a year of change. Discussion with colleagues on a regular basis will support the processes of reflection and implementation. We recommend that you set up a regular schedule with colleagues for follow-up planning and support.

Teachers tell us that they have benefited greatly from regular informal conversations with colleagues and from professional development sessions scheduled every two to five weeks. These discussions can be used to:

♦ discuss progress and problems

♦ plan for events to come (such as a "Portfolio Night")

♦ share ideas, management techniques, and successful solutions to problems

When teachers have time to meet and plan together they can be enormously supportive of one another and can develop many ideas and concrete strategies for resolving implementation problems.

Informing the Community about Work Sampling

When a school or district decides to implement Work Sampling, informing the community about the need for change and the reasoning that culminated in the decision to change will help to ensure successful adoption. The community, as we refer to it, encompasses those groups that have an interest and stake in the school's activities: families of students, district personnel, and district decision-makers. Enlisting the support of the community will help ensure that the Work Sampling System will be well-received. In this section we offer strategies you can use when informing your community about Work Sampling.

First and foremost, explain why the school has decided to implement the Work Sampling System, and what the teachers and the principal perceive as the system's potential benefits. To understand and accept Work Sampling, family members need concrete information about the materials they will receive, about how these materials will illustrate their child's performance and progress, and about the role of the Work Sampling System in maintaining educational standards.

Family members need to be informed that the Work Sampling System Summary Report will take the place of the traditional report card. Families accustomed to graded report cards will need help understanding how students are to be evaluated without grades. If a district implements the system gradually, families will need:

♦ assurance that the implementation plan will not negatively affect their children's education

♦ an explanation of how the new method of assessment will enhance student learning

♦ information about how reporting methods will be affected

Some of this information is provided in the Overview for Families. Written information works best, however, when combined with face-to-face interaction. We recommend family members be offered several opportunities to meet with the school principal and teachers. Also keep in mind that the community at large should be introduced to the system and the materials, and should understand the school's reasons for adopting Work Sampling as its assessment system.

To smooth the transition from one reporting system to another, we suggest that each program, school, or school district design strategies for informing families and the larger school community about the Work Sampling System. The strategies selected by your school should fit the unique circumstances of your district and should reflect the gradual implementation plan you are using. Below are some strategies for informing families and the larger community about Work Sampling.

♦ **Schedule a series of parent meetings led by teachers and the principal or director.** In many schools parent meetings are offered more than once and at different times to accommodate parents' varying schedules. Both the principal and the teachers attend the meeting. Work Sampling System materials are displayed for parents to review, an overview and explanation of the system is provided, and there is time for questions and discussion.

♦ **Send a personalized letter home with the Overview for Families.** For example, one school drafted a letter explaining that the school would be using a new system to evaluate students, described the system briefly, and discussed why the school decided to try it. The letter was signed by all members of the team (principal, classroom teachers, specialist teachers, and special education staff). At the end of the letter, a form asked parents to describe their needs for further information, with check-offs giving specific suggestions.

♦ **Assign the principal or another staff member to respond to parents' questions and concerns.** In some schools the principal holds coffee hours to meet informally with family members who have questions or concerns. In other schools the principal schedules times that he can be reached by phone to answer questions.

♦ **Inform the Parent Teacher Organization and involve PTO members in planning an outreach campaign (such as visits to local service organizations, newspaper articles, and radio spots).** In many schools parents have played an integral role in supporting successful implementation. Groups of parents have attended initial informational meetings about Work Sampling so that they could be resources for other parents. Parents have also assisted school staff in drafting letters to families, planning parent meetings and open houses, and conducting presentations to the School Board.

♦ **Invite families and community members to an open house, to provide contact with teachers and an introduction to performance assessment and the Work Sampling System.** Later in the school year, consider arranging an open house so that students can share their Portfolios with their families.

♦ **Present to the school or community board or other public forum.** Presentations to the school board can involve teachers, parents, principals, district personnel, and even students.

♦ **Create and distribute question-and-answer brochures about the Work Sampling System and its relationship to local concerns.**

♦ **Conduct family conferences at the end of the first collection period.** In most schools using Work Sampling, the first conference follows other informational meetings about Work Sampling. It is still necessary during these conferences, though, to review the main ideas of the system, especially when teachers are sharing Portfolios and Summary Reports for the first time. Some schools have used the first conference as an opportunity to give families a simple questionnaire to solicit feedback about Work Sampling.

In this chapter we have offered tips to help you get started, methods of gradual implementation, ways to work with colleagues, and strategies for informing the community. In closing, we want to remind you to be patient with yourself and enjoy the learning process. Getting started with Work Sampling will be challenging, but we hope that the effort you make will benefit you as a teacher and your students as learners.

CHAPTER 6
Special Topics

This chapter addresses a variety of topics that arise as teachers learn about and implement the Work Sampling System:

- Using Work Sampling in Preschool and Kindergarten Classrooms

- Using Work Sampling in Older Elementary Classrooms

- Using Work Sampling in Multi-Age Classrooms

- Assessing Children with Special Needs

- Involving Special Subject Teachers

- Using Work Sampling for Title I evaluation

Using Work Sampling in Preschool and Kindergarten Classrooms

The Work Sampling System was originally developed as an assessment for preschool and kindergarten children. The earliest version consisted only of a developmental checklist and emphasized the importance of teacher observation in the assessment process. The extension of Work Sampling to the elementary grades highlighted the connections between preschool experiences and the academic learning of later years, and helped teachers recognize how preschool education creates a foundation for later cognitive and academic learning. In this way, the Work Sampling System validates the curriculum of the early years.

The use of Work Sampling in preschool and kindergarten classrooms differs from its use in elementary classrooms in two important ways. First, the Portfolio collection process with very young children requires greater involvement of the teacher. Because the work of preschool and kindergarten children centers on process and exploration, and because children this age do not create many products on their own, their teachers must assume greater responsibility for documenting and representing children's learning processes in order to preserve them in a Portfolio.

Second, the actual implementation of the Work Sampling System in preschool and kindergarten classrooms may vary from implementation at the elementary level. These differences are necessary because preschool and many kindergarten programs have shorter days, and many preschools have fewer school days per week than do elementary programs. Children may attend for half days, or may attend only two to four days per week. Some preschools start later in the fall than elementary programs and they often follow gradual start-up schedules that include home visiting, individual screening, or attendance of part of the class at a time. As a result, teachers have less time to observe, document, and collect information about children, and the amount of information teachers can collect must be adjusted to reflect this.

This section will describe the differences in how the three elements of the Work Sampling System might be used in preschool and kindergarten classrooms.

Guidelines and Checklists

Completion of the Checklists does not differ markedly in preschool and kindergarten classrooms. Preschool and kindergarten teachers tend to be very familiar with checklists and observational records, so this part of the system will probably fit easily into your classroom. Use of the Checklist may help sharpen your observation skills by making you more watchful for behavior related to specific performance indicators. As discussed in the previous section, we encourage you to begin implementing Work Sampling using only two or three domains initially and adding more throughout the year.

Portfolios

Although Portfolios at the preschool and kindergarten level have the same purposes as Portfolios for elementary-age children, the learning characteristics of three, four, and five year olds necessitate changes in focus and methods of collection. Children at these ages learn in very concrete ways. They must actively manipulate objects, and must directly experience events and explore materials in order to learn about them. Exploration is the centerpiece of their learning, but these explorations do not often culminate in the creation of products.

Preschool and kindergarten Portfolio collection differs in three important ways from Portfolio collection with older children:

♦ methods of documentation

♦ collection of Core Items

♦ the role of the child

DOCUMENTATION Preschool and kindergarten Portfolios document the process of learning. In order to document this process, teachers record "word pictures" of a child's participation in classroom activities. A preschool or kindergarten teacher might describe how a child interacts with objects, plays with other children, or moves around the classroom, as shown in Examples 1–3.

EXAMPLE 1   While cutting the outer layer off a ball of play dough with a plastic knife, Mandy explained, "I'm making potatoes. I'm peeling them."

EXAMPLE 2   Exploring with the farm stamps, Luis says, "You press really hard, like this, and then you get a picture."

EXAMPLE 3   Taniesha picks up the tape measure, and measures the length of the 'Discovery Table.' "A mouse is this big," she says, as she pulls the tape about six inches. Taniesha then pulls the tape out "real long" to measure her friend Shaina.

These records are entirely descriptive, without any interpretations or conclusions by the teacher. More than mere observational notes that support Checklist ratings, Portfolio anecdotes or word pictures provide a description not only of what children can do, but of how they do it. They are almost like video clips that capture a moment in the child's classroom experience.

At the preschool and kindergarten level, a major objective of Portfolio collection remains evaluating growth over time. Progress can be demonstrated through documentation of the same areas of learning on repeated occasions. In the following example, the teacher selected as an area of learning for Social Studies "understanding of family and social roles." Her three records follow. Example 4 shows her fall record.

EXAMPLE 4   During the fall, Tom painted at the easel three stick figures. He said that his picture showed his mom, his dad, and himself.

In winter, the teacher made the following anecdotal record (Example 5):

EXAMPLE 5   Tom was playing with 3 other children in the block area. They had made a "house" of blocks and were playing with the Duplo people. Steven said, "Grandma will sleep like this," putting one person in one room, "and the children will sleep in here," putting three people in another room.

He made one person walk up to another on the wall and say, "We're off to New York!" and then he took both of them and made them fly around. He said, "Aaah... going to New York!" as they flew through the air. And "Aaah... we went to New York!" as they landed.

In spring, the anecdotal record reads as follows (Example 6):

EXAMPLE 6   Tom was playing with the doctor's kit in the house area. He held a doll behind the x-ray machine and operated it. He stood the doll in front of the eye chart and recited A–Z (all of the alphabet is on the eye chart). Then he lifted the "hammer" to check reflexes and said, "Do it gently, now." He tapped the doll's knees and feet. Then he said, "Hmm. I think he needs a shot." Tom picked up the syringe, gave the doll a shot and said, "Owww!"

Together, these anecdotal records, Tom's fall, winter, and spring Core Items, demonstrate the growth Tom has made in his understanding of social roles through dramatic play.

Here are some other ways that teachers document learning:

- taking photographs of children at work and writing a narrative to describe the photo

- videotaping activities

- audio taping children's language or singing

- writing down dictations of stories or conversations

Whether the teacher writes a "word picture," takes a photo, or audio tapes a conversation, her documentation itself becomes the Portfolio item. Although many Portfolio items will be teacher narratives or documentation, some of the child's work, such as art work, writing, cutting samples, and collages, can also be included. These products are natural outgrowths of the child's participation in classroom activities.

CORE ITEM COLLECTION Many preschool teachers feel strongly about collecting Core Items for Personal and Social Development and Physical Development & Health. They believe that these domains are so central to the preschool experience that they should be made prominent in the Portfolio. Preschool teachers may decide to document children's play interactions, independence, eye-hand coordination, or balance over the course of the year. If desired, preschool teachers may decide to eliminate two of the other domains in order to keep the workload manageable. Examples of areas of learning for preschoolers in five domains are listed in the Appendix A.

ROLE OF THE CHILD A third characteristic that distinguishes preschool and kindergarten Portfolio collection is the role of the child. Preschool and kindergarten children can review and reflect upon their activities and work, but very few children at these ages can make judgments about the quality of their work and evaluate their progress over time. Therefore, the development of personal standards for school work as a goal of Portfolio collection is less relevant for preschool and kindergarten children than it is for older children.

It is important for preschoolers and kindergartners to know that their work is being saved and reproduced for their Portfolios. These Portfolios should be stored in a visible location, where children can look at them occasionally and share them with their families. They may want to save something they have made by including it in their Portfolio. In this way, Portfolios can become a vehicle for recalling school activities and for beginning to appreciate growth over time.

Children at these ages usually want to take their work home, even when they know they have a Portfolio. Some ways that teachers have handled this issue are to:

♦ photocopy items for the Portfolios

♦ keep one copy of a project—if the child has made two—for the Portfolio and send the other one home

♦ put work on the bulletin board as an intermediary step before putting it in the child's portfolio

♦ send work home with a note asking the family to send it back for the Portfolio collection after they have looked at it with the child

It is important to remember that if the child feels strongly about taking a particular sample of work home, you should allow her to do it. Children will create other work that can be kept for their Portfolios.

Summary Reports

We encourage regular, systematic communication with families about their child's learning in preschool and kindergarten. The Work Sampling System has two different report forms: the Standard Summary Report and the Narrative Summary Report. Some preschool and kindergarten teachers prefer to use the Narrative Summary Report because it more closely resembles the narrative reports they are already familiar with. Regardless of your choice of form, you summarize information from the Checklists and Portfolios at the end of each collection period, evaluate children's performance and progress, and address areas that will be emphasized during the next collection period.

Adapting Work Sampling for Preschool and Kindergarten Classrooms

In some situations teachers of preschool and kindergarten children adapt their use of Work Sampling to fit their program. Very often preschool and kindergarten teachers have two sessions of students, one group in the morning and a different group in the afternoon. Many preschool programs are structured so that teachers see children only two or three mornings or afternoons each week. In these situations teachers can not expect to do the same amount of documentation for each of their students as a teacher who spends all day with one class of children. There are several ways teachers have successfully adapted Work Sampling to accommodate these circumstances.

- Complete Checklists on all students in fewer than seven domains and establish reasonable expectations about the amount of observational data you can record and collect.

- Select only one area of learning for the domains you select for Portfolio collection.

- Combine the domains of Scientific Thinking and Social Studies by identifying one area of learning that integrates the two domains.

The goal of Work Sampling is to get to know your students in order to evaluate their work and effectively plan for their instruction. We feel strongly that teachers in settings such as those described above need to redefine what is meant by full implementation of Work Sampling. If you are with children for less than five full days each week, we encourage you to consider carefully what is necessary to collect in order to know your students well.

Using Work Sampling with Older Elementary Students

Older elementary students (third, fourth, and fifth graders) can take an active role in all aspects of the assessment process. Unlike children in earlier grades, third, fourth, and fifth graders can begin to think and talk about their learning analytically. They can more easily reflect on their work, understand and develop evaluative criteria, set personal goals, and evaluate their performance and progress. Moreover, with the support of their teacher, students this age can handle some of the management tasks related to portfolio collection. In this section we will describe how teachers at these grade levels involve their students in understanding and using each of the elements of Work Sampling.

Guidelines and Checklists

Students in third, fourth, and fifth grade can understand what they are expected to learn. Eight to eleven year olds can participate in conversations about their own learning. Because children at these ages can understand the idea that there are categories (domains and components) of learning, and that there are specific skills and concepts that they are expected to learn, you can introduce them to the structure and organization of the Checklist. For example, a fourth grader can understand that one area of study is mathematical thinking and that there are different units of study within this broad category. In addition, he can begin to recognize that he has greater understanding of number concepts than of spatial relationships. You may want to display the wall chart in a prominent place and use it as the basis for goal-setting discussions.

Many teachers of these levels use daily journals or learning logs with their students. At the end of an activity or at the end of the day they ask students to reflect on their work and their learning, sometimes with a specific focus. For example, a teacher might ask students to reflect on how they collaborated with others during a science investigation, or to describe the strategies they used to solve a set of math problems. Other teachers ask their students to reflect on reading and writing conferences with the teacher and with peers. Students' written reflections provide additional observational data for teachers to use when completing the Checklists.

Portfolios

Third, fourth, and fifth graders can actively participate in Portfolio collection. First, they can understand and contribute to the development of evaluation criteria. Second, they can review and evaluate their own work.

Third, they can make selections for their Portfolios and record their reasons for selection. Finally, they can help with the management and organization of Portfolio collection.

We strongly encourage teachers of all age groups to talk with children about their expectations for student work. Older children especially should be encouraged to engage in detailed and meaningful discussions about the criteria for quality work. Many teachers begin these discussions with the topic of writing because it is concrete and accessible to students. They ask their students to generate a list of the characteristics of a good piece of writing. At the start of the year the list generated by a group of third graders, for example, may be superficial and include only such criteria as staying on one topic; having a beginning, middle, and end; and being interesting. Writing lessons throughout the year can then support students' acquisition of increasingly complex characteristics such as voice, mechanics, and organization. As students acquire an understanding of evaluative criteria, they can begin to develop rubrics for evaluating work. A rubric is a scoring tool that describes levels of accomplishment.

When students have been involved in discussions of evaluation criteria, they have greater interest in reviewing and evaluating their own work. Having developed evaluation criteria, they can be more thoughtful judges of their work and of the work of others. Such opportunities to discuss evaluation criteria and to reflect on their work will engage students metacognitively—that is, it will ask them to think about their own thinking. For many third graders metacognitive processing may be quite challenging. For fourth and especially fifth graders, however, it is an invaluable part of the learning process. Because students at these ages can review and reflect on their work, they can be expected to produce revisions of their work. Often it is valuable to include several drafts of work in the Portfolio, especially when the drafts are annotated with an explanation of the stages in the process.

A third way that older elementary students take an active role in Portfolio collection is through the collection, selection, and annotation of their work. At this age students can comprehend the meaning of areas of learning and can be taught to recognize the relationship between assignments and areas of learning. For students at these ages it is especially important that you include annotation on work when you assign it, stating the purpose of the work and your expectations for it. This will help students with self-evaluation and will help them determine at the time of collection and selection whether the assignment is a potential Core Item. To encourage students to annotate their work, use the large Portfolio Item Record from the Reproducible Masters booklet (see Chapter 3) so that students have ample space to record their reasons for selecting an item for the Portfolio.

Many teachers spend time teaching their students how to file work and how to manage their collection bins. They find that the time they spend up front teaching the routines pays off significantly over the course of the year.

Summary Reports and Conferences

We encourage you to talk with your students prior to completing their Summary Reports. Many teachers of third, fourth, and fifth graders find it valuable to have informal conferences with their students. These informal conferences allow the teacher to share her evaluation with the student, a process that helps demystify assessment for the student and models how they can evaluate their own performance and progress.

Some teachers organize these conferences around Portfolio review. Other teachers focus on goals—having students reflect on goals set earlier and establishing new ones. Teachers report that when students take an active role throughout the assessment process, they are meaningful contributors in the conference process.

For students to be effective participants in conferences, they first need time to review their work, to reflect on their progress, and to identify what they will discuss, the work samples they will share, and their personal goals. Many teachers create conference guidelines that students can use to help them prepare. Some teachers provide class time for students to role-play conferences with peers.

Using Work Sampling in Multi-Age Classrooms

The Work Sampling System is very appropriate for multi-age classrooms. We define multi-age classrooms as those that have students from at least two age or grade levels. Many of these classrooms use Work Sampling as an assessment tool because of its emphasis on the continuum of children's development. By examining the six levels of an indicator presented in the Omnibus Guidelines, teachers can see what comes before and what comes after each indicator.

One of the challenges teachers in multi-age classrooms face is creating curricular and instructional plans for a wide developmental range of students. Multi-age teachers using Work Sampling report that the Omnibus Guidelines help them understand how to modify curricular and instructional plans to accommodate differences in expectations for children at different ages. For example, knowing conventions of print is an important aspect of writing for all grade levels, but the Omnibus Guidelines show how expectations for this skill gradually change as children mature.

Completing Checklists

Although the Omnibus Guidelines present several levels of development at once, the Checklists do not. Teachers in multi-age groups use different Checklists to cover the ages or grade levels represented by their students. Because all of the domains, most of the components, and many of the indicators are the same across several grade levels, the Checklists for different ages or grade levels are very similar. By reading the rationales and examples described in the Omnibus Guidelines, however, teachers of multi-age groups can learn the differences that exist between children of different ages.

Using Portfolios

The structure of Work Sampling Portfolios lends itself easily to multi-age classrooms. Because the areas of learning for Core Item collection are defined broadly rather than in terms of grade-specific skills or concepts, multi-age teachers can select the same areas of learning for all of the grades represented in their classroom. Although Portfolio collection is structured in the same way for all students, children are free to represent their learning in ways that reflect their own levels of development.

Assessing Children with Special Needs

The Work Sampling System has been used successfully to assess children with special needs who are included in regular education classrooms. In fact, several features of the Work Sampling System make it particularly appropriate for the assessment of children with special needs. First, Work Sampling takes an individualized approach to learning and assessment. Children are not compared to one another, but are compared to standards of performance identified in the Developmental Guidelines. Moreover, because Work Sampling evaluates progress as well as performance, it allows children with special needs to demonstrate growth even in areas where their performance is delayed.

The Work Sampling System's emphasis on ongoing assessment embedded within the classroom curriculum is also particularly relevant for children with special needs, many of whom have difficulty performing "on demand." In order to obtain an accurate picture of their strengths and weaknesses, it is critical to observe them over time and in a variety of circumstances. The emphasis Work Sampling places on repeated observation of learning within the classroom context ensures a comprehensive picture of each child's typical behavior.

Work Sampling's focus on classroom-based assessment and the use of assessment information to inform instruction makes it very compatible with the Individual Educational Plans (IEPs) required for children with special needs. IEPs provide detailed assessments of the child's needs and equally detailed plans for instruction, which are updated regularly. Work Sampling's individualized profile of each child's development, created through extensive collection and observation of student work and behavior in seven domains, is a very powerful method for informing the IEP. In addition, Work Sampling assists teachers in planning appropriate and meaningful curricula that promote the movement of children toward their greatest potential.

Many teachers have successfully linked Work Sampling with IEPs. Figure 1 shows how one preschool teacher linked IEP language goals to Work Sampling performance indicators.

Just as curricular adaptation may be necessary for a child with special needs to participate fully in learning activities, adaptations may also be needed in the Work Sampling System. The severity of a child's handicapping condition will be a major determinant of the necessary adaptations.

Individual Education Plan

Student: _Tom_   Date of Birth: _5/14/94_   IEP From: _1/2/99_   To: _2/1/00_

Goals and Objectives   Domain: _Speech_   Sequence: _1.1_

Goal 1.1 – Tom will expand his expressive language, using language for a variety of purposes.

Objectives and Evaluation Procedure and Schedule

Objective 1.1.1 – Tom will be able to state how things are different when given a picture clue as well as when no clue is provided.

Evaluation Procedure:

Evaluation Schedule:

Objective 1.1.2 – Tom will demonstrate an understanding of prepositions (i.e., in, on, under, over, etc.).

Evaluation Procedure:

Evaluation Schedule:

Goals and Objectives   Domain: _Speech_   Sequence: _1.2_

Goal 1.2 – Tom will improve his speech sound production in order to speak clearly enough to be understood without contextual clues.

Objectives and Evaluation Procedure and Schedule

Objective 1.2.1 – Tom will correctly articulate the /th/ in the initial (think), medial (toothpaste) and final (with) positions in targeted and spontaneous speech.

Evaluation Procedure:

Evaluation Schedule:

Objective 1.2.2 – Tom will use -ing endings in targeted and spontaneous speech

Evaluation Procedure:

Evaluation Schedule:

Guidelines and Checklists

As teachers use the Work Sampling System with children with special needs they most often make adaptations to the Checklists. Modifications may include interpreting indicators in a more inclusive way, deleting certain indicators or components, and supplementing the Work Sampling System with other, more specialized assessments.

In many places, it is possible to change the language of the performance indicators to encompass varied expressions of the indicator and the use of adaptive equipment. For example, in the domain of Language and Literacy, the first indicator under the component of speaking in first grade is "Speaks clearly and conveys ideas effectively." "Speaking" can be interpreted as "communicating" in order to reflect the fact that children with special needs may communicate in ways other than speaking (such as with gestures, signs, facial expressions, and communication boards). The language used in the Guidelines indicators is designed to be inclusive so that a child's development can be noted even when a handicapping condition is present (for example, the word "communicates" is used instead of "verbalizes"; and "notices" is used instead of "sees").

Sometimes particular indicators, components, or domains will assume greater importance for children with disabilities. For example, for children with physical impairments, learning how to ask for assistance and how to decline assistance appropriately are central to the development of independence. Similarly, the domain of Personal and Social Development assumes increased emphasis for children with behavioral or emotional disabilities.

Some components or performance indicators may not be appropriate for individual children and should be omitted. For example, most of the performance indicators in the Physical Development & Health section may not be appropriate for children with moderate to severe cerebral palsy. These indicators would be omitted and replaced with more relevant performance indicators or a different assessment. A child with a moderate to severe mental impairment may require elimination of performance indicators requiring higher-level abstract thinking skills, such as "Makes predictions based on data" in Mathematical Thinking.

Obviously, there are limits to the applicability of Work Sampling for some children with disabilities. Given the variety of needs even among children with the same disability, no single assessment can address all needs. Children with special needs may require additional assessment in some areas. For example, a child with motoric involvement may require intervention to improve oral-motor ability in order to help the child speak more clearly. In that case, a performance indicator could be added to encompass the area of oral-motor control. Similarly, a severe visual impairment warrants the assessment of mobility. When development in a given domain is very different or delayed, a specialized instrument administered by a therapist or special education consultant may be necessary to supplement information obtained through Work Sampling. When a child's functioning is below that of a three year old, other assessments are more effective and informative than the Work Sampling System.

Teachers frequently ask whether they should always use the Checklist that corresponds to a child's chronological age. This decision should be made in conjunction with family members and special education consultants. An important factor to consider is whether the child has a general developmental delay and is performing at a consistent level across the seven Work Sampling domains, or whether the child's performance varies widely from one domain to another. For example, if a child is experiencing a general developmental delay, using the grade level Checklist that corresponds to a child's chronological age may not be appropriate because all indicators would be rated "Not Yet." If all of the indicators are far beyond the child's current capabilities, then the Checklist would not demonstrate the child's progress, nor would it inform instructional planning. In such cases, it is more useful to use a Checklist that more nearly reflects the child's developmental age. In this way, the child's growth can be reflected as the year progresses.

In contrast, for children functioning near their age level in several domains, it may be most appropriate to use the Checklist that corresponds to their chronological age. This Checklist could be supplemented with additional assessments in areas of delay and with information from the Guidelines that describes younger children. It is important, though, that teachers do not underestimate a child's capabilities by using a Checklist that most closely reflects the child's weakest area.

Portfolios

Portfolio collection provides specific information about how a child learns and works. It also provides a focus for discussion between a classroom teacher and other team members (for example, consultants, therapists, and psychologists). By documenting how the work was completed (noting adaptations, amount of help required), the teacher collects valuable information to share with other team members who may have much less contact with the child.

Summary Reports

Teachers complete Summary Reports the same way for children with and without special needs. Some children with special needs will have a particularly uneven developmental profile and may show frequent discrepancies between performance and progress. A child with a moderate degree of mental impairment may be delayed according to the Guidelines, but his progress may still be remarkable. When a child needs support in order to perform at a certain level, that information can be indicated on the Summary Report. For example, one might note "after brainstorming and discussing a story with a peer tutor, Susie is able to write a three-part story."

Working on a Team

We recommend that the classroom teacher collaborate with special education teachers and consultants. By using the child's Portfolio and Checklist, the teacher can communicate clearly with specialists and family members about how the child performs in the classroom. Because the classroom teacher spends more time with the child, she has a wealth of specific knowledge about how the child approaches learning. The rich, detailed, individualized portraits that Work Sampling provides make the system a valuable addition to the educational assessment of children with special needs.

Involving Special Subject Teachers

The role of the special subject teacher (the specialist) in the Work Sampling System depends on how the special subject teacher functions in your district. Many aspects of this role vary depending on such factors as:

♦ whether the district employs specialists

♦ the curriculum areas taught by specialists

♦ the frequency and duration of the specialist's contact with students

♦ the size of the specialist's caseload

♦ whether the specialist is responsible for student evaluation

The determination of the appropriate role special subject teachers should serve with Work Sampling can be made only after consideration of district specifics and of the contractual realities that influence how specialists currently function.

Work Sampling is a method of classroom-based performance assessment that relies heavily on classroom teachers' expertise and professional judgment regarding student performance across all domains of learning. We believe that each domain is an important and necessary curriculum area that can and should be addressed by classroom teachers. For this reason, the Guidelines and Checklists for the Arts and for Physical Development & Health are based on classroom teachers'—not specialists'—level of knowledge. The performance indicators in these two domains reflect the types of skills, performances, and accomplishments that teachers observe in the classroom. Therefore, classroom teachers can be expected to complete Checklists in these domains without the input of special subject teachers. However, we do not view this as the best method of obtaining a complete picture of the child's performance and progress.

A more effective route to learning about children and negotiating between classroom teachers and specialists is the route of teacher/specialist collaboration. Both classroom teachers and specialists benefit from each other's expertise and their rich collaboration can take many forms. Optimally, the classroom teacher and the specialist will share their knowledge about students. In some districts special subject teachers have developed special subject Checklists to address the specific skills covered in their classes. In other settings, specialists use their own skill-based inventories to meet their evaluation needs. When the information they collect is shared with classroom teachers, Checklist ratings become more accurate as they reflect more detailed and comprehensive observations. Specialists who see many children for short class periods, however, find it difficult to collect and organize observations for Checklist ratings. Under these circumstances, it may be best for classroom teachers to discuss students' performance and progress with specialists before completing the Checklist and the Summary Report.

Depending on the time available for joint planning, teachers and specialists may also collaborate to plan activities that can result in items for the Portfolio. Sharing knowledge about a domain among classroom teachers and specialists may result in activities that are more in-depth and meaningful. Themes and investigations carried out in the classroom can be enriched by extension into special subject areas. Similarly, the content of activities in the special class can illuminate concepts presented in the classroom. We discourage classroom teachers from turning over Checklist sections or entire domains to the specialist for evaluation. Rather, to maximize the knowledge of specialists, we suggest that teachers and specialists collaborate to provide children with the richest possible experience.

The Special Subject Report form (see Chapter 4) has been designed to facilitate communication between specialists and classroom teachers. This form lists all seven domains and allows special subject teachers to check the domains that they want to evaluate. They write brief narratives that include information for the classroom teacher. It is a four-part, carbonless form with copies for the classroom teacher, the special subject teacher, the family, and the school.

Using Work Sampling for Title I Evaluation

Although the Work Sampling System is primarily an instructional assessment system that utilizes curriculum-embedded methods of record keeping and evaluation, Work Sampling data can be combined in order to make Title I student evaluations.

When Work Sampling is used for Title I evaluation, the Checklist and Portfolio ratings are first translated into Title I ratings. Then they are combined into a single Title I rating for each domain that is included in the Title I report.

Translating Work Sampling Data into Title I Ratings

Checklists

To translate data from the Checklist into Title I terminology, the Checklist ratings are summarized as follows:

WORK SAMPLING CHECKLIST	TITLE I
All ratings "Proficient"	"Advanced"
Majority of ratings are "Proficient" with some "In Process" and no "Not Yet" ratings	"Proficient"
Combination of "Not Yet", "In Process," and "Proficient," or all "In Process," or a combination of "Not Yet" and "In Process" ratings	"Partially Proficient"

Portfolio

Performance on the Portfolio is rated "As Expected" when students' work meets or exceeds expectations. To translate Portfolio data into Title I ratings, the Portfolio performance ratings that are shown on the Summary Report must indicate whether the child's work is meeting or exceeding expectations. When the "As Expected" rating means that a child's performance has exceeded expectations, it is essential that the teacher indicate this by marking a plus sign (+) alongside the rating.

WORK SAMPLING PORTFOLIO	TITLE I
"As Expected"/Exceeds Expectations (+)	"Advanced"
"As Expected"/Meets Expectations	"Proficient"
"Needs Development"/Below Expectations	"Partially Proficient"

Overall Title I Rating

An overall Title I rating of "Advanced" for a particular domain requires an "Advanced" rating on the Checklist (all ratings "Proficient") and an "Advanced" rating on the Portfolio ("As Expected"/Exceeds Expectations).

CHECKLIST	PORTFOLIO	TITLE I OVERALL RATING
"Advanced"	"Advanced"	"Advanced"

The overall "Proficient" rating for a particular domain is given for any of these three possible combinations of ratings.

CHECKLIST	PORTFOLIO	TITLE I OVERALL RATING
"Advanced"	"Proficient"	"Proficient"
"Proficient"	"Advanced"	
"Proficient"	"Proficient"	

"Partially Proficient" for a particular domain is given as an overall rating when any of the following three combinations of ratings are present.

CHECKLIST	PORTFOLIO	TITLE I OVERALL RATING
"Proficient"	"Partially Proficient"	"Partially Proficient"
"Partially Proficient"	"Proficient"	
"Partially Proficient"	"Partially Proficient"	

Conclusion

In this section we have described how Work Sampling can be used with different groups of students, in multi-age classrooms, and by special subject teachers. Although some of these topics were addressed briefly in Chapters 2, 3, and 4, we elaborated on them here because of their importance to successful implementation of Work Sampling. As you learn to use Work Sampling, we hope that you find the information provided in this chapter and throughout this book helpful. We are confident that you will make many new discoveries about Work Sampling, and we invite you to share them with us.

APPENDIX A

Suggestions for Core Items—Preschool and Kindergarten

To help you get started with Portfolio collection, we have provided a list of effective areas of learning for preschool and kindergarten and included examples of children's work that represent each area of learning. In some cases the examples (Core Items) are general and in others they are quite specific. We hope these ideas support your work.

Suggestions for Core Items—Preschool and Kindergarten

Language and Literacy

AREA OF LEARNING	CHILD'S WORK/REPRESENTATION
Using symbols (e.g., symbols, drawing, emergent writing) to communicate ideas	• Scribbles created to express an idea • Child's writing (name or words) on art work • Photo of letters or symbols written in finger paint or in wet sand • Samples of copied words or written words with representational drawing or invented spelling
Communicating (verbally, manually, with gestures) to express ideas and thoughts	• Anecdotal record of story or thoughts child has expressed during group time, told to the teacher, or overheard as child talked to a friend • Record of instructions child gave to help start a game, settle an argument, or help a friend understand something • Audiotape of child telling about a school or family event
Writing (and/or dictating) to communicate ideas	• Signs made for block structures • Shopping lists made during dramatic play • Letters to friends or family members • Invitation to come to a class event • A dictated story that accompanies a drawing • Dictation of a child's description of scribbles or symbols • Copies of pages from a journal
Understanding and responding to a story	• Anecdotal record of a child retelling a story to a friend • Anecdotal notes about child acting out a story in dramatic play or on the playground • Child's depiction of a story through drawing or painting • Photo with anecdote of child "reading" a story using pictures as prompts • Record of child's responses to questions about a story • Audiotape of child retelling a story
Shows interest and understanding about books and reading	• Photo of child in reading corner for "choice time" • Photo of child at listening center • Anecdotal record of child's responses to books, questions about books or requests for books to be read • Record of child's use of books to obtain information about how to build a bridge or a castle • Record of child's conversation with others about books or stories • Child's dictated thoughts about a story

Mathematical Thinking

AREA OF LEARNING	CHILD'S WORK/REPRESENTATION
Understanding and applying classification and seriation skills	• Record of child sorting beads • Photo of child's arrangement of rods, buttons, or crayons in order of size • Photo of child putting away blocks or other equipment according to size, shape, or use • Anecdotal record of child's comment about the rule used for classifying • Anecdotal record of child's comments at snack or out on the playgournd that demonstrate understanding of seriation or classification • Child's drawing that shows classifying skills (these are all toys, this is my family, or these are all the kinds of leaves we collected) • A collage of categorized items (e.g., shapes, colors, foods, animals, or "the things we do on the playground")
Understanding and using number concepts to solve problems	• Anecdote describing child's method of arranging cups and napkins for snack • Description of child counting children at sand table to see if there is room for a friend • Record of child's solution to a question about distributing class supplies for a project • Anecdotal record of child's comment about the rule used for classifying • Record of child's counting children at circle and remarking that "there are more girls than boys"
Understanding and applying size and measurements concepts	• Record of child's comments comparing sizes of blocks • Photo with note of child measuring own height or the growth of a plant • Anecdote depicting how child compared heights of classmates • Photo of child measuring amounts of ingredients during a cooking project, potting plants, or making play dough • Child-created measuring tape for determining the length of a block structure or the snack table • Photo of child using balance scale
Using sorting, classifying, and patterning skills	• Photo of pattern created with pattern blocks or other manipulatives: sample of patterning using collage materials • Anecdotal record of comments about a pattern or classification grouping within the class ("all the people with red socks should sit over there and people with other colored socks sit here") • Record of clapping pattern or motor pattern • Photo of beads, rods, or buttons arranged in a pattern or sorted according to a specific attribute • Photo of pattern created with finger paint or in shaving cream • Photo of peg board patterns • Paper replicas of created patterns

Suggestions for Core Items—Preschool and Kindergarten

Scientific Thinking

AREA OF LEARNING	CHILD'S WORK/REPRESENTATION
Using senses to explore and observe the natural and physical world	• Anecdotal record or child's comments when playing with water or sand toys, pounding play dough, exploring glue, finger paints, or shaving cream • Record of child's responses to group recall of sounds heard on the woods walk or sites seen on the library walk • Child's dictated observation of the class pet, seeds sprouting, or objects on the magnet board • Photo of child's exploration of a bird's nest
Observing and predicting (or guessing) in an investigation	• A record of seed growth including child-made chart and about what helps the plant to grow • Dictated guess about what will float and what will sink—and why • Record of child's prediction about weight of objects • Record of child's guesses or predictions during a class brainstorming discussion • Interview with the child about predictions of what the bunny will eat and how to find out if the prediction is accurate
Experimenting and solving problems during exploration	• Child-created chart that describes what the class pet eats and drinks for a week and determination for what to feed it next week • Chart or record of plant growth including experimentation with amounts of sun, water, plant food • Photo with accompanying note showing the child's experimentation at the water table with different sized tubes to determine the one that makes the water flow fastest, the child's prediction, and the child's description of the result
Observing and describing the environment	• Drawing of child's collection of leaves • Drawn and dictated observations of the behaviors of the class pet • Photo and anecdote of child's observations of what is heard when listening through a stethoscope or looking through a magnifying glass • Child's description of how play dough feels, or how a new kind of cracker or fruit tastes • Photo and record of child's observation when blowing bubbles

Social Studies

AREA OF LEARNING	CHILD'S WORK/REPRESENTATION
Gathering and interpreting information about families and the community	• Painting or collage of family members • Drawing of trip to a hospital or police station • Drawing and writing about a family vacation • Photo depicting child's role play of a family member in the housekeeping area • Photo of child's block structure of the airport, their house, or church
Collecting and interpreting information about people's roles in a community	• Record of child's "interview" with the school custodian or principal, doctor, or a shoe salesperson • Child's response during a brainstorming session about the jobs of community workers • Anecdote describing the child's reenactment of a visit to the grocer or the pharmacist • Photo of child's train made from chairs or big blocks, diagram of a shoe store created with unit blocks
Developing knowledge and understanding about self and family	• Drawing or painting of child's depiction of family working or playing • Dictated story about a family party, visit, or trip • Child's book or collage of family members and their activities • Photo and note showing the child's reenactment of family interactions • Anecdote of child's description of how the work gets done at his house
Recognizing and understanding similarities and differences among people	• Drawing of friends who are different from each other • Child's comment, as recorded and initialed on the experience chart, about the ways people are different from or similar to each other • Anecdote documenting a snack table discussion about similarities and differences in families' activities

Suggestions for Core Items—Preschool and Kindergarten

The Arts

AREA OF LEARNING	CHILD'S WORK/REPRESENTATION
Participating in visual arts (or dramatic arts, or music, or dance/creative movement)	• Drawings (e.g., with pencils, chalk, markers, or crayons) • Paintings (e.g., with tempera, watercolors, or finger paint) • Photo of clay or play dough sculptures • Photo of child dancing or singing • Anecdote or audiotape of child-created song • Photo of child dramatizing with puppet or felt board • Collage with dictation of child's explanation of how it was created
Using the arts to represent ideas	• Drawings • Paintings • Photo of child telling a story through dance or movement • Anecdote or audiotape of child's musical retelling of a story • Audiotape of child singing about a class or family event
Exploring different artistic media	• Samples of child's work with a variety of art media • Collage with anecdotal notes of child's verbal explanation about the collage • Sample of child's cut-out magazine pictures or use of scissors to create a design • Photo of child's creative dancing or puppet show story
Exploring and using a single art medium	• Examples of child's work in easel painting or marker drawings throughout the year • Photos and anecdotal record of child's progress in communicating through dance or dramatization • Photos of child's representations made with clay or play dough • Collage work collected over the year • Audiotapes of child singing over the course of the year • Audiotapes of child using a classroom instrument over the year such as rhythm sticks, a triangle, or a kazoo

APPENDIX B

Suggestions for Core Items—Elementary Grades

To help you get started with Portfolio collection, we have provided a list of effective areas of learning for elementary grades and included examples of children's work that represent each area of learning. In some cases the examples (Core Items) are general and in others they are quite specific. We hope these ideas support your work.

Language and Literacy

AREA OF LEARNING	CHILD'S WORK/REPRESENTATION
Communicating ideas verbally	• An audiotape of the student doing an oral research presentation describing a scientific investigation • Dictation of the student's spoken language • Artwork with dictation of the child's description of the work • Dictation of the student's contributions to a class discussion • An anecdote that captures a direct quotation of student's language • An audiotape or dictation of an interview with the student
Using strategies to read for meaning—decoding and expressing	• An audiotape of the student reading aloud accompanied by the teacher's description of strategies being used • A running record or miscue analysis of text read by the student with a guide to help parents understand it • An interview with the student about his reading strategies
Comprehending and interpreting text	• A book report • An illustration of a story with writing or dictation • A story map of a book • Written or verbal responses to questions about a story or other text • A written or dictated letter to the author about one of the author's books • A written or dictated review of a book • A re-write or re-telling of a story or the ending to a story
Writing to express ideas	• A story, poem, or fable written by the student • A journal entry • A script for a skit or puppet show • An article for the class newspaper • A letter • A research report • A sign for a block structure or model

Suggestions for Core Items—Elementary Grades

Mathematical Thinking

AREA OF LEARNING	CHILD'S WORK/REPRESENTATION
Using strategies to solve number problems	• The student's drawing, chart, graph, calculations, and solution to a word problem, with an explanation of the process in the student's words • An anecdotal record of a student's approach to solving a number problem • A videotape or an audiotape, showing the student's approach to solving a number problem • A student-created word problem(s) that illustrates a number sentence or equation
Using strategies to solve problems involving geometrical concepts	• A student's pictorial representation (or photo) and verbal description of the solution to a problem using tangrams, pattern blocks, Pentominoes or other geometry materials • An anecdote of the student's process and solution to a geometry problem • A student's written description of her process and solution to a geometry problem • A photo or student-drawn representation of a solution to a geoboard problem • A photo or sketch of two and three-dimensional shapes made from pipe cleaners or straws • Student's analysis of the use of shapes in the environment or in the construction of a building
Solving problems involving number concepts and arithmetic operations	• Photos or student-drawn representations of numbers or operations, using manipulatives • Samples of written computations • A teacher-written anecdote or the student's written description about the student's use of number concepts and operations • A photo or anecdote of the student using Cuisenaire Rods to represent numbers and to perform numerical operations • Collage of magazine pictures showing different quantities of objects, with number sentences written to accompany them • Photo or pictorial representation of the value of sets of coins
Applying the concept of patterns and relationships to problem-solving	• Photo or student-made replica of a copied, original, or extended pattern • An anecdote of a student's recognition of a geometrical, numerical, or natural pattern • Dictated or student-written analysis of the patterns and relationships in a numerical sequence, a two or three-dimensional design, or a naturally occurring arrangement • Artwork that incorporates sorting, patterning, sequencing, balance, and symmetry
Applying measurement concepts to solve real world problems	• Photograph, with dictated or student-written explanation, of a student using unifix cubes to compare heights of classmates • An anecdote describing a student's method of doubling the measurements in a recipe • Student's calculations made while figuring how many pounds of hamburger to get for the class picnic • Diagram or drawing that shows how much wood is needed to complete a wordworking project

Mathematical Thinking

AREA OF LEARNING	CHILD'S WORK/REPRESENTATION
Applying estimation strategies in measurement, computation, and problem-solving	• Student's description of the strategies used to estimate the number of objects in a container • A photograph with anecdotal note describing a student pacing off an estimated 100 yards for a running race • A student's estimated range of numbers that could be the answer to a word problem, along with the actual solution • A written or dictated estimate, with the reason for that estimate, of how long it will be before all the snow melts from the playground or how long it will take for the plant to produce a flower

Suggestions for Core Items—Elementary Grades

Scientific Thinking	
AREA OF LEARNING	**CHILD'S WORK/REPRESENTATION**
Observing, recording, and describing phenomena	• A drawing or painting, with written or dictated description of a classroom pet, a natural object, or plant • A written or dictated description of an observed event or process • A sketch of an object, as seen under a magnifying lens or microscope, with labels to identify parts • Comparative drawings that show differences among trees, animals, people, rocks, shells, or feathers
Collecting and communicating scientific data about change over time	• Excerpts from a science log, tracking the growth of a plant over time • A series of drawings showing the metamorphosis of a caterpillar or tadpole • A series of descriptions of mold over several days • A collection of data describing cloud color, size, formation, and accompanying weather conditions over time
Interpreting and explaining information generated by scientific investigation	• Written or dictated explanations after observing animal or plant behavior in different situations • Pictures and explanations of changes in a cake before and after baking or an oil/water mixture before and after stirring • Photos of model bridges made in different ways, the results of weight-bearing tests, and written or dictated interpretation of the findings • Audio or videotaped presentation of findings from an investigation about the absorbency, buoyancy, and fluidity of different liquids
Investigating a question by predicting, testing, explaining, and drawing conclusions	• Written or dictated prediction to a question about the causes of natural disasters, along with written, drawn, or dictated information from research that supports or negates the prediction • An anecdotal record of a student's questions and efforts to find answers • A student's description of an experiment designed to answer a classmate's question about food preferences of different wild birds • An excerpt from a science log, showing three possible ways to collect information to answer a question about electricity
Planning and conducting an experiment to answer a question or to test a hypothesis	• Photo and anecdotal note of student conducting informal experiments at the water table • Student-written or dictated descriptions of two ramps built in the block area in order to test which toy car rolled the farthest • Student's written description and steps of an experiment designed to compare the weights of different substances • A written summary of a scientific experiment with insects, including the student's hypothesis and newly discovered information

Social Studies

AREA OF LEARNING	CHILD'S WORK/REPRESENTATION
Collecting and understanding information about self and family	• Student-written or dictated description of her/himself and her/his family • Drawing that reveals knowledge of family terminology and functions • A life book or timeline that tracks the student's life or the life of a family member • A photograph of the student with a written, taped, or dictated autobiography
Understanding human interdependence in communities (e.g., family, classroom, school community, nation)	• Written or dictated story depicting characters who depend on one another • Drawings and descriptions of various jobs and their importance in the community • A written or taped analysis of a book or story about people who work together to achieve a goal • Anecdotal record of student participation in a classroom economy • Text and interpretation of an interview with a community leader
Collecting, understanding, and interpreting information about the relationship between people and their environment	• Anecdotal evidence of a student's knowledge about pollution: verbal contributions to discussions, description of recycling efforts made by the student, newspaper articles the student brought in • Photograph with accompanying description of a model of the local community showing how and where people live and work • Drawings of people's home who live in different climates • Interviews with people about the effects of local factories on their lives and a summary of the information gathered through the interviews • A research report about eco-systems
Using maps and other geographic representations	• Anecdotal note of a student's use of a map, atlas, or globe to locate a city, state, country, or body of water • A student's hand-drawn map, made to give directions to her house or to find objects in a scavenger hunt • A photograph of a three-dimensional model of the school yard, the neighborhood, or community that shows actual geographic features • A record of comparisons between old and modern maps of the same area
Collecting, understanding, and interpreting information related to social studies topics	• Information and summary from interview with a senior citizen about long ago life • Research report about an historical figure or event, a political controversy, or a different culture or country • Drawing or text, summarizing a video about different kinds of families, an incident of discrimination, or a human conflict • Dialogue of conversation about different celebrations, different eating habits, different viewpoints about a group of people • An historical fiction story about an era or conflict in the past
Understanding and interpreting information about the relationship between people and their surroundings	• Research report about how a historical group of people used resources from the environment to shape their culture • Drawings or paintings depicting how people live and work (e.g., the homes of people who live in the desert, transportation methods used by people who live in the Arctic region, how the river is used for employment) • A story written by the student describing life in early America

Suggestions for Core Items—Elementary Grades

The Arts

AREA OF LEARNING	CHILD'S WORK/REPRESENTATION
Using the arts to represent ideas	• A painting that tells a story • A drawing with written or dictated text • A tape of a song made up by a student to describe a field trip • A videotape of a student-created skit
Responding to, interpreting, and analyzing artistic experiences	• Writing about personal reactions to the art seen on a museum field trip • A drawing that expresses how an artistic work or performance made the student feel • A record of comments from a discussion of a play the class saw • Videotape of children recreating the choreography of a dance they saw performed by a professional dance troupe • A student's written notes from an interview of another student about an artistic event they both attended
Understanding the arts as an expression of history and culture	• A reproduction of a mask, weaving, or style of painting from a different culture • Written or dictated explanation about why an art form was practiced by an ancient culture • A photo of a banner or flag designed by the student to represent the unique qualities of his family, school, or town
Exploring and controlling an artistic medium	• Paintings collected at various times throughout the year • Sculptures made from different materials collected over the course of the year • Collages collected over the course of the year • Crayon drawings made over time • Audiotape of a student playing a musical instrument at different times during the year

---

APPENDIX C

Example of Teacher's Letter to Parents

Here is the text of one teacher's letter to families, sent home with the Summary Report. The purpose of the letter is to explain the specific curriculum goals within each domain.

Dear _____,

To help you understand your child's fall Summary Report, I will describe our curriculum areas, classroom activities, and the topics we have studied so you can understand better what your child is doing in school.

- ◆ Personal and Social Development—I strive to create an environment that gives children opportunities to be active, independent learners as well as responsible members of the classroom community. Your child's report will inform you about your child's approach to learning, social skills, and participation in the group.

- ◆ Language and Literacy—In our classroom, group discussions are very important. Some topics we have discussed this fall are: problems and solutions in stories, things we know about clocks, reasons why scientists might go to a jungle, ways we can help a new student feel comfortable in our class, and fairness on the playground.

  Children have many chances to read each day: some are informal and unstructured, while others are focused and instructional. Many different types and levels of books are available in the room.

  Writing occurs daily in our classroom. My goals for writing are for children to feel comfortable expressing their ideas in writing, show interest in writing, compose organized stories that vary in topic or style, and develop increasing accuracy in spelling and using conventions of print (e.g., periods, commas, capitalization, etc.).

- ◆ Mathematical Thinking—Math activities emphasize solving different kinds of problems and using a variety of strategies to solve problems. During the fall, the children explored math problems related to double-digit numbers and shapes. They used a variety of materials to help them solve problems such as Cuisenaire rods, Unifix cubes, pattern blocks and tangrams. We also worked on telling time, measuring, and graphing.

- ◆ Scientific Thinking—Our science curriculum has included a study of the jungle habitat as well as ongoing investigations of the natural surroundings of our school. I look at your child's interest in and curiosi-

Example of Teacher's Letter to Parents

ty about the topic, your child as an observer and investigator, and how your child applies and uses scientific information.

- Social Studies—Our Social Studies experiences emphasize understanding people and the world they live in. As we study different habitats, we explore what people need in order to survive and how different environments affect the people who live, work, or visit there.

- The Arts—In our classroom children can choose a variety of expressive activities that help them share and integrate what they know. For example, music drama, puppetry, dance, drawing, painting, sculpting, inventing, and building are some of the ways children might represent their knowledge of predator/prey relationships in the jungle. I am also interested in your child's responses to the artistic expressions of others, such as a band concert given by older students.

- Physical Development and Health—An underlying belief of our classroom is that healthy physical development and an awareness of personal health and safety issues are critical to successful academic progress. In first grade, self confidence about one's physical skills contributes to children's sense of competence.

Little if anything in this Summary Report should be a surprise to your child. I encourage you to read the report with your child. Some questions you might ask to encourage conversation and to learn about your child's assessment of his or her own learning this fall include:

- Why do you think the teacher thinks you are a good scientist (problem-solver, reader, friend)?

- Tell me about a time when you became excited (frustrated, scared, happy, proud, sad, nervous) at school.

- Can you give me an example of what the teacher is talking about (referring to a specific comment on the Summary Report)?

- What do you think would help you with this problem at school?

- Did the teacher forget to tell me anything you think is important ?

I hope this letter has helped you gain a picture of our classroom and school activities. Please feel free to call me or write a note if you have any questions, comments, or concerns.

Sincerely,

— *Charlotte Stetson*

Brattleboro, VT

APPENDIX D

Examples of Completed Summary Reports

CHILD	Kenneth Hampton	AGE/GRADE Pre-Primary
TEACHER	Rider	DATE 3/5/95
SCHOOL	Westview Early Childhood Center	
ATTENDANCE: DAYS TARDY		DAYS ABSENT

The Work Sampling System.
Summary Report

FALL ☐
WINTER ☑
YEAR-END ☐

GENERAL COMMENTS: Give reasons for "Needs Development" and/or note special strengths and talents in each domain. Also give explanation if progress is other than expected. Describe plans for supporting child's growth.

I Personal & Social Development
Self concept
Self control
Approaches to learning
Interaction with others
Social problem-solving

Kenny is excited about learning activities in the classroom. At times he can interact well with other children and adults. Kenny has made little progress in learning how to resolve conflicts, follow directions, and use words to express anger and continues to need my support in these areas. One way I am helping him is through small group activities that focus on feelings.

II Language & Literacy
Listening
Speaking
Reading
Writing
Research (3-5)

Kenny loves books, listening to stories, and is just starting to work on writing. He uses his name card to practice writing letters. When speaking, he struggles to put words together and to verbally communicate with others. As we have discussed, he is receiving some outside support to help him develop these skills.

III Mathematical Thinking
Mathematical processes
Number and operations
Patterns, relationships, and functions
Geometry and spatial relations
Measurement
Data collection and probability (K-5)

Kenny is very interested in quantities and numbers. He can easily recognize and copy simple patterns. Kenny can also accurately count with 1-to-1 correspondence up to 5.

IV Scientific Thinking
Inquiry
Physical science (K-5)
Life science (K-5)
Earth science (K-5)

Kenny enjoys using his senses to explore the world around him. He is very observant, draws pictures of what he sees, and tries to use his words to describe or question what he discovers. Kenny is also beginning to understand and interpret information on a chart.

V Social Studies
People, past and present
Human interdependence
Citizenship and government
People and where they live

Kenny is beginning to understand family roles. He talks of his family often. There was concern for a few months (Nov.-Jan.) as Kenny did not adjust well to the new baby at home. He has shown considerable progress and is beginning to talk about how he takes care of the baby.

VI The Arts
Expression and representation
Understanding and appreciation

Kenny loves music and finger plays. He is very responsive to them and this could greatly aid his language development. Kenny also enjoys acting out stories.

VII Physical Development & Health
Gross motor development
Fine motor development
Personal health and safety

Kenny is right on target for a four-year-old. He can jump, run, hop and climb with great balance and coordination. He is working on his fine motor skills by working with puzzles, blocks and manipulatives.

DOMAINS & COMPONENTS

PROGRESS — Other than Expected / As Expected
PERFORMANCE — PORTFOLIO — Needs Development / As Expected
CHECKLIST — Needs Development / As Expected

SEE REVERSE FOR HOW TO READ THE SUMMARY REPORT

4th Edition   ©1997, 2001 Rebus Inc

WHITE – FAMILY   YELLOW – OFFICE   PINK – TEACHER

The Work Sampling System®
Summary Report

CHILD: Serena Porter
AGE/GRADE: Third Grade
TEACHER: Mr. Groves
DATE: 2/29/96
SCHOOL: George Washington Elementary School
ATTENDANCE: DAYS TARDY: 0   DAYS ABSENT: 1

FALL ☐
WINTER ☑
YEAR-END ☐

DOMAINS & COMPONENTS

I Personal & Social Development
Self concept
Self control
Approaches to learning
Interaction with others
Social problem-solving

II Language & Literacy
Listening
Speaking
Reading
Writing
Research (3-5)

III Mathematical Thinking
Mathematical processes
Number and operations
Patterns, relationships, and functions
Geometry and spatial relations
Measurement
Data collection and probability (K-5)

IV Scientific Thinking
Inquiry
Physical science (K-5)
Life science (K-5)
Earth science (K-5)

V Social Studies
People past and present
Human interdependence
Citizenship and government
People and where they live

VI The Arts
Expression and representation
Understanding and appreciation

VII Physical Development & Health
Gross motor development
Fine motor development
Personal health and safety

SEE REVERSE FOR HOW TO READ THE SUMMARY REPORT

4th Edition   ©1997, 2001 Rebus Inc.

WHITE – FAMILY   YELLOW – OFFICE   PINK – TEACHER

PERFORMANCE
CHECKLIST — Needs Development / As Expected
PORTFOLIO — Needs Development / As Expected

PROGRESS
As Expected / Other than Expected

GENERAL COMMENTS: Give reasons for "Needs Development" and/or note special strengths and talents in each domain. Also give explanation if progress is other than expected. Describe plans for supporting child's growth.

Serena gets along well with her classmates and teachers. She works out conflicts in appropriate ways. She is confident in her ability and participates in class discussions. Serena still has problems with organizational skills -- she needs reminders to get started, to stay on task, to complete her assignments. The interventions I've tried so far have not helped. My goal during the next few months will be to go over her work with her daily and give her time after school to complete her assignments. Her portfolio reflects her good thinking, but also shows her difficulty in completing tasks.

Serena continues to progress in her ability to read grade level texts independently and with comprehension. She has special ability in her writing. Not only does she use conventionally spelled words, she also uses capitalization and punctuation correctly. Her stories are well organized and filled with humor.

Serena has good problem solving strategies. She can mentally and quickly work out solutions to problems involving addition, subtraction, multiplication and division. She was able to quickly grasp the concept of using parentheses in problems to change the answer. My goal for her during the next few months is for her to complete math assignments that require several steps and to record her thinking in writing when solving mathematical problems.

Serena uses scientific thinking skills when conducting scientific investigations and research projects. Serena compiled a list of facts she learned about fish during our river study. She did these from memory and stated that fish need water to get oxygen. Her description of how a river starts included parts of the water cycle and the fact that the treatment plant adds chlorine and fluoride to the water.

Serena is a keen observer and remembers many details from our trips. She wrote a lengthy detailed piece about our trip to the water treatment plant. She remembered and wrote about many of the jobs and equipment we saw there. She again mentioned that chemicals were added to the water to clean it. She is able to show through discussion, writing and drawing the differences between the present and the past.

She uses her ability to draw and paint to share knowledge. An example of this is her picture of clothing and transportation used in Pittsburgh long ago. She performed a dance with precision and enthusiasm for our African American history program. She also perfored songs with the class.

Her fine and gross motor skills are highly developed as evidenced by her small precise writing, her building of trees and bushes for our river model and her agility during physical education classes.

APPENDIX E

Glossary of Terms

Area of Learning—a strand of a curriculum domain that guides the collection of Core Items.

As Expected (performance)—a performance rating on the Summary Report that indicates that the child's performance as seen in the Checklist or Portfolio meets or exceeds age- or grade-level expectations.

As Expected (progress)—a progress rating on the Summary Report that indicates that the child has grown appropriately according to the teacher's professional judgment and knowledge of child development.

Checklist—*see Developmental Checklist*

Checklist Ratings—*see In Process, Not Yet, Proficient*

Collection Period—a duration of time during which data are collected in an ongoing manner in order to make an evaluation. Work Sampling has three collection periods: fall, winter, and spring.

Component—*see Functional Component*

Core Items—Representation of a particular area of learning within a domain. Collected from five domains three times a year, Core Items are designed to display both the quality of children's work and their progress in domain-related knowledge and skills.

Curriculum-embedded—an assessment that uses students' actual performance in the regular classroom routine as the "data" for evaluation.

Criterion-referenced—an assessment that evaluates a student's work with reference to specific criteria rather than with reference to other students' work.

Developmental Checklist—a list of performance indicators for each grade level that are organized by curriculum domains and are used to collect, organize, and record teachers' observations.

Developmental Guidelines—a book that describes age- or grade-level expectations for the performance indicators; contains a rationale and examples for each indicator.

Domain—a broad area of the curriculum.

Glossary of Terms

Examples—descriptions of ways that children demonstrate what they know and can do related to each performance indicator in the Developmental Guidelines.

Functional Component—a subset of a domain comprised of several performance indicators.

Guidelines—*see Developmental Guidelines*

Indicator—*see Performance Indicator*

Individualized Items—Portfolio items that capture the child's unique interests and experiences, and reflect learning that integrates many domains of the curriculum.

In Process—a Checklist rating that indicates that the skill or knowledge represented by a performance indicator is intermittent or emergent, and is not demonstrated consistently.

Needs Development—a performance rating on the Summary Report that indicates that the child's current performance does not meet age- or grade-level expectations.

Not Yet—a Checklist rating that indicates that a child cannot demonstrate the skill or knowledge represented by a performance indicator.

Omnibus Guidelines—two volumes (P3–3, K–5) that each display six years of Developmental Guidelines on facing pages, arranged to show year-to-year progress.

Other than Expected—a progress rating on the Summary Report that indicates that a child's progress is either above or below teacher expectations.

Performance—refers to the level of a student's behavior, skills, and accomplishments at a particular point in time.

Performance Assessment—refers to assessment methods that rely on students demonstrating their knowledge or skills in applied situations.

Performance Indicator—a skill, behavior, attitude, or accomplishment that is evaluated in the classroom.

Proficient—a Checklist rating that indicates that the skill or knowledge represented by a performance indicator is demonstrated consistently, and is firmly within the child's repertoire.

Progress—growth over time.

Portfolio—purposeful collection of children's work.

Rationale—a brief explanation of an indicator that includes reasonable age- or grade-level expectations.

Summary Report—a report completed three times during the school year that integrates information from the Developmental Checklist and Portfolio with teachers' knowledge of child development in order to evaluate a student's performance and progress.

Summary Report Performance Ratings—*see As Expected (performance), Needs Development*

Summary Report Progress Ratings—*see As Expected (progress), Other than Expected*

Glossary of Terms

Index

A

Accordion Files **61, 73**

Anecdotal Notes **29, 40, 55, 80, 83, 121, 122, 185**

Areas of Learning
see also Core Items, Portfolio, Portfolio Collection
analyzing using various charting methods **91**
choosing Core Items **101**
criteria for effectiveness **63, 84–86**
definition **62**
developing **87–92, 120**
difference from Checklist indicators **86**
for planning curriculum and instruction **89**
getting started **87, 120**
number in the Portfolio **84**
planning **65**
reflecting concepts or processes **86**
relation to classroom activities **90, 96**
relation to curriculum **85**
relation to domains **87**
relation to skills and concepts **88**
relevant for all students **85, 122**
represented in Core Items **90, 96, 101**
responsibility for selecting **62**
same for all students in the classroom **65**
selecting effective areas of learning **87**
showing progress **63, 65, 85, 88**
suggested areas of learning **201–212**

Assessment
achievement tests **2**
authentic performance assessment **2, 4**
collection of children's work **7**
curriculum-embedded **2, 48**
documentation **4, 51, 129**
evaluation **4, 129**
observation **7, 11**
ongoing and continuous **5**
performance assessment **2, 4**
relation to effective instruction **2, 96**
role of context in **2, 4, 23**
student awareness of **44**
student involvement in **176, 177**
summarization **7**

Audiotapes **32, 79, 186**

B

Binders **38, 74**

Booklet of Reproducible Masters, *see Reproducible Masters*

Boxes **74**

Brief Notes **28, 36, 40, 55**

Butcher Paper **33**

C

Calendars **33**

Carpenters' Aprons **33**

Checklist
see also Guidelines, Observation, Documentation
and children with special needs **194–196**
as documentation **11**
choosing appropriate age/grade level **54, 195**
completing **10, 19–47**
components **16**
difference from Portfolio **60, 86**
differences between collection periods **46, 51**
domains **16, 122**
evaluating performance in **135, 139**
evaluating progress in **53, 135**
evaluation in **11, 16**
features **10**
for planning curriculum and instruction **50**
how long to complete **54**
how long to learn **53**
in multi-age classrooms **56, 192**
in observation **7, 11**
in preschool **184**
indicators **16**
introduction **11–18**
making final ratings **46, 48**
making preliminary ratings **41–43, 46, 48**
overview **10**
page reference of indicators to grade-level Guidelines **16**
purposes of **12**
ratings **16, 42**
reasons for three collection periods **53**
relation to other Work Sampling elements **3, 7**
reliability **51**
reviewing periodically **41–43**
reviewing to plan observation **39, 44**
sharing the Checklist with families **52, 53**
space for ratings **16**
space for written comments **16, 43**
specialists **52, 197**
status at year-end **53**
storage **38**
student involvement in **43–44, 189**
student's identifying information **16**
translating to Title I ratings **199**
using **10, 19–47**
using Guidelines as reference **16, 46**
validity **51**
Wall Chart of Performance Indicators **21, 43**
when to complete **19**

Checklist Performance Rating, *see Summary Report*

Checklist Ratings, *see Checklist*

CHILD DOMAIN PROCESS NOTES 34

Child Involvement, *see Student Involvement*

Children, *see Students*

Collection of Children's Work, *see Portfolio Collection*

Collection Periods
    evaluating progress in the fall collection period **161**
    in the Portfolio **58, 68**
    influence on Checklist ratings **46, 51**
    number of Portfolio items **69**
    on the Checklist **16**
    reasons for three collection periods **53**
    relation to other Work Sampling features **4**

Components
    definition **13**
    in grade-level Guidelines **13, 15**
    in the Omnibus Guidelines **13, 18**
    on the Checklist **13, 16**
    on the Summary Report **132, 133**
    relation to domains **14**
    relation to indicators **14**
    variation in different age/grade levels **13**

Computers, hand-held **34**

Conferences with Families
    see also Family Involvement, Student Involvement, Summary Report
    Checklist in **52**
    eliciting information from families **157**
    Portfolio in **118**
    preparing for **157**
    student involvement in **118, 159**
    student-led conferences **159**
    Summary Report in **157, 167, 191**
    to help introduce Work Sampling **182**

CORE ITEM COLLECTION PLAN **93**

CORE ITEM PLANNING WORKSHEET **91**

Core Items
    see also Areas of Learning, Portfolio, Portfolio Collection
    areas of learning **62–63, 84–95**
    as representations of areas of learning **90, 96, 101**
    choosing **101**
    Core Item Collection Plan form **61, 73, 93, 94, 95, 112, 120**
    Core Item Planning Worksheet form **88, 91, 92**
    definition **62**

developing areas of learning **87–92**
difference from Individualized Items **68**
domains **61, 62, 64, 68, 73, 84, 122, 187**
features **63–66**
functions **68**
getting started **87**
managing Core Item collection **93–95**
number of items **68, 69, 75**
planned in advance **65**
planning **120**
planning for Core Item collection **65, 68, 84–95**
relation to collection periods **68**
role in the Work Sampling Portfolio **7, 58**
showing performance **64**
showing progress **63, 65, 85, 88**
showing representative work **64**
storage **61, 73**
student involvement in **102, 104**
suggested areas of learning **201–212**

Criterion-Referenced, *see Guidelines*

Curriculum-Embedded Assessment, *see Assessment*

D

Date Stamps **76**

DEVELOPMENTAL CHECKLIST **16**

Developmental Checklist, *see Checklist*

Developmental Guidelines, *see Guidelines*

Diagrams **31, 82**

Documentation
    see also Documentation Methods and Tools, Observation, Portfolio Collection, Storage
    annotating Portfolio work **105–111**
    attachments to Summary Report **157**
    attachments to the Portfolio **117**
    Checklist as **11**
    Child Domain Process Notes form **34, 37**

difference between fact and opinion **23**
difference between informal and formal records **51**
Domain Process Notes form **34, 36**
establishing realistic expectations **25, 48**
for planning curriculum and instruction **50**
General Process Notes form **35, 37**
getting started **176, 177**
how to observe and record **39–45**
identifying records for the Summary Report **47, 52**
in assessment **4, 51, 129**
including opinions in **24**
managing **48, 54**
methods **28–32**
of curriculum **107, 110, 157**
of multiple indicators **55**
of observations after the fact **27**
of observations while participating in the action **25**
of observations while stepping out of the action **26**
of points to communicate to families **118**
of Portfolio work context **109, 110**
of selection of Portfolio work **109, 110**
planning for **39–41, 175, 177**
preparing for **22–38**
preparing methods and tools **24–38**
Process Note forms **34–37, 175, 177**
reasons for recording observation **23, 51**
relation to fair and objective evaluation **165**
reviewing for Summary Report completion **138, 160**
role of context in **25–28, 40, 48**
Roster Process Notes form **36, 37**
student involvement in **43–44, 189**
support from colleagues **55**
Teacher File **32, 38, 42, 44, 46**
time requirements **48**
tools **32–36**
using to make preliminary Checklist ratings **41**
value of descriptive writing **28**
value of tallying **28**
when to document **19**

Documentation Methods and Tools
see also Documentation, Portfolio Collection, Storage
anecdotal notes **29, 40, 55, 80, 83, 121, 122, 185**
audiotapes **32, 79, 186**
brief notes **28, 36, 40, 55**
butcher paper **33**
calendars **33**
carpenters' aprons **33**
date stamps **76**
diagrams **31, 82**
hand-held computers **34**
index cards **33, 40**
legal pads **32**
mailing labels **32**
masking tape **33**
matrices **30, 36**
multiple drafts **80**
My Portfolio Item Record form **105**
photographs **31, 79, 186**
planning and preparation **40, 175, 177**
Portfolio Item Record self-stick notes **81, 83, 105, 110**
Process Note forms **34–37, 175, 177**
rating scales **29**
recording forms or worksheets **78**
running records **29**
self-stick notes **33, 35, 81, 83, 105, 110, 118**
sketches **31, 82**
still cameras **33**
tallies **30**
tape recorders **33**
Thoughts About My Portfolio form **115**
time samplings **31**
video cameras **34**
videotapes **32, 79, 186**

DOMAIN PROCESS NOTES 34

Domains
Child Domain Process Notes form **34, 37**
definition **13**
descriptions of **5–7**
Domain Process Notes form **34, 36**
for Core Items **61, 62, 64, 68, 73, 84, 122, 187**
for Individualized Items **67, 68, 73, 122**
getting started with only some domains **173–176**

in grade-level Guidelines **13, 15**
in the Omnibus Guidelines **13, 18**
in the Portfolio **61, 62, 64, 67, 68, 73, 84, 122, 187**
observation options **40**
on the Checklist **13, 16, 122**
on the Summary Report **132, 133**
relation to areas of learning **87**
relation to components **14**
relation to indicators **14**
relation to other Work Sampling features **3**

E

Evaluation
differences between Core and Individualized Items **117**
in assessment **4, 129**
involving students **158**
of the Checklist **11, 16**
of the Portfolio 1**00, 113–119, 120, 121**
of the Portfolio for the Summary Report **116–117**
relation to observation **164**
role of judgment in **164**
standards of comparison **135, 164**
student review and evaluation of the Portfolio **113–116**
Summary Report **133**

Examples, *see Indicators*

F

Fall Collection Period, *see Collection Periods*

Family Involvement
see also Conferences with Families, Student Involvement, Summary Report
eliciting information from families **157**
example of letter to families **213–214**
informing the community about Work Sampling **180–182**
Overview for Families **180, 181**
Parent Teacher Organization **181**
Portfolio Nights **118, 179**
responding to questions **181**

sharing the Checklist with families **52, 53**
sharing the Portfolio with families **118–119, 124, 179**
Student anf Family Comments form **158**
student-led conferences **159**
Wall Chart of Performance Indicators **21**

File Cabinets **38, 74**

File Folders **38, 61, 73, 77**

Functional Components, *see Components* **5**

G

GENERAL PROCESS NOTES 35

Getting Started
becoming familiar with the Guidelines **20, 175, 177**
collecting Portfolio Core Items **87**
completing the Summary Report **160**
developing areas of learning **87**
establishing realistic expectations for recording observations **25, 48**
exploration **177**
extending knowledge of observation **22–24**
gradual implementation **173–178**
informing the community about Work Sampling **180–182**
one element at a time **176–177**
preparing for observation **20–38**
preparing observation methods and tools **24–38, 175, 177**
tips for learning Work Sampling **172**
with only some domains **173–176**
with Portfolio collection **120, 175**
with Summary Reports **176**
writing narratives on the Summary Report **155**

GRADE-LEVEL DEVELOPMENTAL GUIDELINES 14

Grade-Level Guidelines
see also Guidelines, Omnibus Guidelines
components **15**

domains **15**
examples (for indicators) **15**
indicators **15**
page reference of indicators on Checklist **16**
rationale (for indicators) **15**

Guidelines
see also Grade-Level Guidelines, Omnibus Guidelines, Checklist, Observation, Documentation
adding examples **21**
and children with special needs **194–196**
becoming familiar with **20, 175, 177**
criterion-referenced **15**
developmentally appropriate expectations in **11**
ensuring valid and reliable Checklist ratings **51**
features **10**
for planning curriculum and instruction **20, 50, 54**
for reference in completing Checklists **46**
how long to learn **53**
in multi-age classrooms **56, 192**
in observation **7**
in preschool **184**
introduction **11–18**
mastery of **39, 44**
overview **10**
purposes of **12**
relation to other Work Sampling elements **3, 7**
reviewing to focus observation **28**
standards in **11, 164**
student involvement in **43–44, 189**
support from colleagues **20**
using **10, 19–47**
using Omnibus Guidelines to adjust age/grade level expectations **54**
Wall Chart of Performance Indicators **21, 43**
when to use **19**

H

Hanging Files **74, 77**

I

Index Cards **33, 40**

Indicators
definition **13**
difference from Portfolio areas of learning **86**
documentation of multiple indicators **55**
examples **14**
in grade-level Guidelines **13, 15**
in the Omnibus Guidelines **13, 18**
making preliminary ratings **41**
on the Checklist **13, 16**
rationale **14**
relation to components **14**
relation to domains **14**
variation in different age/grade levels **17**
Wall Chart of Performance Indicators **21, 43**

Individual Education Plans **193**

Individualized Items
see also Portfolio, Portfolio Collection
definition **66**
difference from Core Items **68**
domains **67, 68, 73, 122**
features **66–68**
functions **68**
number of items **68, 69, 75**
planning **68**
relation to collection periods **68**
role in the Work Sampling Portfolio **7, 58**
selecting **102**
showing approach to learning **66**
showing integrated knowledge **67, 122**
showing significant accomplishments **66**
showing special interests and talents **66**
storage **61, 73**
student involvement **102, 104**

L

Language and Literacy, *see Domains*

Legal Pads **32**

M

Mailing Labels **32**

Masking Tape **33**

Mathematical Thinking, *see Domains*

Matrices **30, 36**

Milk Crates **74, 77**

Multi-Age Classrooms
Guidelines and Checklists in **56, 192**
Portfolio in **192**
Work Sampling in **3, 192**

MY PORTFOLIO ITEM RECORD **105**

N

Narrative
space for comments on the Checklist **16, 43**
writing the narrative on the Summary Report **144–156, 166**

NARRATIVE SUMMARY REPORT **133**

O

Observation
see also Documentation, Documentation Methods and Tools, Guidelines, Checklist
applying understanding of **44–45**
as fundamental Work Sampling process **7**
definition **22**
difference between fact and opinion **23, 50**
ensuring fairness of **50**
extending knowledge of **22–24**
getting started **20–38, 175, 176, 177**
Guidelines and Checklists in **7**
how to observe and record **39–45**
in assessment **7, 11**
in preschool **184**
information obtained **22**
managing **48, 54**
observing while stepping out of the action **26**
ongoing processes **23, 39, 41**
planning for **39–41**
preparing methods and tools **24–38**

reasons for recording observation **23, 51**
reflecting after the fact **27**
reviewing the Guidelines **28**
role of context in **23, 25–28, 40, 48**
student involvement in **43–44, 189**
support from colleagues **41, 55**
time requirements **48**
what to observe **39, 41, 49**
when to observe **19, 40**
while participating in the action **25**

Omnibus Guidelines
see also Guidelines, Grade-Level Guidelines
components **18**
domains **18**
examples (for indicators) **18**
highlighting continuum of development **17**
in multi-age classrooms **56, 192**
indicators **18**
rationale (for indicators) **18**
to adjust age/grade level expectations **54**
to plan curriculum and instruction **56**
two volumes **17**
variations of indicators in different age/grade levels **17**

OMNIBUS GUIDELINES 17

OVERVIEW FOR FAMILIES 180

P

Parent Teacher Organization **181**

Peformance Indicators, *see Indicators*

Performance
as seen in the Checklist **10, 135, 139**
as seen in the Portfolio **64, 135, 141**
difference from progress **160**

Performance Assessment, *see Assessment*

Performance Ratings, *see Summary Report*

Personal and Social Development, *see Domains*

PHOTOGRAPHIC PORTFOLIO ITEM RECORD 80

Photographs **31, 79, 186**

Physical Development and Health, *see Domains*

Planning
annotating Portfolio work at time of assignment **107, 110**
considering methods to portray learning **77–84, 97**
Core Item Collection Plan form **93, 94, 95, 120**
Core Item Planning Worksheet form **88, 91, 92**
curriculum and instruction **11, 20, 39, 50, 54, 60, 89, 96–98, 121, 123**
for Core Item collection **65, 84–95, 120**
for observation and documentation **39–41, 44, 48, 176, 177**
managing Core Item collection **93–95**
Portfolio collection **68, 73–95**
precedures to collect student work **75–77, 99, 101**
preparing observation methods and tools **24–38**
preparing to complete Summary Reports **46**
preparing to share Portfolios with families **118**

Plastic Tubs **74**

Pocket Folders **73**

Portfolio **179**
see also Portfolio Collection, Core Items, Individualized Items, Areas of Learning, Storage
accessibility to students **74**
and children with special needs **196**
areas of learning **62–63, 84–95**
attaching additional information **117**
collection periods **68**
Core Item Collection Plan form **61, 73**
Core Item domains **61, 62, 64, 68, 73, 84, 122, 187**
Core Items **7, 62–66**
creating individual Portfolios **73–75, 120, 175**
difference between Core and Individualized Items **68**
difference from Checklist **60, 86**

difference from Teacher File **38, 121**
different standards of evaluating Core and Individualized Items **117**
evaluating **113–119**
evaluating for the Summary Report **116–117**
evaluating for Title I **199**
evaluating performance in **135, 141**
evaluating progress in **135**
family involvement **118–119**
features **58**
for planning curriculum and instruction **60**
in conferences with families **118**
in multi-age classrooms **192**
Individualized Item domains **67, 68, 73, 122**
Individualized Items **7, 66–68**
introduction **59–69**
number of items **68, 69, 75**
overview **58**
Photographic Portfolio Item Record form **80**
photographs of student work **79**
Portfolio Domain Labels **74**
Portfolio Item self-stick notes **81, 83, 105, 110**
Portfolio Nights **118, 179**
purposes **60**
relation of Core Items to areas of learning **90, 96, 101**
relation to other Work Sampling elements **3, 7**
sharing the Portfolio with families **118–119**
sharing with other teachers **125**
showing approach to learning **66**
showing integrated knowledge **67, 122**
showing performance **64**
showing progress **60, 63, 65, 70, 85, 88**
showing quality of student work **60**
showing representative work **64**
showing significant accomplishments **66**
showing special interests and talents **66**
status at year-end **124**
storage **61, 73–75, 175**
storage of Portfolio items **61, 73**

storage of possible Portfolio items **76**
structure **61**
student involvement in **60, 70, 81, 118, 189**
student review and evaluation **81**
using **58, 70–119**

Portfolio Collection
see also Portfolio, Core Items, Individualized Items, Areas of Learning
annotating work **70, 101, 105–111**
areas of learning **62–63, 84–95**
as fundamental Work Sampling process **7**
choosing Core Items **101**
clarifying expectations **98**
collecting work **70, 120**
collection bin **76, 120**
collection periods **68**
considering methods to portray learning **77–84, 97**
Core Item Collection Plan form **93, 94, 95, 112, 120**
Core Item Planning Worksheet form **88, 91, 92**
Core Items **62–66**
dating work **76, 101**
developing areas of learning **87–92**
discussing expectations with students **99**
discussing purposes of activities with students **99**
evaluating **100, 120, 121**
for planning curriculum and instruction **60, 89, 96–98, 121, 123**
getting started **87, 120**
grading of Portfolio work **121**
how much to collect **76**
how to annotate work **107**
how to collect and select work **96–112**
in assessment **7**
in kindergarten **201–206**
in preschool **122, 185–187, 201–206**
in primary grades **207–212**
Individualized Items **66–68**
introduction **59–69**
managing Core Item collection **93–95**
managing selection **112**
My Portfolio Item Record form **105**

ongoing processes **76, 121, 122**
overview **58**
planning **73–95**
planning for Core Item collection **65, 84–95**
planning for Portfolio collection **68**
planning procedures for collecting student work **175**
planning procedures to collect student work **75–77, 99, 101**
Portfolio Collection Tally form **112**
providing constructive feedback **100**
purposes **60**
relation of Core Items to areas of learning **90, 96, 101**
selecting Individualized Items **102**
selecting work **70**
showing performance **64**
showing progress **60, 63, 65, 70, 85, 88**
showing quality of student work **60**
specialists **124, 198**
student involvement in **60, 70, 81, 98–100, 102, 103–105, 176, 187**
student review and evaluation **81, 113–116**
students choosing own Core Items **102, 104**
students selecting own Individualized Items **102, 104**
suggested areas of learning **201–212**
talking with students about their work **99**
teaching students about portfolios **98**
Thoughts About My Portfolio form **115**
using **58, 70–119**
variety of ways for student to express learning **97**
when to annotate work **71, 107**
when to collect work **71, 100**
when to select work **71, 101–103**
work folder **76, 120**

PORTFOLIO COLLECTION TALLY **112**

PORTFOLIO DOMAIN LABELS **74**

PORTFOLIO ITEM RECORD SELF-STICK NOTE **105**

Portfolio Item self-stick notes **81, 83, 105, 106, 110**

Portfolio Nights **118, 179**

Portfolio Performance Rating, *see Summary Report*

Process Notes
Child Domain Process Notes form **34, 37**
Domain Process Notes form **34, 36**
General Process Notes form **35, 37**
Roster Process Notes form **36, 37**

Progress
as seen in the Checklist **11, 53, 135**
as seen in the Portfolio 6**0, 63, 65, 70, 85, 88, 135**
Core Items **63, 65**
difference from performance **160**
evaluating in the fall collection period **161**

Progress Rating, *see Summary Report*

R

Rating Scales **29**

Rationale, *see Indicators*

Reproducible Masters
Core Item Collection Plan form **61, 73, 93, 94, 95, 112, 120**
Core Item Planning Worksheet form **88, 91, 92**
My Portfolio Item Record form **105**
Photographic Portfolio Item Record form **80**
Portfolio Collection Tally form **112**
Process Notes **34–37, 175, 177**
Thoughts About My Portfolio form **115, 158**

Roster Process Notes **36**

Running Records **29**

S

Self-stick notes **33, 35, 81, 83, 105, 106, 110, 118**

Scientific Thinking, *see Domains*

Sketches **31, 82**

Social Studies, *see Domains*

Special Needs
    choosing appropriate age/grade
        level for Checklist **54, 195**
    Individual Education Plans **193**
    Portfolio **196**
    Summary Report **196**
    using Omnibus Guidelines to adjust
        age/grade level expecations **54**
    Work Sampling and children with
        special needs **193–197**
    working on a team **196**

SPECIAL SUBJECT REPORT 167

Special Subject Teachers, *see Specialists*

Specialists
    and the Checklist **52, 197**
    and the Portfolio **124, 198**
    and the Summary Report **167, 198**
    in the Work Sampling System
        197–198
    Special Subject Report form **52,
        167, 198**

Spring Collection Period, *see Collection
    Periods*

STANDARD SUMMARY REPORT 132

Standards
    and the Summary Report **164**
    differences in evaluating Core and
        Individualized Items **117**
    in evaluation **135, 164**
    in the Guidelines **11, 164**
    in the Portfolio **87, 116, 117, 165**
    local standards **87, 117**
    national and state standards **3, 10,
        11, 164**
    standards of comparison **135, 164**

Still Cameras **33**

Storage
    accordion files **61, 73**
    boxes **74**
    collection bin **76, 120**
    file cabinets **38, 74**
    file folders **38, 61, 73, 77**
    hanging files **74, 77**
    milk crates **74, 77**
    of Checklists **38**
    of observation records **38**
    of Portfolio items **61, 73–75**
    of Portfolios **61, 73–75, 175**
    plastic tubs **74**

pocket folders **73**
Portfolio Domain Labels **74**
Teacher File **32, 38, 42, 44, 46,
    121, 175, 177**
three-ring binders **38, 74**
work folder **76, 120**

Student Involvement
    accessibility of the Portfolio **74**
    awareness of assessment process
        44
    choosing own Core Items **102, 104**
    in conferences with families **118**
    in kindergarten **104, 113**
    in observation and documentation
        43–44
    in Portfolio collection **187, 189**
    in preschool **104, 113**
    in primary grades **104, 114**
    in Summary Report **158**
    in the assessment process **176, 177**
    in the Checklist **43–44**
    in the Portfolio **60, 70, 98–100,
        102, 103–105, 124**
    My Portfolio Item Record form **105**
    Portfolio Nights **118, 179**
    reviewing and evaluating the
        Portfolio **81, 113–116**
    selecting own Individualized Items
        102, 104
    Student and Family Comments
        form **158**
    student-led conferences **159**
    Thoughts About My Portfolio form
        115, 158
    Wall Chart of Performance
        Indicators **21, 43**

Students
    developmentally appropriate
        expectations **11**
    transfers to other schools **17**
    types of activities engaged in **11**

Summarization
    see also Summary Report
    as fundamental Work Sampling
        process **7**
    in assessment **7**

Summary Report
    see also Summarization
    addressing age/grade level
        expectations **54**
    and children with special needs
        196

as replacement for conventional
    report cards **8**
attaching additional information
    157
Checklist performance rating **139,
    162**
child's identifying information **132,
    133, 137**
choosing standard or narrative **137,
    188**
comments **132, 133, 166**
completing **128, 136–159**
completing performance and
    progress ratings **138–144**
components **132, 133**
conferences with families **157, 167,
    191**
differences among collection
    periods **168**
domains **132, 133**
evaluating the Portfolio **116–117**
examples of completed Summary
    Reports **215–216**
features **128**
functional components **132, 133**
getting started **160, 176**
getting started writing narratives
    155
how long to complete **166**
how much to write **153–155**
identifying records for completing
    47, 52
introduction **129–135**
language in the narrative **147–152**
narrative comments **132, 133, 166**
Narrative Summary Report **133**
organizing narrative comments **155**
overview **128**
performance ratings **132, 134, 139,
    141, 160, 161, 162**
Portfolio performance rating **141,
    162**
preparing to complete **46, 138, 160**
preschool **188**
progress rating **132, 134, 143, 160,
    161**
purposes of **130**
relation to other Work Sampling
    elements **3, 8**
reviewing collected information
    138, 160
sharing with child and family **156–
    159**

Special Subject Report form **167, 198**

specialists' contributions to **167, 198**

Standard Summary Report **132**

Student and Family Comments form **158**

student involvement **158**

translating Portfolio rating to Title I ratings **199**

types **132, 133**

using **128, 136–159**

what to include in narrative comments **144–147**

when to complete **136, 160**

writing narrative comments **144–156, 166**

Summary Report Manager software **128, 137**

SUMMARY REPORT-STUDENT AND FAMILY COMMENTS **158**

T

Tallies **30**

Tape Recorders **33**

Teacher File **32, 38, 42, 44, 46, 121, 175, 177**

Teacher Folder, *see Teacher File*

Teachers
diverse contexts **8**
diverse teaching styles **2, 8, 28, 38**
expertise and judgment **8**
of special subjects, *see Specialists*
sharing the Portfolio **125**
support from colleagues *20, 41, 55, 87–92, 124, 175, 179*
working on a team for children with special needs **196**

The Arts, *see Domains*

THOUGHTS ABOUT MY PORTFOLIO **115**

Three-Ring Binders **38, 74**

Time Samplings **31**

Title I **199–200**

V

Video Cameras **34**

Videotapes **32, 79, 186**

W

Wall Chart of Performance Indicators **21, 43**

WALL CHART OF PERFORMANCE INDICATORS **21**

Winter Collection Period, *see Collection Periods*

Work Sampling System
advantages and benefits **2–3**
age/grade levels **4**
collection of children's work in **7**
collection periods **4**
domains **3, 5–7**
elements **4, 7**
for Title I evaluation **199–200**
fundamental processes **7–8**
in multi-age classrooms **3, 192**
in preschool and kindergarten **184–188**
in primary grades **189–191**
informing the community about Work Sampling **180–182**
introduction **2–4l**
observation in **7**
performance assessment in **4–5**
purpose **7**
special needs **193–197**
specialists in **197–198**
summarization in **7**
with diverse student populations **3**